D0757644

TRANSITION The London Art Scene in the Fifties

John Deakin: Photograph of a plaster maquette by William Turnbull, in the artist's north London garden, 1951. Private collection

TRANSITION

The London Art Scene in the Fifties

MARTIN HARRISON

MERRELL
in association with
Barbican Art

First published 2002 by
Merrell Publishers Limited
42 Southwark Street
London SE1 1UN

in association with

Barbican Art Galleries
London

Published on the occasion of the exhibition
Transition: The London Art Scene in the Fifties
31 January – 14 April 2002
Barbican Gallery, Barbican Centre, London

The exhibition was organized by Barbican Art Galleries
Guest Curator: Martin Harrison
Barbican Curator: Tomoko Sato
Exhibition Organizer: Louise Vaughan
Curatorial Assistant: Elina Middleton-Lajudie

Barbican Centre is owned, funded and managed by
the Corporation of London

Distributed in the USA by Rizzoli International
Publications, Inc. through St. Martin's Press,
175 Fifth Avenue, New York, NY 10010

ISBN 1 85894 172 5 (hardback)
ISBN 1 85894 173 3 (paperback)

Produced by Merrell Publishers Limited
Designed by Martin Harrison, with Tony Waddingham
Edited by Iain Ross and Anthea Snow

Printed and bound in Italy

Full information for images that appear in the
exhibition are given in the Biographies and Checklist
section, pp. 176–88. Bracketed numbers in the
captions indicate a cross-reference to that section.
Picture credits for all images are listed on p. 192.

Front jacket/cover: Jack Smith in his 'studio', 1956
(p. 12, detail)

CONTENTS

6 Foreword

7 Author's Acknowledgements

8 Lenders to the Exhibition

9 Art Partners

11 In Transition

22 Shadows and Utopias

46 Disruption

72 New Realisms

92 Opposing Forces

122 Cities/Bodies

148 Continuum

173 Notes

176 Biographies and Checklist

189 Selected Bibliography

190 Index

192 Picture Credits

Foreword

Transition: The London Art Scene in the Fifties is a logical follow-up to two exhibitions organized by the Barbican, *A Paradise Lost* (1987) and *The Sixties Art Scene in London* (1993), which surveyed British art of 1935–55 and the 1960s respectively. Taking a fresh look at the 1950s, a decade often eclipsed by World War II and the 'Swinging Sixties', the exhibition redefines the position of this decade in the history of British art. Recent years have seen increasing interest in the period, manifested by the current revival of Fifties fashion and design, as well as by such scholarly publications as Margaret Garlake's *New Art New World: British Art in Postwar Society* (1998). In addition, major retrospectives in 2001 of Michael Andrews (Tate Britain) and Frank Auerbach (Royal Academy of Arts) provided great opportunities to reappraise the achievements of two influential figures of British Art who emerged in the 1950s. *Transition* is a timely contribution to the further understanding of developments in post-war British art.

As the title *Transition* indicates, the exhibition identifies the 1950s as a period of unprecedented changes, preparing the way for the future. It was a period of rebuilding after the devastation of the War, a time to look forward and to progress. Under increasing American influence, popular consumerism and material culture began to make an impact on British life. However, the decade was also marked by political pessimism. Much of the world was divided into the two camps of the Cold War and was conscious of living under a nuclear threat. While the map of the world was being redrawn, a new generation of immigrants, encouraged to seek work in the West, began to arrive on the shores of Britain, gradually changing the texture of British society. In the context of this rapidly changing world, *Transition* explores the decade's creative innovators and how they prepared the way for the avant-garde of the Sixties, which would establish British art as one of the most influential forces in the international art scene.

In some senses, our world at the start of the twenty-first century has much that resonates with that of fifty years ago. Despite the fall of the Berlin Wall, which virtually ended the Cold War, world politics continues to be tense. America is a dominant force in the world economy, politics and popular culture. The new materialism as it emerged in the 1950s is at its zenith with credit card debt never higher; and the advancement of technology and media, which challenged traditional notions of art fifty years ago, continues to provide options for creative expression. It is interesting to contemplate where our world will go in the next decade, while looking back half a century to a decade of great transition.

In organizing this exhibition, we have been supported by a number of individuals and institutional colleagues, whom we acknowledge on page 7. Our special thanks go to Martin Harrison, the Guest Curator of this exhibition, who has worked tirelessly on our behalf. With his typical versatility, Martin has not only researched and selected the exhibition, but also designed this book and written its main essay.

Our thanks also extend to John Hoole, former Art Galleries Director, who initiated this project with Martin.

We are particularly grateful to all the lenders of this exhibition (listed on page 8) and to Resource: The Council for Museums, Archives and Libraries. Without their generosity and organizational support, this exhibition could not have materialized.

Carol Brown
Head of Art Galleries
Barbican Centre

Tomoko Sato
Curator
Barbican Art Galleries

Author's Acknowledgements

First, I wish to add my grateful thanks to all of the private collectors and public institutions, listed overleaf, who have kindly loaned works to the exhibition. Within these and other organizations many individuals have helped in my research and I want to record my appreciation of the following: Douglas Dreishspoon (Albright-Knox Art Gallery, Buffalo); Beth Miller (Yale Center for British Art); Lisa Webb (Leicestershire Museums, Arts and Records Service, Leicester); Isobel Johnstone (Arts Council Collection, Hayward Gallery, London); Adrian Glew and Victoria Lane (Tate Archive, The Condé Nast Publications Ltd, London); Emma Chambers (College Art Collections, University College, London); Lisa Hodgkins, Francesca Harrison and Christopher Pipe (Vogue Library); Juliet Thorp and Darlene Maxwell (Royal College of Art, London); Andrew Hunter (Gainsborough's House Museum, Sudbury); Ann Bukantas (Ferens Art Gallery, Kingston upon Hull); Isobel Hunter (Archivist, The National Gallery, London); Patrick Elliott, Richard Calvocoressi, Keith Hartley and Fiona Pearson (Scottish National Gallery of Modern Art, Edinburgh); and Alison Cowling (Northampton Museums and Art Gallery). Pat Jordan Evans of the Bohun Gallery was extremely helpful, as were Gerard Faggionato (Faggionato Fine Arts, London); Alan Cristea (Alan Cristea Gallery, London); Thomas Lighton (Waddington Galleries, London); and Chili Hawes and Karen Boston (October Gallery, London). Jane England made every effort to make paintings available to me, and I am also grateful to her for the exemplary catalogues she has produced of Fifties artists. Julian Hartnoll, a friend since the 1960s, has been constantly supportive, not least in allowing me extensive access to the archives of John Bratby.

Many individuals not listed as lenders have contributed enormously to this project, and special thanks are due to Michael Ashburner; Els Baeten; Elizabeth Beatty; Peter Blake; Denis Bowen; Barbara Braithwaite; Campbell Bruce; Nichola Bruce; Jon Catleugh; James Chesterman; Alfred Daniels; Ted Dicks; Joanna Drew; Mary Facetti; Annie Freud; Ken Garland; Philippe Garner; Mike Goldmark; Derrick Greaves; Alfred Rozelaar Green; Richard Hamilton; Ben Harrison; Brett Harrison; Richard Hollis; Don Hunstein; Ann Jellicoe; Julie Lawson; Julian Lax; James Meller; George Melly; Juliet Morchoisne; Lynda Morris; Jenny Mortimer; Robin Muir; Myles Murphy; Bernard Perlin; Monica Pidgeon; Toni del Renzio; Yvonne Robinson; Sylvia Sleigh; Richard Smith; Roger Spear; Jacqueline Stanley; Silvie Turner; Tony Waddingham; Nick Wadley; Victoria Walsh; and Professor Henry Walton. For digital camera technology, invaluable for recording artworks, my thanks to Graeme Chapman and Sara Cubitt of Olympus Optical Co. (U.K.) Ltd.

A simple list of names scarcely indicates the extent of my indebtedness to those I have mentioned above, nor, especially, to the artists in whose company it has been a privilege to share; to all of them I reiterate my sincere thanks. It remains to single out five friends: Richard Lannoy freely shared his experience of the Independent Group, which was a particularly gracious gesture in view of his forthcoming, and eagerly awaited, autobiography; he also informed this project in a much wider sense and all of our meetings were a great pleasure. Polly Hope most generously made available to me the library of her late husband, Theo Crosby, which was an invaluable resource, and Mary Spear similarly allowed me complete access to the archives of Ruskin Spear. Sadly, Leslie Duxbury died while this volume was on press, and I want to record my warm memories of an enjoyable and informative day spent with him. Lastly, I must mention the late David Sylvester, to whom all art historians are indebted for the art criticism that is his legacy. I knew him only in the last two years of his life, but throughout his illness I was never made to feel, though such was surely the case, that he had more pressing matters on hand: he was an inspiration.

The curatorial staff at the Barbican Art Galleries have ensured that our collaboration was, for me at least, a rewarding experience, and I wish to thank warmly Carol Brown, Tomoko Sato, Elina Middleton-Lajudie and Louise Vaughan. At Merrell Publishers, Matt Hervey, Iain Ross and Anthea Snow were extremely sympathetic collaborators. Finally, I wish to add a special acknowledgement to John Hoole, who was the director of Barbican Art Galleries in 1999 when he invited me to be the Guest Curator of what became *Transition*. I shall remain indebted to him for his advice and encouragement, and I hope he feels that the result goes some way to justifying the faith he showed.

Martin Harrison

Lenders to the Exhibition

Barbican Art Galleries would like to thank all those lenders listed below and those who wish to remain anonymous.

GERMANY
Museum Kunst Palast, Düsseldorf

ITALY
Germano Facetti

SPAIN
Andrée and Oscar Quitak Collection

UNITED KINGDOM
Arts Council Collection, Hayward Gallery, London
Michael Ashburner
Peter Blake
Sandra Blow
Dorothy Bohm
Bradford Art Galleries and Museums, Bradford
Sarah Braun
Rosemary Butler
Jon Catleugh
John Chillingworth
Brian Clarke
College Art Collections, University College, London
The Condé Nast Publications Ltd, London
Robyn Denny and The Redfern Galllery, London
England and Co. Gallery, London
The Estate of Francis Bacon, courtesy of Faggionato Fine Arts, London and Tony Shafrazi Gallery, New York
Private collection, courtesy of Faggionato Fine Arts, London
Ferens Art Gallery, Hull City Museums and Art Gallery, Kingston upon Hull
Annie Freud
Government Art Collection, London
Margot Hamilton Hill, ARCA
Rita Donagh
The Estate of Nigel Henderson
Laing Art Gallery, Tyne and Wear Museums, Newcastle-upon-Tyne
Richard Lannoy

The Artworks Loan Scheme, Leicestershire Museums, Arts and Records Service, Leicester
Roger Mayne
The Museum of London, London
Biddy Noakes
Northampton Town and County Art Society, Northampton
Jasia Reichardt
Royal College of Art Collection, London
Jack Smith
Mr & Mrs A.H. Sandford-Smith
Scottish National Gallery of Modern Art, Edinburgh
Alison and Peter Smithson, Architects, London
Southampton City Art Gallery, Southampton
Mrs Mary Spear
Swindon Museum and Art Gallery, Swindon Borough Council
The David Sylvester Literary Trust, London
Tate, London
William Turnbull, courtesy of Waddington Galleries, London
The Trustees of the Museums and Galleries of Northern Ireland (Ulster Museum)
National Museums and Galleries on Merseyside, Liverpool (Walker Art Gallery)
The Whitworth Art Gallery, University of Manchester, Manchester
Anna Yandell
York City Art Gallery, York

UNITED STATES OF AMERICA
Albright-Knox Art Gallery, Buffalo NY
Magda Cordell McHale, Buffalo NY
Irving Penn, New York NY

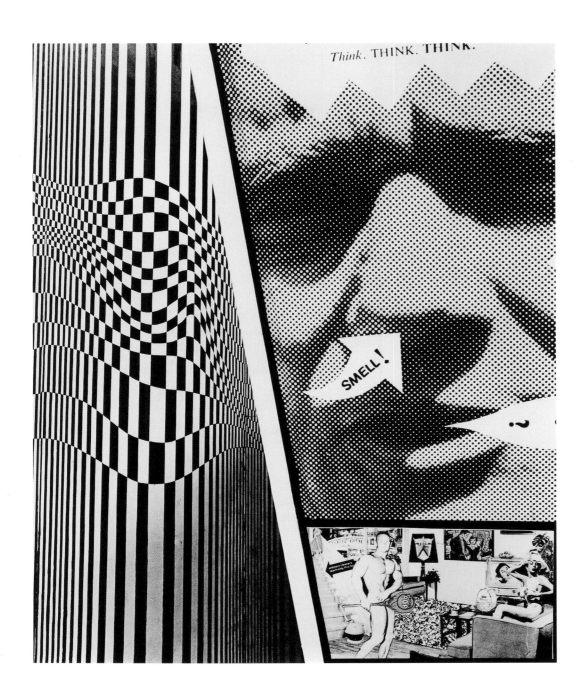

Richard Lannoy: Photograph of the installation by Richard Hamilton, John McHale and John Voelcker for the exhibition *This is Tomorrow*, Whitechapel Art Gallery, 1956. Collection of the artist

Art Partners

The Barbican would like to thank its current Art Partners

Linklaters
Clifford Chance
Merrill Lynch
Bloomberg
BP
Slaughter and May
Richards Butler

IN TRANSITION

'Sunday in London in the rain: the shops are shut, the streets almost deserted; the aspect is that of an immense and well-ordered cemetery. The few passers-by under their umbrellas, in the desert of squares and streets, have the look of uneasy spirits who have risen from their graves': this is not a description of a putative Neo-Romantic or Social Realist painting, but a passage from *Notes on England*, written by Hippolyte Taine in 1872. In 2000 the painters Richard Smith and Robyn Denny had arranged to meet at the Delfina Gallery, in Bermondsey. Heading for the bright, white, art space through a warren of dank and grubby Victorian railway arches near London Bridge, Smith was reminded of how dark and dreary London, still under the pall of gloom evoked by Taine, had appeared to him in 1950. He was reminded of a vision he had in the Fifties of discovering a resplendent art environment in London: in shabby, grey, austerity-era Britain he had sought a luminous and dynamic modernity.

For Smith, the experience of living and working through the Fifties was analogous to a journey from darkness into light. He entered the Royal College of Art (RCA) in 1954, just after the Kitchen Sink painters had left. One of his tutors, John Minton, had taught the Social Realists and commented on them: 'Doom being in, and Hope being out, the search amongst the cosmic dustbins is on, the atomic theme is unravelled.'[1] This barbed appraisal resonated with the generation of Smith and Denny, for whom Social Realist painting was parochial and drab – literally as well as metaphorically low-key. The flats of Hans and Elsbeth Juda in South Kensington, and Richard and Terry Hamilton in Highgate, were oases of modern design, and Smith found encouragement in his visits to them; but the lure of New York's light and spacious loft studios proved irresistible. In 1959 he left for the USA on a Harkness Travelling Fellowship and, unusually for a British painter (Bernard Cohen, David Hockney and Malcolm Morley are the other notable exceptions), has subsequently spent most of his life there.

The transition to which the title of this exhibition refers is intended to signify the unprecedented changes that occurred in British art between 1950 and 1960. The Fifties began during the Cold War, with the Labour government, having nationalized much of Britain's industrial base and established the welfare state, entering its last year in power. In 1957 Prime Minister Harold Macmillan's vaunted 'most of our people have never had it so good' speech ushered in burgeoning consumerism; by the end of the decade Britain was economically stable and relatively affluent, but, like the rest of the world, still under the threat of nuclear annihilation.

After peace was declared in October 1945, Britain embarked on a programme of recovery and reconstruction. But, faced with a crippled economy and devastated infrastructure the euphoria of victory rapidly subsided: in 1946 the popular Victoria and Albert Museum exhibition *Britain Can Make It*, which aimed to promote improved design standards in export goods, was sarcastically re-christened 'Britain Can't Have It' by many among its huge audience. The arts had been disrupted, but the six-year wartime hiatus ultimately acted as a spur to fundamental change, which was accelerated by the post-war collapse of social, political and ethical certainties. The Suez débacle marked the end of imperialist dreams in 1956; the same year was also a turning point in British art of the Fifties: it witnessed, for example, the first large-scale exhibition of American Abstract Expressionism in Britain, the first Social Realist writings of the Angry Young Men, and a fledgling mass-media-based Pop Art. Such disparate impulses cannot be embraced under a single heading as either the logical consequence of a political crisis or as a reaction to conservative values; nor were they the only tendencies in British art.

(opposite) **Anthony Bisley**: Robyn Denny and Richard Smith painting at the RCA, 1957. Collection of Robyn Denny

Photographer unknown: Jack Smith in his 'studio', 1956. From a magazine illustration pasted in one of John Bratby's scrapbooks. Private collection courtesy of Julian Hartnoll

Stylistic heterogeneity does not lend itself to facile chronological or thematic classification, and pioneer projects that explored the art of the Fifties dealt with this by narrowing their frames of reference. *The Forgotten Fifties* (Graves Art Gallery, Sheffield, 1984) and *The Fifties* (The British Council, 1998) concentrated on Social Realism and on the St Ives painters respectively. *Transition* is concerned primarily with works that relate to either the urban environment or the human body, and is dominated, therefore, by figurative art; Margaret Garlake's *New Art New World: British Art in Postwar Society* (1998) is an indispensable guide to the broader picture. In the subtitle of *Transition*, 'London' was substituted for 'British' because it more accurately indicated its scope, not for reasons of provocative metrocentrism. Most of the artists represented here lived, during the period under review, in London. The more talented students from provincial art schools also tended to gravitate to one of the leading London schools to complete their studies. Jack Smith, for example, moved from Sheffield College of Art to St Martin's School of Art in 1948, and continued at the RCA from 1950. Asked whether he agreed with Bryan Robertson's remark that cultural life in the provinces was a 'desolate and lonely wilderness', he replied, 'I feel that the wilderness starts ten miles from the centre of London in any direction'.[2]

Transition is biased towards those artists for whom 'the creative act is nourished by the urban environment they have always lived in',[3] a view advocated by the influential critic Lawrence Alloway, who was committed to the plurality of city culture and 'non-pastoral, pro-urban, technological art'.[4] London's social life, and in particular the Bohemian underworlds of Soho and Fitzrovia, was a lure for many of the painters featured in *Transition*; like Baudelaire, they flourished 'among the roofs and towers ... the restless workshop ... the many-masted city'. Rural England, however, continued to exert its opposite attraction: Michael Ayrton left the city in 1952 and wrote to a patron: 'In the matter of Geography! Ayrton has retired from the Great Metropolis to Pastoral Solitude in the hope that by Meditation, Peace and Economy he may restore his Equilibrium.'[5] The urbanists took a negative view of this kind of exodus, which, they contended, was to reject a vital source of inspiration: as Theo Crosby remarked of another self-imposed retreat into the countryside, it was a journey to 'the boondock from which no-one ever returns'.[6]

There were several attempts in the twentieth century to define schools of artists under the banner of the capital city. The London Group was founded in 1913 by Camden Town Post-Impressionists and younger Vorticists, the city's avant garde in dissent from the Royal Academy of Arts's hegemony. A jubilee exhibition of the group's work, held at the Tate Gallery in 1964, included several of the artists featured in *Transition*, such as David Bomberg (who had been a founder member), John Bratby, William Gear, Ceri Richards, Julian Trevelyan, Keith Vaughan, Brian Wall and Carel Weight. The Ecole de Londres proposed in 1948 by David Sylvester (then based in Paris and at his most Francophile) was taken up in the following year by Patrick Heron, who sought to bridge abstract and figurative art in an eclectic School of London in which St Ives artists were prominent, but Bacon and Freud more marginal. These initiatives gathered limited support, but in 1976 R.B. Kitaj gained a more positive response with his School of London, essayed in *The Human Clay*, an exhibition he selected for the Arts Council that argued cogently for the value of sustained prowess in draughtsmanship. His school encompassed some of the 'ten or more people in this town, or not far away, of world class'. In 1987 the term was adopted in two major exhibitions organized by the Royal Academy of Arts and by the British Council respectively to denote a smaller group comprising Bacon, Freud, Auerbach, Kossoff and Andrews, augmented in the latter instance by Kitaj himself.

Ruskin Spear: *Home Guard's Dream*, 1940. Watercolour on paper, 30 × 42 cm. Collection of Mrs Mary Spear

Humphrey Jennings wrote to his wife at the end of the War: 'England has, you will find, changed a great deal ... the young coming up are pretty determined – and people in general have had a good think.'[7] The leading artists in Britain in 1945 were, by general consensus, Paul Nash, Henry Moore, Ben Nicholson, John Piper and Graham Sutherland. But Francis Bacon's *Three Studies for Figures at the Base of a Crucifixion* (1944), exhibited at the Lefevre Gallery in 1945, violently disrupted both geometric abstraction and Neo-Romanticism and announced a more disturbing leader of the avant garde. *Transition* concentrates on the generation of artists that came to prominence in London in the period after 1945. During the planning stage of the exhibition *This is Tomorrow* in 1956, the Director of the Whitechapel Art Gallery, Bryan Robertson, wrote to the organizer, Theo Crosby, to say that while he did not wish to appear 'like an old fogey' he urged the inclusion of 'a contribution from the Hepworth–Nicholson faction'.[8] Crosby ignored the suggestion, and these distinguished artists are similarly absent from *Transition*. In 1954 Eduardo Paolozzi epitomized the reaction against the elder statesmen of art when he described Henry Moore as 'a continual source of visual surprise and inspiration', but qualified his praise with, 'However, he is still a man of the 30s and the idea of holes in wood for sculpture is not for us today'.[9]

Eduardo Paolozzi: *Untitled*, 1955.
Wax (presumed not to be extant, dimensions unknown)

Following the International Surrealist Exhibition, organized by Herbert Read and Roland Penrose at the New Burlington Galleries in 1936, Surrealism belatedly engaged many British artists; brought to an abrupt halt by the onset of war, after 1945 it lost its impetus. Julian Trevelyan, whose paintings had been included in the exhibition, cited the War as the reason for its demise: 'It became absurd', he commented, 'to compose Surrealist confections ... when German soldiers with Tommy-guns descended from the clouds on parachutes dressed as nuns',[10] an event satirized in Ruskin Spear's *Home Guard's Dream*. Yet the tenets of European Surrealism persisted:

Richard Lannoy: Lee Miller with Richard and Terry Hamilton at a party at the Penroses', 1951 (no. 62)

they were a constant in the paintings of Francis Bacon, who was fond of describing himself as a 'medium for accident and chance', and Eduardo Paolozzi has always located his own work within a Surrealist context. Although it gradually diversified, the Institute of Contemporary Arts (ICA) was dominated initially by Surrealist sympathizers such as E.L.T. Mesens, Robert Melville and Herbert Read; Roland Penrose and Peter Watson were, in addition, on hand to top up Arts Council funding when required. Penrose's collection, which included important works by Picasso, Ernst, Miró, de Chirico and Tanguy, was a vital resource for artists affiliated to the ICA at a time when modern art of any kind was virtually absent from public collections.

In 1945 younger exponents of Neo-Romanticism had to come to terms again with Picasso. The popular exhibitions of Picasso's and Matisse's work at the Victoria and Albert Museum in 1945–46 brought the 'Picasso question' into sharp focus: 'After Picasso and Matisse', John Minton despaired, 'there is nothing more to be done.'[11] But with European travel feasible again, British artists were able to break out of their enforced isolation from Continental influences. Initially, Paris was the favoured destination: Eduardo Paolozzi, William Gear, William Turnbull, Adrian Heath and Nigel Henderson made frequent or extended visits there, formative for all of them, and Raymond Mason moved there permanently in 1946. The Anglo-French Art Centre, founded by Alfred Rozelaar Green in the old St John's Wood Art School in 1946, was another locus for French and other European influences: during its two-year existence, André L'Hôte, Jean Lurçat, Germaine Richier and Fernand Léger all visited London to exhibit or lecture there.

The Festival of Britain in 1951 was intended to boost morale in a nation only slowly climbing out of austerity, and to act as a beacon of the promised new prosperity. Timed to mark the centenary of the Great Exhibition of 1851 at the Crystal Palace, several of the exhibits, such as the Arts Council's *Masterpieces of Victorian Photography*, the ICA's *Ten Decades: A Review of British Taste* and Julian Trevelyan's mural of the Crystal Palace, addressed this theme. The Great Exhibition had aimed to advertise Britain's products and celebrate its empire, unscathed by the revolutions that had shaken Continental Europe. But behind the country's power and prosperity lay extremes of social inequality and deprivation. One way in which Dickens addressed this problem in his novels was by elevating the disenfranchised poor to sainthood; a century later the Marxist art critic John Berger similarly deified the workman. In this context it was ironic that the Labour party, which had planned the festival, lost power in the 1951 elections.

There was no consistent pattern to the political affiliations of artists in the Fifties. The idealism of middle-class left-wing intellectuals of the 1930s had largely dissipated, so that in 1951 the return of a Tory government, which remained in control throughout the decade, was generally met with nothing stronger than resignation. At the ICA, the most avant-garde of London's art institutions, the Senior Secretary, Brenda Pool, tried to persuade the young gallery assistant, Richard Lannoy, to join the Labour party; but while not unsympathetic, he was not alone in responding to the defeat of socialism with indifference. Despite the short-lived support of John Berger for Social Realism, its chief exponents, John Bratby, Jack Smith, Edward Middleditch and Derrick Greaves, did not share his faith in Marxism, nor, apart from Bratby, did they sustain their interest in Social Realism beyond 1956. A broader realism was proposed by David Sylvester and others. The confrontation between Berger and Sylvester was fought not only over a definition of realism but also from the opposite poles of art as socialism and art as existentialism: Berger believed that art must morally elevate the spectator, while for Sylvester it had been liberated by Sartre from any a priori function to exist as *art*, rather than as history or as dogma.

Photographer unknown: Party at the Anglo-French Art Centre, *c.* 1947. Collection of Anna Yandell

The membership of the Artists International Association (AIA), a body formed in 1933 in the context of the social and political conflict of the Depression, spanned realism, Surrealism, and abstraction, and by 1936 totalled more than six hundred artists, the majority of whom were British. The AIA remained active until 1971, but its radicalism declined after the War, a shift that was confirmed by the removal of the association's political clause in 1953. The new mood was anticipated in a statement published by the AIA Exhibition Committee in a newsletter of 1949, which was anxious to declare that the association's gallery had 'no political basis whatever'.

Among the signatories to this was the curator and critic Lawrence Alloway. Three years later Alloway became a member of the Independent Group at the ICA. Fiercely committed to intellectual and artistic freedom, and operating at the margins of the art establishment, the Independent Group remained fundamentally apolitical. It did, however, launch a revisionist assault on established art theory. The idea that all images may convey meaning, that analysing a science-fiction movie could reveal as much about the culture that produced it as does a Renoir painting, was revolutionary in Britain and was to have a profound impact: this Brutalist challenge to Oxbridge hegemony was to alter the basis of art discourse and, to a certain extent, facilitated art that was freer from class imperatives.

Kurt Schwitters: *Difficult*, c. 1942–43.
Collage, 79.4 × 61 cm. Albright-Knox Art Gallery, Buffalo NY
(Gift of the Seymour H. Knox Foundation, Inc. 1965)

Francis Newton Souza: *The Emperor*, 1958 (no. 94)

The insularity of British art increasingly preoccupied artists and critics in the Fifties. From 1952 Bryan Robertson mounted, at the Whitechapel Art Gallery, a range of exhibitions that promoted a more international outlook. He expressed concern in 1946 about a 'nationally conscious' school of painting, and drew attention to the dangers of 'erecting artificial barriers against outside influence'.[12] But given the low international standing of British art, the desire for regeneration is understandable: the extent to which external influences were resisted remains a debatable topic. In the 1930s Franz Kline and Mark Tobey both lived and worked in England largely unnoticed, but this was at an early stage in their careers. Kurt Schwitters lived in almost complete oblivion in England from 1940 until his death in 1948; however, three contemporary Jewish refugees, Jankel Adler, Josef Herman and Franciszka Themerson, were supported and admired. The immigration of Afro-Asian artists after 1946 is, however, a more vexed issue, since some of these artists have testified to having suffered from racist attitudes. The reorientation of British art in the Fifties, from the influence of France to that of the United States, was itself affected by questions of national identity, and by an innate tendency to translate foreign influences in an indigenous manner. Between the two Tate Gallery exhibitions of American art in 1956 and 1959, the breakdown of anti-American prejudice gave a fresh impetus to gestural abstract art in Britain, a development that impinged on artists both inside and outside the present study. The Independent Group had already embraced transatlantic art and culture, and the legacy of their researches combined with art practice in significant ways after 1956.

A pervading theme in *Transition* concerns the response to photography. The Fifties are often seen as the decade that laid the foundations for British art of the 1960s, but many artists were preoccupied with retrieving the threads of Modernism that had been severed in 1939. One of the most significant developments in art to be truncated by the War was the influence of photography and films. In the 1930s Walter Sickert based many of his late masterpieces on photographs, Henry Moore took up photography at the same time to record his sculpture, and William Coldstream, who recognized Degas's indebtedness to the snapshot, briefly abandoned painting to join John Grierson's General Post Office film unit in 1934. In the same decade John Piper and Paul Nash both took photographs that informed their topographical or Surrealist interests, and Francis Bacon used an x-ray radiograph as source material for one of his paintings. Photography was debated in front of a packed house at the ICA in 1952, by which time it had also become an important topic at the Slade School of Fine Art. Less expectedly, John Minton identified the influence of photography on his Social Realist protégés, bemoaning the impact of 'The cinema eye, the over-exposed photograph'.[13] The dialogue with photography was not, however, universal: it plays no discernible part, for example, in the work of one of Britain's leading painters, Frank Auerbach, who has also maintained a lifelong resistance to television.

To divide art into decades is, of course, to apply an artificial construct, and sacrifices accuracy to convenience. A definition of British art in the Fifties would need to encompass at least Neo-Romanticism, Social Realism, Geometric and Painterly Abstraction, and Pop Art. Certain paintings incorporated elements of more than one of these idioms, or artists might begin their careers by adhering to a currently fashionable style before finding their own direction: many viewers familiar with the sculptures made by Bryan Kneale since the 1960s might be surprised by the realist portraits he painted in the Fifties. As it opened up again to Continental influences, the complexity of the London art scene was increasingly evident. Patrick Heron (important as a critic and as a painter) visited Paris in 1949, and William Gear lived there from 1948 to 1950; they were conduits for the filtration into Britain of the work of the Ecole de Paris, whose paintings

Hans Hammarsköld: Bryan Kneale, 1955. The Condé Nast Publications Ltd, London

An unpublished variant from a series of portraits of Kneale that Hammarsköld took for Vogue. Hammarsköld's photographs were exhibited at the ICA in 1955.

Nicolas de Staël: *Le Ciel rouge*, 1952. Oil on canvas, 130.8 × 162.9 cm. Collection Walker Art Center, Minneapolis (Gift of the T.B. Walker Foundation, 1954)

De Staël, who committed suicide aged forty-one in 1955, and was the subject of a major retrospective at the Whitechapel Art Gallery in 1956, was an influential figure in Britain throughout the Fifties. John Berger was a strong supporter of de Staël, especially when, immediately after painting *Le Ciel rouge*, his work became more overtly figurative.

offered an alternative to the perceived crisis in figuration, to the anthropocentrism that equated depictions of the figure with humanism. The allusions to identifiable subjects in Nicolas de Staël's Tachiste paintings, as well as their bold impasto, were adopted by many British artists; the de Staël exhibition at the Matthiesen Gallery in 1952 impressed certain painters previously hostile to abstraction, such as Keith Vaughan. Vaughan's struggle to reconcile abstraction and figuration epitomized the dilemma of many of his contemporaries – Heron himself, and Roger Hilton, for example, alternated between these two modes: their indecision is ultimately what provoked unfavourable comparisons with the work of their American counterparts. The vigour and spontaneity of gestural Action Painters such as Georges Mathieu (who was included in the ICA exhibition *Opposing Forces* in 1953) inspired many of the younger British artists emerging in the mid-Fifties, a tendency that increased under the impact of the scale, confidence and physical presence of the American Abstract Expressionist paintings shown at the Tate Gallery in 1956.

A phenomenon that, while not exclusive to British painting, was prevalent across a range of artists in the early Fifties was a predilection for pulsating colour, a luminescence that may relate to the flickering waves of incandescent and neon lighting; its powerful emergence may indicate a reaction to wartime 'blackout' restrictions as well as to contemporary dullness. In France only the paintings of Pierre Soulages and Alfred Manessier were comparable; the glow of Manessier's pigments is integral to stained glass, the medium in which light is transmitted through coloured glass held in black armatures, and in which he was a designer. It is evident in certain abstract paintings by Gear, Heron and Hilton in which the unfixed, oscillating viewpoints and illusory space also relate to 'afocalism' as defined by David Sylvester (see p. 50 for a related phenomenon, the kinetic 'flicker' of Francis Bacon's paintings). The interpenetration

Patrick Heron: *Two Women in a Café*, 1950 (no. 53)

Arguably Heron's early masterpiece, in which he has integrated the influence of Braque, Matisse and ideogrammatic Klee with spirit and confidence.

Willem de Kooning: *Woman*, 1950.
Oil, cut and pasted paper, on cardboard, 37.5 × 29.5 cm. The Metropolitan Museum of Art, New York, from the collection of Thomas B. Hess (Gift of the heirs of Thomas B. Hess, 1984) (1984.613.6)

In its unalloyed expressiveness and brash conviction – T.J. Clark calls it vulgarity – *Woman* clearly exemplifies the distinction between British and American painting in the Fifties.

of light and dark, which connects to contemporary social fluctuations and instability, has a further modern, urban analogy with the spatial and temporal 'porosity' observed by Walter Benjamin in the city of Naples.

After 1959 the reputations of some of the artists featured in *Transition* declined. The attention paid to Pop and Op Art in the 1960s eclipsed the priorities of the 1950s, and the onset of Minimalism, Performance and Conceptual Art by the end of the decade marginalized much, if not most, representational art. In 1969 John Bratby, by then long displaced from the avant garde, cited Roy Lichtenstein and Yoko Ono as examples of the current 'disbelief in painting' and Duchamp as 'the chess-player and nihilist'.[14] In the context of the renewed interest in draughtsmanship in the Post-Modern 1980s, *The Forgotten Fifties* exhibition was less anachronistic than would have been

Wols (Wolfgang Schulze): *Oui, Oui, Oui,* 1946–47.
Oil on canvas, 79.7 × 65.1 cm. The Menil Collection, Houston

the case a decade earlier, and it probably contributed to the increasing viability of the 'Modern British Art' market in the salerooms. In 1987 the critic Peter Fuller founded the magazine *Modern Painters*, and concurrent with the revived awareness of the excellence of British figurative art other milestones were reached, such as the expanded School of London exhibition *The Pursuit of the Real*, which toured to the Barbican Art Gallery in 1990.

At the Royal Academy of Arts in 1832 the architect Sir John Soane exhibited a painting of the rotunda of the Bank of England. It was imagined in ruins. In the all-too-prescient belief that his vision of a 'New Rome' would perish, he had engaged J.M. Gandy to paint his then newly completed dome. To this projection of romantic ruin he appended a line spoken by Prospero in *The Tempest*: 'Yea, all of which it inherit shall dissolve.' In the event, much of Soane's bank was obliterated by extensive rebuilding in the 1920s, pre-empting the wartime destruction of a third of the fabric of the City. London as palimpsest, as the site for cycles of renewal, becomes, then, a principal theme of *Transition*.

SHADOWS AND UTOPIAS

'LONDON, cathedral of black bones ... where streets glint, grudgingly, like shabby coins

and, much-pummelled, the body's putty sags' – *Nigel Henderson*

'The powerful attraction that Blake's genius radiates today ... has led,

by way of Palmer and his other disciple, Edward Calvert, the exponent

also of a kind of biblical arcadia, to a revived interest in the whole,

unequalled achievement of the Romantic school.' – *Robin Ironside*

'... the Festival had a real and lasting effect on private life in Britain.

Clothes, streets, houses and thousands of things in daily use have

slowly got brighter and lighter ever since ... .' – *Barbara Jones*

David Bomberg: *Evening in the City of London*, 1944 (no. 15)

David Bomberg's *Evening in the City of London* (1944), the most moving of all paintings of wartime Britain, fixes the heart of the capital at a moment of enforced transition, as the tabula rasa envisaged by Soane. Bomberg was himself a fire-watcher and his mutilated City glows at the red end of the spectrum – the red of embers and the heraldic red of London. The raised viewpoint – Bomberg was allowed into a church tower to make a preliminary charcoal sketch[1] – provides a haunting perspectival sweep across effaced buildings to St Paul's Cathedral, dark and brooding on the horizon, a defiant survivor looming above the debris, damaged but not obliterated. Wren's cathedral had itself replaced the medieval church destroyed in the Great Fire of London, the dramatic palimpsest of 1666. St Paul's distinctive dome, a symbol of continuity for Bomberg, was the first such structure to be built in London; the influence of Bramante's St Peter's Cathedral, Rome, had filtered through to Paris, which Wren visited in 1665. The alien dome's enduring potency as a symbol was again exemplified in London in 1951 with Ralph Tubbs's saucer-shaped Dome of Discovery for the Festival of Britain, and the form controversially re-emerged further downstream on the bank of the River Thames to be identified with the new millennium.

Bomberg had lived in London since the age of five, when his family moved from Birmingham to Whitechapel. *Evening in the City of London*, together with his vigorous charcoal sketches of the blitzed City, drawn between 1944 and 1946, were more than topographical documents: they were deeply felt personal statements. They occupy an important position in Bomberg's turbulent career, marred as it was after 1914 by intermittent periods of doubt and lack of support. Soon after war was declared in 1939, Bomberg lobbied to be appointed an official war artist; he was unsuccessful, but as a sop he was commissioned in 1942 to paint a bomb store near Burton-on-Trent. The remarkable oil studies he made there are replete with the pregnant destructive power of the one-thousand-pound bombs neatly but ominously stacked in their subterranean vault. The studies erupt, their splintered, jagged forms slashed with intense blue and scarlet: he was painting beyond the nominal subject to distil the violent potential of weapons of mass destruction. This direct engagement with the consequences of war was the antithesis of the morale-boosting, reassuring picturesque favoured by the War Artists Advisory Committee (WAAC); Bomberg's request to return to make a large oil painting was refused, and the studies were never hung in the WAAC exhibitions at the National Gallery. But the *Bomb Store* studies did, at least, help to lift Bomberg out of a creative impasse, and seven years of renewed invention followed, distinguished by masterpieces that ranged from the flower paintings of 1943 to the Devon and Cornwall landscapes of 1946–47.

One of the greatest British artists of the twentieth century, Bomberg died in 1957 in poverty and neglect. He had been a founder member of the London Group in 1914, and such paintings as *In The Hold* (1913–14) and *The Mud Bath* (1914) briefly secured him a place at the head of Britain's avant garde. But service in the trenches, and the stylistic compromise he was forced to accept over his Canadian War Memorial commission in 1917, seemed to shatter his confidence. His artistic integrity and dogged individualism precluded any easy or lucrative paths, and admiration for the dynamism of his urban Vorticism turned to incomprehension when he began to paint careful, modest, naturalistic landscapes. A pivotal trip to Spain in 1929 set him on a new course, however, and here he began to develop his mature style, characterized by the vigorous brushwork and 'eloquence of paint' of *Self-Portrait* and *Red Hat* (both of 1931). The importance of the work did not, however, translate into recognition, and as far as the art market was concerned, Bomberg slipped further into obscurity.

Leon Kossoff: *City Building Site*, 1959 (no. 61)

In 1945 repeated attempts to alleviate his family's poverty by securing a teaching post were rewarded by his appointments as a part-time lecturer at Borough Polytechnic and as a teacher of draughtsmanship, one day a week, at the Bartlett School of Architecture, University College, London. The Bartlett appointment, considering Bomberg's disavowal of perspective, was perhaps the more surprising, but he was employed there on the advice of Sir Charles Reilly, former head of the Liverpool University School of Architecture. Reilly, notwithstanding his academic, Beaux-Arts principles, apparently recognized Bomberg's interest in the structure of buildings, as well as the inherent grasp of mass and volume exemplified in his drawings of bombed London. Professor Albert Richardson, who became head of the Bartlett School in 1945, encouraged Bomberg to take his students on trips to sketch London buildings, since he shared the view expressed by Bomberg's wife, Lilian, that 'a sense of form is so important a necessity in their field'.[2]

Lilian Bomberg also drew attention to the significance, especially for her husband's later paintings, of the optical theories of George Berkeley, Bishop of Cloyne. From Berkeley's 'view that the eye is a feeble and limited instrument of perception'[3] it followed that two-dimensional vision must be augmented, 'that the sense of Touch and associations of Touch produce on sight the illusion of the third dimension'.[4] This emphasis on the tactile was central to Bomberg's passionate crusade to realize mass and volume on a flat surface. The density of paint in his late works does not, however, obscure its fluidity: within the accretive layers of impasto the rapidity and conviction of their execution ensures the extraordinary energy of the surface.

Among Bomberg's pupils, Frank Auerbach and Leon Kossoff responded to his inspirational teaching by extending his ideas: the tribute they paid him was to pursue their individual paths,

Leon Kossoff: *St Paul's Building Site*, 1954 (no. 59)

Frank Auerbach: *Earl's Court Buiding Site*,
1955 (no. 5)

Frank Auerbach: *Building Site, Victoria Street*,
1959 (no. 6)

Frank Auerbach: *Primrose Hill*, 1959 (no. 7)

pushing beyond Bomberg's achievements to extremes he had not imagined. With the same unwavering commitment, their art has constantly regenerated itself until the present day. From 1948 until 1953 Auerbach and Kossoff studied and painted together, first at St Martin's School of Art and then at the Royal College of Art (RCA); but they also attended (Auerbach from 1947 and Kossoff from 1950) Bomberg's evening classes at Borough Polytechnic. Bomberg's methods were unconventional – his lessons on the elucidation of sight from the memory of touch were transmitted by osmosis rather than verbally – but he inspired veneration among those receptive to his ideas. Auerbach has spoken of the 'atmosphere of research and radicalism that was extremely stimulating'[5] at Borough Polytechnic, and Kossoff acknowledged, 'it was through my contact with Bomberg that I felt I might actually function as a painter'.[6]

Auerbach and Kossoff shared Bomberg's steadfast belief that a painting is an independent image, that it exists as an autonomous object. In view of the high international reputations that Auerbach and Kossoff have justly won, it should be stressed that they have achieved their present status by evolving quite distinct styles – they should not, as one critic rightly insisted, be seen as Siamese twins. But both were, and remain today, painters of London. Auerbach, who had 'a strong sense that London hasn't been properly painted'[7] in the way that Paris or New York had, commented, 'I hate leaving my studio ... I hate leaving London'.[8] Kossoff, who was born on the City Road, close to St Paul's Cathedral, said, 'Ever since the age of twelve I have drawn and painted London'.[9] They re-cast Bomberg's early dictum 'I want to translate the life of a great city, its motion, its machinery, into an art that shall not be photographic, but expressive'[10] for an age more ambivalent about the machine aesthetic and the 'steel city'.

Cityscapes and construction sites (and occasionally demolition sites) were predominant among the most important paintings by Auerbach and Kossoff in the Fifties; their other principal subject, the isolated existential figure (even, in Kossoff's case, when it is part of a bustling crowd) was less prominent before the 1960s. This thematic consistency had its subjective motivations, but it can also be read as a metaphor for the rebuilding of London – in lineal descent, therefore, from Bomberg's anguished painting of a city in ruins. Kossoff's *St Paul's Building Site* (1954), surely lays claim, in this respect, to its art-historical lineage. Although the palette of both artists subsequently became more vivid, in the Fifties their cityscapes emerged – or their original visualization of them re-emerged in the studio – from within thickly encrusted layers of paint, as though the re-conceptualization of a fact might be rendered more real by invoking the physical approximation of the earth and concrete that were the substance of their subjects.

Shadow of War

The origins of British Neo-Romanticism can be traced to 1924 and the discovery by Graham Sutherland, William Larkins and Paul Drury of the drawings of Samuel Palmer. But as a cohesive movement it began in the 1930s: confronted with European abstract and Surrealist tendencies in art that they felt could not be assimilated into British traditions without modification, Graham Sutherland, Paul Nash and John Piper sought inspiration in the indigenous early nineteenth-century Romanticism of Blake, Palmer, Turner and Fuseli. Piper's *British Romantic Artists*, published in 1942, included paintings by Nash, Sutherland and Frances Hodgkins, and made explicit the continuity between the nineteenth and twentieth centuries. The yearning for an idyllic agrarian past that saw artists turn towards the British landscape acquired a new intensity with the onset of war: with both the national fabric and cultural heritage under threat, Britain's topography assumed an increased significance. The record of destruction was taken up immediately after the first major urban air raids, and in October 1940 Piper was sent by Kenneth Clark to paint the still-smouldering ruins of Coventry Cathedral. Doleful catalogues of loss followed, including James Pope-Hennessy's *History Under Fire*, with photographs by Cecil Beaton, and the *Country Life* publication *Britain Under Fire*, both in 1941, and *The Bombed Buildings of Britain*, edited by J.M. Richards, in 1942.

Four of the first volumes of *Penguin Modern Painters*, published in 1943 and 1944, were devoted to Sutherland, Nash, Piper and Henry Moore. This popular series was edited by Kenneth Clark, who had appointed all four as war artists; at the cessation of hostilities in 1945 the same four were widely regarded as among Britain's leading six or seven artists. But their status was soon under threat from a generation of critics impatient with what they interpreted as parochialism. In *Nine Abstract Artists* (1954) the twenty-eight-year-old Lawrence Alloway was as contemptuous of the 'official war-artists' as he was of the 'new generation (Vaughan, John Craxton, Minton). Both the loyal men and the dreamy boys developed an imagery of landscape which implied a kind of dark, meditative patriotism. The sceptred isle became an armoured womb'.[11]

John Piper suggested that 'British romantic movements are too vague and prolific to chart.'[12] As if to confirm this, Robin Ironside, in *Painting Since 1939*, proposed a definition of Neo-Romanticism that managed to embrace Stanley Spencer, Ceri Richards, Ben Nicholson, Francis Bacon and Lucian Freud. Ironside's pamphlet was not published until 1947, when, ironically, Neo-Romanticism was about to enter into decline. He identified a 'Rising Generation' of artists

Lucian Freud: *Portrait of John Minton*, 1952. Oil on canvas, 40 × 25.4 cm. Royal College of Art Collection, London

Jankel Adler: *Woman with Raised Hands*, 1948–49.
Oil on wood, 78 × 58 cm. The Israel Museum, Jerusalem
(Gift of Mr Ludwig Jesselson, New York)

whose indebtedness to senior figures established a hierarchy of descent: thus, he explained, Keith Vaughan paid tribute to Moore and to Sutherland and Piper, John Minton to Palmer, Robert Colquhoun and Robert MacBryde to 'surrealistic influences from Europe'. Among all of the younger Neo-Romantics, the most overt debt was to Graham Sutherland; in particular to the most intensely poetic of his drawings of the natural landscape imbued with undertones of foreboding, made between 1938 and 1941.

In 1942 Colquhoun and MacBryde moved into a studio at 77 Bedford Gardens, Kensington, where they were soon joined by John Minton. All three were talented, but in search of a style. A promising student at Glasgow School of Art in the 1930s, Colquhoun had been influenced by both the palette and the sharp angularity of Wyndham Lewis. At Glasgow he began a lifelong relationship with Robert MacBryde, and won a travelling scholarship that enabled them to tour France and Italy in 1938 and 1939. At the same time Minton was in Paris with Michael Ayrton, where both came strongly under the influence of the Paris-based, Russian-born Neo-Romantics Eugene Berman and Pavel Tchelitchew. In 1941 Jankel Adler (1895–1949) was invalided out of the Polish Army in Glasgow; he moved to London two years later and took a studio above Minton, Colquhoun and MacBryde in Bedford Gardens. Adler was an experienced artist who

John Minton: *Children of the Gorbals*, 1945 (no. 76)

had been friendly with Paul Klee and had absorbed Picasso's monumentalism; for his young colleagues he was a respected conduit for European Modernist influences.

Minton had forged a bleak urban Romanticism about 1940, on to which he began to graft figures whose anatomical idiosyncrasies were derived from Picasso by way of Adler. *Children of the Gorbals*, like *Children by the Sea* (1945) and *Rotherhithe from Wapping* (1946), was painted at the height of Adler's influence, evident in its rich colour and the conventionalized mannerisms of the drawing. In these urban arcadias Minton's disengaged figures intensify the melancholic atmosphere. The subject of *Children of the Gorbals* may have been suggested by the Sadler's Wells ballet *Miracle of the Gorbals*, which opened in London in October 1944; although Minton visited Glasgow during Christmas 1944 the stuccoed Georgian building in the background of his painting is distinctly un-Glaswegian, though comparable to one of Edward Burra's sets for the ballet.

Robert Colquhoun: *Woman with a Birdcage*, 1946 (no. 24)

Robert MacBryde: *Still Life, c.* 1947 (no. 64)

Robert Colquhoun's first one-man show in London was held at the Lefevre Gallery in 1943. The work of the 'Two Roberts', as Colquhoun and MacBryde were known, was highly regarded in post-war London, but the esteem in which they were held was short-lived. This is less a reflection on their merits than on their timing, for no sooner did their work elicit admiration than a reaction set in against Neo-Romanticism, inextricably associated with wartime gloom. Although as colourists they would appear to be beyond criticism, both artists were attacked for the excessive flatness of their paintings, which was attributed to a combination of the influence of Adler and Picasso and a native neo-Celticism. Bryan Robertson, who admitted Colquhoun had been 'marking time in his painting', generously mounted a retrospective at the Whitechapel Art Gallery in 1958, by which time the painter was widely ignored. Robertson's catalogue preface noted Colquhoun's 'by no means straightforward vision of women', who were 'seen with a masculine gaze and commented upon by a masculine intelligence'.[13] Among Colquhoun's most important paintings, which mostly date from the late 1940s, many were of women. The figure in *Woman with a Birdcage* (1946) is represented as tense, angst-ridden, isolated; in the contemporaneous *Two Scotswomen* (1946), the angular, Picasso-esque figures appear anxiously self-absorbed, psychologically though not physically dissociated. Although MacBryde's paintings never achieved this level of originality, and lacked the psychological penetration, the tendency to classify him as the junior partner of Colquhoun should not obscure a considerable talent. MacBryde was an eclectic, and his Cubist still lifes (his other subjects were too obviously derived from Colquhoun's) were often rendered in supercharged Fauve colours or incorporated disorientating Surrealist shadows. In *Still Life* (*c.* 1947) his palette includes the subtly modulated acid yellows and olive greens that distinguished many of his paintings, and which may have helped divert attention from the rather obviously gendered symbolism of sliced melons and cucumbers.

Keith Vaughan: *Assembly of Figures 1*, 1952 (no. 105)

Michael Ayrton: Illustration for *Poems of Death*, 1945. Lithograph, 13 × 20 cm. Private collection

In 1946 Minton left the Bedford Gardens studio and moved to Hamilton Terrace, St John's Wood, where he shared a house and studio with Keith Vaughan. Having passed through stages of overt influence from Moore, Nash, Sutherland and Adler, Vaughan found his true subject, the male body, in about 1947. Less gregarious than Minton, Vaughan was a quietly serious crusader for the male nude in art. He developed an austere rendering of tentative, vulnerable and sometimes awkward forms with which to express his engagement with the male figure. His project, however compromised, required considerable courage, and, with the exception of Francis Bacon, it was not until the paintings of David Hockney in 1960 that this subject was addressed in British art.

Vaughan's wartime service with the Royal Army Medical Corps was identified by David Mellor as the source of his project 'to tend the male body'.[14] But although Minton painted London's Docklands, and Leslie Hurry made a drawing called *Atom Bomb* (1946), the second wave of Neo-Romantics seldom tackled contemporary social or political realities: instead, from 1947, many of them joined an escapist exodus to the Mediterranean. Michael Ayrton's sinister, etiolated, wartime grotesques are too subjective to convey more universal meaning, and the powerful Gothicism of his illustrations for *Poems of Death* (1945) ultimately too melodramatic. Eviscerated, skeletal forms did, nevertheless, force their way into artistic consciousness at the end of the war, possibly in response to the revelations of the Holocaust and Hiroshima. In Paris in the late 1940s Eduardo Paolozzi 'saw a great deal of Isabel Lambert', who was a close friend of Giacometti and 'introduced [Paolozzi] to a great many people at that time'.[15] He presented Lambert with the skeleton of a bat, an object she invested with a talismanic quality and which subsequently accompanied her everywhere. Her *Skeleton of Two Birds and a Fish* (1948) suggests that the theme preoccupied her at that time. Lambert was a prolific designer for the ballet, and the exaggerated gestures of her spiky, bony figures indicate the underlying frame. Her ballet designs recall those of Michael Ayrton, whom she knew through her marriage to Constant Lambert in 1947: this is probably, however, a case of the two artists sharing a common source, since Lambert, too, was close to Tchelitchew and Berman in pre-war Paris.

Isabel Lambert (later Isabel Rawsthorne): *Skeleton of Two Birds and a Fish*, 1948 (no. 86)

Reg Butler: *Birdcage*, 1951.
Forged welded iron, height 426.7 cm. Kenwood House,
London

Photographed (like all the black-and-white illustrations
of Butler's work in this book) by Butler himself, at the
Festival of Britain site on the South Bank. *Birdcage* is
now re-sited at Kenwood House, London.

60 Paintings for '51: Utopian Visions

A great popular success – it attracted over eight million visitors between May and September
1951 – the Festival of Britain presented a vision of a utopian future, a tonic to a nation that,
though its economy was reviving, was still subject to rationing. The Modernism of its art and
design was too compromised to meet with unanimous approval: to the critic Toni del Renzio,
the festival marked only 'deliverance from Europe with its resolute rejection of an international
character'.[16] Del Renzio's sardonic comment was significant, for in 1951 he was becoming
associated at the Institute of Contemporary Arts (ICA) with the architects of New Brutalism,
who rejected both the mainstream Modernism and Neo-Regency whimsy of the festival's
architecture as 'ephemeral and trivial'.[17]

The various festival buildings incorporated murals by John Piper, Victor Pasmore and Graham
Sutherland, whose vast *Origin of the Land* was also dismissed by del Renzio as 'the most
impressive failure of the Southbank'.[18] The interior of the Riverside Restaurant was envisaged by
its designer, Jane Drew, as an opportunity to collaborate with artists, and incorporated work by
Ben Nicholson and Barbara Hepworth, as well as Eduardo Paolozzi's *The Cage* (1951). An
important element of the festival was the collaboration of architects, artists and designers, and
it was fitting, if ironic, that the last large-scale attempt in Britain at this kind of co-operation to
date, the International Union of Architects Congress in 1961, was held on the site of the festival's
long-demolished Dome of Discovery.

As part of the festival celebrations, the Arts Council invited contributions to an exhibition to be
called *60 Paintings for '51*. The brief specified a painting of at least 60 × 45 in. (152 × 114 cm)
and the dimensions, with materials still scarce owing to financial stringencies, were a factor in
directing many artists towards working on a larger scale than hitherto. Josef Herman's epic
South Wales (since destroyed), a tableau of monumental and indomitably heroic miners, was
one of the few paintings in the exhibition that directly addressed the daily realities of working-
class life: not surprisingly, in his *Looking Forward* exhibition the following year, John Berger
included five of Herman's paintings. Herman's *Miners*, the huge mural he painted for what he
described as 'very much a Bauhaus thing',[19] the festival's 'Minerals of the Island' pavilion, took
ten months to complete and does survive (in the Glyn Vivian Gallery, Swansea); the preliminary
sketch *Miners (Study for Festival of Britain Mural)* (1950) was the final of several versions, and
the one from which the finished mural was executed.

A Polish refugee, like Jankel Adler, Herman arrived in Glasgow in 1940, where he renewed his
acquaintance with Adler, whom he had met in Warsaw in 1936. Herman moved to London in 1943,
the year of his first London exhibition, in which he shared the space at the Lefevre Gallery with the
then virtually unknown L.S. Lowry. The following year he made his first visit to Ystradgynlais, a
South Wales mining town, where he initially set up a studio in a local inn. The drawings he had
made in Glasgow were based predominantly on memories of the people he had known in Warsaw,
but, as he recalled, 'when I arrived in Ystradgynlais ... my world opened'.[20] He lived in the town
until 1955, transposing the solid forms of Millet's peasants into the Welsh valleys. In 1938 Herman
had moved to Brussels, where he was befriended by the Belgian Expressionist Constant Permeke
(1886–1952), whose paintings of similarly stocky peasants clearly influenced him. But he identified
personally with the struggle of the Welsh industrial townspeople, as the force of his work
demonstrates. In an interview with the *Jewish Chronicle* he related without self-pity how 'In 1942
I learnt that my whole family were exterminated in one day',[21] a personal tragedy that reveals a clue
to the universality of the œuvre of this displaced emigré artist.

Josef Herman: *Miners*, 1950 (no. 52)

Of the Neo-Romantics, Ayrton, Vaughan, MacBryde, Colquhoun and Minton were all included in *60 Paintings for '51*. But like the festival itself the exhibition was broad in scope, and among leading artists, Patrick Heron, Peter Lanyon, Bryan Wynter, Ivon Hitchens, Ben Nicholson, Claude Rogers, Rodrigo Moynihan, Prunella Clough, Victor Pasmore and William Scott were also represented. Five of the paintings were purchased for the Arts Council's permanent collection, and the selection of *Autumn Landscape* (1950; see illus. p. 39) by William Gear caused the type of press scandal that has continued to attend public purchases of 'difficult' abstract art. Gear, who studied under Leger in 1937, had recently returned from a two-year stay in Paris where he exhibited with the CoBrA group alongside the Tachistes Soulages and Hartung, a contact that was exceptional among his British contemporaries. Gear's paintings are often compared to those of Jean Bazaine, but they are freer and more lyrical in execution. His fractured semi-abstract forms are rendered in fulgent colours, bounded by dark armatures. Their dynamism and vibrancy is severely reduced in reproduction, which may account for Gear's otherwise inexplicable recent neglect; he is due a major retrospective.

Alan Davie, like Gear born in Scotland and an unusually vigorous abstract painter, was not included in *60 Paintings for '51*. In 1948 a travelling fellowship from Edinburgh School of Art enabled him to hitch-hike across Europe, where he saw the (pre-web, pre-drip) Jackson Pollocks at the Venice Biennale; *The Saint* (1948; see illus. p. 40), painted in Venice, was an immediate response to this cathartic experience. Soon afterwards Davie eliminated all figurative references from his work, although, as in *Woman Bewitched by the Moon no. 2* (1956; see illus. p. 41), he had a predilection for appending oblique titles to works after they were completed. In the early 1950s Davie pushed the gestural aspect of his work to extremes, placing his masonite board on the floor and painting rapidly and spontaneously with broad brushstrokes. The desire to release his intuition was further encouraged by his reading of *Zen in the Art of Archery* in about 1955, though improvisation was second nature to this accomplished jazz saxophonist and pianist.

Ceri Richards: *Trafalgar Square*, 1950. Oil on canvas, 151 × 244 cm. Tate, London

This was the version of *Trafalgar Square* that Richards painted for *60 Paintings for '51*; the smaller *Trafalgar Square II* (no. 87) is in the collection of the Walker Art Gallery, Liverpool. Trafalgar Square's importance as a focal point of the capital was celebrated by many artists. Piet Mondrian began a painting of it in 1939 that he completed in New York in 1943. The former Vorticist William Roberts, who died in 1980, remained active in the Fifties and taught drawing at the Central School of Arts and Crafts throughout the decade; in respect of its urban bustle, Roberts's *Trafalgar Square* (1952) is comparable to the Ceri Richards. Both the Richards and the Roberts are in striking contrast to Edward Middleditch's *Pigeons in Trafalgar Square* (1954; see illus. p. 77); Middleditch's starkly depopulated conception is emotionally intense, with a shadowy, *film-noir* mood of desolation.

William Gear: *Autumn Landscape*, 1950 (no. 43)

Alan Davie: *The Saint*, 1948 (no. 29)

Alan Davie: *Woman Bewitched by the Moon no. 2*, 1956 (no. 30)

Davie is another artist who can only be classified as an independent. Even to call him an abstract painter is misleading, for his paintings are replete with symbols, images and nebulous forms – Celtic, fantastic, supernatural, prehistoric, pagan. He describes the process of painting as a 'search for freedom, for the miraculous',[22] and his combination of chaos and meticulousness was outlined in a note he made about contemporary music in his diary for 1948: 'the great innovation is in the intelligent use of "unresolved" moments.'[23]

During the War Ceri Richards was based in his native Wales, where he was head of Cardiff College of Art, but in 1945 he returned to live in London, near Wandsworth Common. The move coincided with a change in style, when Richards added to his vivid Matisse-like colours forms in extravagant, swirling motion. He had a fondness for painting in series, and the *Trafalgar Square* (1950; see illus. p. 38) exhibited in *60 Paintings for '51* was one of at least nine versions. Margaret Garlake has suggested that the appeal of *Trafalgar Square* for the Modernist middle ground lay in its attractive palette and definable subject, which outweighed criticism of the flattened picture plane and distorted drawing;[24] nevertheless, the abiding public response to the Arts Council's exhibition was that it was élitist and over-intellectual. The flatness evinced by *Trafalgar Square* was a constant in Richards's paintings, and recalls the elegant relief constructions and collages that constituted most of his output in the 1930s, when he exhibited in *Objective Abstraction* at the Zwemmer Gallery (1934) and with the Surrealist Group at the London Gallery (1936–37). *Trafalgar Square* is assembled in a collage-like manner, the component elements animated by Richards's nervy but assured draughtsmanship. The London subject was unusual in the festival exhibition, and his painting of one of the main hubs of the capital's leisure activity may be compared with Gerald Wilde's *Piccadilly Circus* (1946; see illus. p. 45).

A Special Case: Gerald Wilde

Gerald Wilde qualifies as a special case for many reasons, not least because his work – which has been called Abstract Expressionist and Neo-Romantic – firmly resists classification. He remains, as he was in his life, difficult to pin down. A diffident – if sometimes also difficult – character, he frequented Soho bars, drinking to excess, yet appeared barely self-sufficient in his personal life. Denied establishment recognition almost as much as was David Bomberg, he was, entirely characteristically, omitted from *60 Paintings for '51* yet commissioned to supply the cover for the exhibition catalogue.

But Wilde was no artistic naïve. He studied at Chelsea School of Art, first under Percy Jowett and then, in about 1932, with Graham Sutherland, who, he said, 'gave me a place in his teaching room and was always ready to help me'.[25] Henry Moore, who was also on the staff at Chelsea at that time, became a lifelong friend. In 1942 he began another long-term friendship with the poet Tambimuttu, who published Wilde's remarkable illustrations in *Poetry London*, drawn in styles that range from the residually Sutherland-esque to a bold, free Expressionism.

Wilde's most important paintings date from about 1943 to the mid-Fifties. In reviews of Wilde's 1955 retrospective at the ICA, the word 'genius' was invoked by both John Berger and Toni del Renzio, and in *Ark* 16 magazine David Sylvester called him an 'unsung genius'.[26] *The Alarm*, which he painted in two versions in 1947, one in gouache (no. 109) and one in oil, is among the works that justify these claims. It is impossible to apprehend precisely the subject of *The*

Gerald Wilde: *The Alarm*, 1947 (no. 109)

Alarm. Both versions contain enervated and roughly schematized figures. The sketchily delineated buildings in the top-left corner of the gouache, and the vague wall-shapes and swathe of vivid scarlet and red in the oil version, support the suggestion of a reference to a wartime conflagration: while serving with the Pioneer Corps, Wilde apparently helped to demolish blitzed London buildings, and the germ of the *The Alarm* could have been a scene he witnessed. If that was the case, perhaps an alarm bell had sounded a disaster; but Wilde painted from the subconscious, and what he got on to canvas was not so much an actual event but the ensuing psychological stress – a state of chaos or tension – of being alarmed.

In an essay on *The Alarm*, William Feaver noted that Wilde's paintings evince a debt to Sutherland, Colquhoun, Gear and Bacon. Bomberg's *Bomb Store* studies could be added to this list, were it not extremely unlikely Wilde had seen them in 1947. Feaver also described *The*

Gerald Wilde: *Beast in Landscape*, 1949 (no. 110)

Alarm as a 'marvellous example of intuition overcoming received technique', noting that 'the paint lies thin and perfunctory on the armature of an idea'.[27] *Beast in Landscape*, painted in 1949, belongs to a brief period when Wilde painted quite thickly in oils. Here he wrenched the dense impasto into urgent and convulsively rhythmical forms, the ominous, shadowy, black 'beast' counterpoised against painterly gestures of vibrant crimson and deep red. Again, the exact theme is unclear, but Wilde appears to have poised the image on the threshold of an act of bestial violence. *Mob Metamorphoses* (*c.* 1946) is another anguished nocturne, a site of urban panic in which a jostling, fearful crowd appears to be fleeing an unspecified menace. In *Piccadilly Circus* (1946) Wilde's passionate engagement with painting is reflected in a simultaneously chaotic and rhapsodic appreciation of another hub of London, on the border of his Soho haunts. Wilde sweeps the viewer past a standing figure, a bus – perhaps – and a Belisha beacon into a swirling vortex and up into what is almost a plan view of the

Gerald Wilde: *Piccadilly Circus*, 1946 (no. 108)

metropolitan maelstrom. Lawrence Alloway believed it absurd for Erno Goldfinger and E.J. Carter, in a County of London plan, 'to print a photograph of Piccadilly Circus and caption it ARCHITECTURAL SQUALOR'.[28] He, on the contrary, called the neon spectacle 'the best night-sight in London': Wilde, who relished the anonymity of passing unnoticed through bustling, crowded streets, was the prescient painter of urban dramas.

DISRUPTION

'Watch it. This really is the enemy, this illusion of inevitability which the academic historian imposes on flickering events ... .' – *Victor Willing*

'The post-war flush of painters has now thinned out ... in painting and sculpture, two more powerful figures have emerged – Bacon and Butler. These two, and l'art brut, have undermined the cosy English basis of Sutherland and Craxton.'
– *Theo Crosby*

'For most students the experience of an art school, and particularly the Slade, involves a change in the conception of figurative quality. At that moment, with Coldstream's arrival, attention was concentrated at the Slade on just this issue.' – *Lawrence Gowing*

Victor Willing: *Act of Violence*, 1952 (detail; no. 111)

Nervous System: Francis Bacon and the Intensified Instant

Francis Bacon's paintings are manifestations of his struggle to create a living presence on canvas, a presence apart from the nominal subject, emerging from the marks of the brush to exist independently. In his re-visioning of the Grand Manner, photography and the cinema were central to the anti-narratives of his realism. He credited photography with having released art from the function of illustration, yet also declared that 'Ninety-nine per cent of the time I find that photographs are very much more interesting than abstract or figurative painting. I have always been haunted by them'.[1] For much of his life, however, he risked diminishing his stature by admitting this. But Bacon had no formal training, and his preparation depended as much on his absorption of photography's iconography of gesture as on his encounters with the history of art. His plundering of photography's lexicon of attitudes was, however, a means to an end – the emergence of new, more 'real' images. He deplored the 'mixed-media jackdaws' who used photographs too literally, their factual accounts insufficiently 'digested and transformed':[2] while the camera produced 'diverted illustrations', in his paintings Bacon aimed 'to trap this living fact alive'.[3]

Bacon was never grounded in the procedures of drawing from a live model, but this avoidance of the English linear tradition was turned by him to good account, for it liberated him from many of its conventions. His alternative Modernism was articulated, for example, in his uninhibited handling of pictorial space, on the disjunction of flat planes and perspectival space-frames. The space of a Bacon painting is the space of a Beckett play, a psychological arena. Working from photographs or reproductions obviated the need to struggle with the third dimension. And though he was required to develop his own methods of applying and working with paint, he exploited his limitations so successfully that Robert Melville could call him 'the greatest painter of flesh since Velasquez'.[4] But the idea that Bacon was entirely self-taught was a fallacy that he abetted by the mercurial and selective recounting of his autobiography. The importance of the period in the early 1930s of close contact with the Australian Cubist painter Roy de Maistre should not be underestimated, and de Maistre's paintings further reveal that his influence was not limited to technical advice.[5] Lucian Freud, Bacon's close friend for many years, studied from 1939 at the East Anglian School of Painting and Drawing, run by Cedric Morris and Arthur Lett-Haines, first at Dedham then at Hadleigh: the experience he gained with Morris was, notwithstanding the singular talent that eventually emerged, similarly crucial in his formative years.

In his youth Bacon spent two years in 'the great capitals of Europe, savouring their turmoil and decay'.[6] This period, in the late 1920s, coincided with the rise of photojournalism and the picture press. Bacon's knowledge of modern art was probably, at this stage, quite limited, but what he saw in abundance and responded to intuitively was the 'news' imagery of people and societies in motion, nations on the edge of conflict, of powerful figures exposed in unguarded moments. Miniature-camera technology also facilitated the rise of sports photography, another source extensively mined by Bacon. Eadweard Muybridge's analytical studies of animals and humans in movement provided Bacon with an image bank to which he returned continually; scientific and medical photographs – stark and brutally factual – suggested many of his nerve-jangling effects. The Picasso exhibition at Galerie Rosenberg in Paris in 1927 may have determined Bacon to become a painter, but in the following year, when Buster Keaton cast a press photographer as the hero of *The Cameraman*, he valorized an almost equally potent contemporary visual reference. Bacon was as alert to photography and to the cinema as instruments of Modernism as he was to the creative fertility of Picasso.

Francis Bacon: *Head Surrounded by Sides of Beef*, 1954. Oil on canvas, 129.9 × 122 cm. Harriott A. Fox Fund, 1956.1201. Photograph © 2001, The Art Institute of Chicago. All rights reserved

Deakin's portraits of Bacon with carcasses (opposite) did not suggest the inclusion of the motif in *Head Surrounded by Sides of Beef*, for Bacon had already included sides of meat in *Painting* (1946), one of his favourite early works.

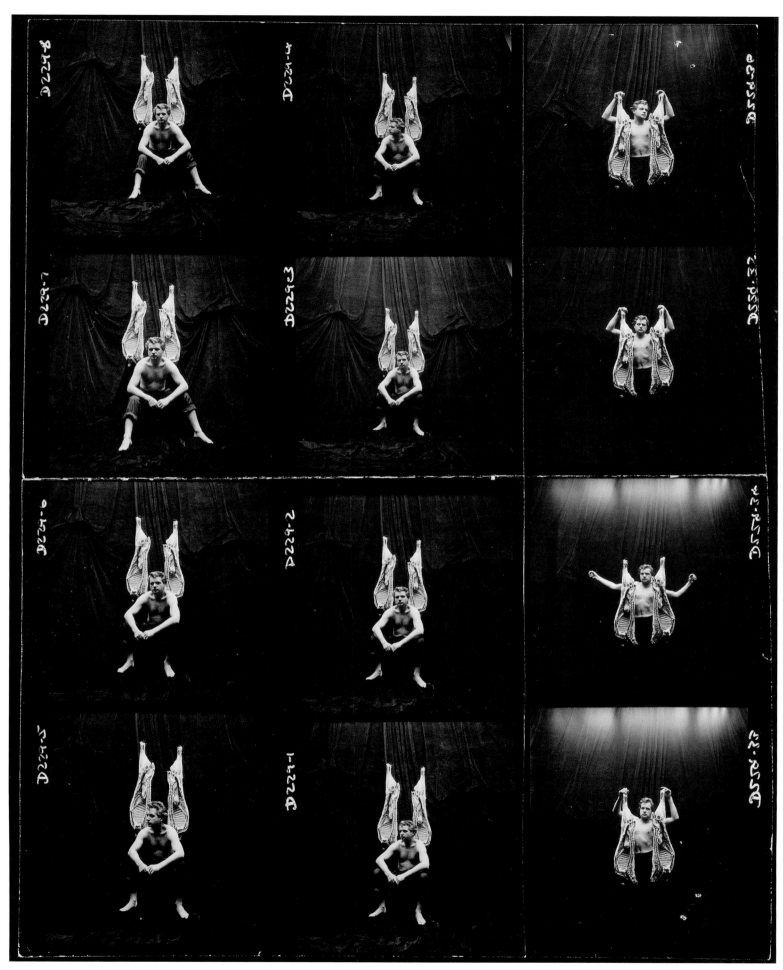

John Deakin: Francis Bacon (original contact sheet), 1952 (no. 33)

Bacon's abiding fascination with the cinema is most famously evident in his obsession with screaming figures, inspired by the horrified nanny in the Odessa steps sequence in Eisenstein's *Battleship Potemkin*, which he claimed to have seen shortly after the film's release in 1926. The intensity of his reaction to this scene is surely due in part to his identification with the plight of a nanny-reared child hurtling towards extinction, a political metaphor for the end of an order that resonated with his own socially privileged upbringing. Bacon's relationship with his childhood nurse, Jessie Lightfoot, was unusually close. She shared in his various ménages in London from about 1930, part surrogate mother, part co-conspirator; when she died in 1951 Bacon was devastated. The image recurs frequently in his paintings, notably in the screaming *Pope* figures painted after 1950, where it becomes an autobiographical transposition of distraught nanny and authoritarian father-figure.

Bacon's only memory of meeting Virginia Woolf was at a lunch in the 1930s, when, he told his friend Dennis Wirth-Miller, she 'just shouted right the way through'.[7] But in 1926, in her prescient essay 'The Cinema', Woolf, despite her ambivalence towards Modernism, had described the potential of certain cinematic devices that would have held considerable significance for the artist. Deprecating the industry for following the safe and parasitic option of reworking the linear narratives of literary 'classics', Woolf observed the capacity of film to operate in another dimension, 'more real, or real with a different reality from that we perceive in daily life'. She was impressed by a specific sequence in Robert Wiene's *The Cabinet of Dr Caligari* (1919–20) and described it in equally Baconian terms as an accidental shadow that 'seemed to embody some monstrous diseased imagination of the lunatic's brain'.

In his catalogue essay to accompany Bacon's first American retrospective, at the Solomon R. Guggenheim Museum, New York, in 1963, Lawrence Alloway quoted Panofsky to explain how Bacon painted human movement as 'the result of a continuous transition from one state to another.' He described how Bacon had 'made this theme his own, with his studies of transitional human movements flickering through the wrecked Grand Manner'.[8] The notion of 'flicker' is a Baconian paradigm. A quintessentially modern concept, it can be related to the cinema – colloquially the 'flicks' or 'flickers' observed in the pulsing of primitive film projectors. Bacon, who lived in a time of religious doubt, of the collapse of the grand narrative, was acutely aware of the paradox inherent in his ambition to locate his work within the Grand Manner. He read Aeschylus and Shakespeare, but also Joyce and Eliot, who wrote for a post-Freudian age of uncertainty, of questioned identity. He painted the human character breaking up in Eliot's age of anxiety, flickering between ignorance and enlightenment like the symbolic darkness and light of Conrad's *Heart of Darkness*.

Bacon's desire to 'return the viewer more directly to the nervous system' can also be compared to the flickers of the 'Dreamachine' developed by Brion Gysin and Ian Sommerville from W. Grey Walter's neurological research into the brain's alpha rhythms.[9] The altered states of consciousness induced by the machine operate in the shadowlands of perception, the elusive territory inhabited by Bacon's transitory, dissolving figures. In the transgressive *Untitled (Two Figures in the Grass)* (c. 1952) the boundaries of the poignantly crouching forms are ambiguous, the background violently smeared with broad, free brushstrokes: the bodies appear to fuse, to merge together, 'a kind of live phantasmal tissue'.[10] Melville's analogy with human biology

Francis Bacon: *Untitled (Two Figures in the Grass)*, c. 1952 (no. 9)

Francis Bacon: *Study for a Portrait of Van Gogh VI*, 1957. Oil on canvas, 198.1 × 142.2 cm. Arts Council Collection, Hayward Gallery, London

Beginning in 1956, Bacon made eight paintings based on a postcard reproduction (the original was destroyed in World War II) of Van Gogh's *The Painter on the Road to Tarascon* (1888).

The Van Gogh paintings represented a major departure for Bacon – not least in their powerful colour – and were not well received at the time. The change from a monochromatic palette has been related to the influence of the increase in colour printing in magazines; it may equally well have been triggered by Bacon's frequent visits to Tangier from 1955, and in the Van Gogh series was partly dictated by the colours of the original.

In *Study for a Portrait of Van Gogh VI*, Bacon, in spite of his admiration for the artist's letters, evidently strove to minimize the narrative connotations of the subject; this was consistent with one of the fundamentals of his art – the firm resistance of the anecdotal.

extends to some of Bacon's contemporaries. The web-like armatures of William Gear, for instance, may be compared to arteries, surrounding forms that pulse, like blood coursing through the body – another kind of flicker. Bacon lamented the absence of a modern equivalent of Greek mythology and sought to revivify traditional iconographies. Walter Benjamin located the decline of the uniqueness of works of art, of what he called their 'aura', in the rise of photography and mechanical reproduction; it is paradoxical then, considering Bacon's sources, that he as much as any twentieth-century painter attempted to return the auratic, as well as the aura, to art.

The inclusion of Bacon's *Crucifixion* (1933) in Herbert Read's influential book *Art Now* (1933), marked the beginning of his public recognition. Sir Michael Sadler, Master of University College, Oxford, commissioned Bacon, on the strength of the reproduction in Read's book, to paint his portrait, which formed part of another *Crucifixion* (1933) and was based on an x-ray photograph of his head. In Sadler, Bacon had found his first important patron, but the exhibition he mounted in 1934 was either ignored or savaged in the press. After this discouragement a long hiatus ensued, during which he painted only intermittently, and it was not until an exhibition at the Lefevre Gallery in April 1945 (together with Frances Hodgkins and Graham Sutherland) that he began to make a noticeable impression on the art world. He later dissociated himself from paintings that pre-dated *Three Studies for Figures at the Base of a Crucifixion* (1944), which shocked and puzzled viewers at the Lefevre Gallery. *Figure in a Landscape* (1945), also exhibited at the Lefevre Gallery, was based partly on a photograph of his lover and patron Eric Hall sleeping in a deckchair in Hyde Park: the figure, decapitated in Bacon's radical cropping, the enigmatically clasped hands, ambiguous machine-gun and metal fence anticipate many of his preoccupations, his free play with space, subtle gestures and predilection for internal frameworks.

By 1953, when he painted *Man with Dog*, Bacon's techniques had acquired an assurance that belied the late start to his career. Thinner and drier than before, the paint is fluidly applied to achieve an almost monochrome tonality derived from black-and-white photography. Ronald Alley noted that the stance of the blurred dog in motion was based on the same Muybridge photograph as two earlier Bacon paintings – Muybridge was occasionally a 'trigger of ideas' as well as a reference. Alley also observed the parallel between Bacon's composition and Giacomo Balla's *Leash in Motion* (1912), which had been exhibited at the Tate Gallery in 1952.[11] Neither Aaron Scharf nor Van Deren Coke[12] went so far as to suggest that the Futurist *fotodinamismo* of Anton and Arturo Bragaglia influenced Balla's painting, but there is an intriguing correspondence with the Bragaglias' investigation of 'movementism', the kinetics of the body-in-space, that is relevant not only to the Futurists but extends to Bacon himself.[13] The blurring of Bacon's dog is adroitly executed, its form so vaporous, so ectoplasmic, that it threatens to disappear like a chimera through the iron ribs of the drain-hole cover it is approaching (a typically enigmatic inclusion: this and the kerb are the only 'solid' forms in the painting); the leash is delineated in delicate drops of white paint, a bravura, iridescent counterpoint. From 1936 at the latest Bacon frequently painted dogs, but as a sufferer from asthma since childhood he was unable to be in their presence: his ambivalence towards them is manifest in the shadowy intangibility of *Man with Dog*, a shrouded monochrome that eloquently expresses the sustained or expanded potential of painting in the age of photography.

Francis Bacon: *Man with Dog*, 1953 (no. 10)

Camera-Shutter Existentialists[14]

Bacon's unsettling provocations began to have an effect on a younger generation of artists, most conspicuously on a group of students attending the Slade School of Fine Art.[15] By 1949 Bacon's paintings were being exhibited regularly in London, at the Hanover Gallery and elsewhere, and widely discussed. Their physical presence was reinforced in lectures and seminars given at the Slade and the Royal College of Art (RCA) by David Sylvester: although Sylvester did not write about Bacon until 1952, he was close to him at this time and in 1950 shared living premises with the artist. Photography was not merely an important topic of debate at the Slade; it dominated, as Sylvester recounted in his 'Curriculum Vitae',[16] the intense discussions on art at the school. Lucian Freud lectured one day a week at the Slade, and Bacon and Sutherland were occasional visitors. Sylvester, who had grasped the significance of photography for Bacon's work, began to collect his own clippings of images from newspapers and magazines, and to show them in his lectures.

The interest in photography was highly selective, and tended not to draw on the work of mainstream professionals of that time, such as Cecil Beaton or Bill Brandt. Nigel Henderson, for example, admired Brandt's earlier social reportage of 'the uncompromising severity of the social caste system' but found the wide-angle nudes of the Fifties sterile.[17] While Bacon allowed that 'some photographers are artists', he was 'not particularly interested in that aspect of photography'. Painters tended to seek a more elusive quality in photographs, the 'slight remove from fact', as Bacon put it, found in images mediated through the reductive tonalities of black-and-white newspaper and magazine reproductions. Peter Rose Pulham, who had been an inventive and experimental fashion and portrait photographer in London from 1932 until 1937, when he left to become a painter in Paris, was equally well informed about both media. He returned to London during the War and had met Bacon by 1943.[18] In Paris Pulham had become immersed in the Surrealist milieu.[19] His paintings, initially indebted to Ernst and de Chirico, changed radically following the contact with Bacon: his amorphous anatomies have affinities with Bacon's *The Crucifixion* (1933) and *Studio Interior* (c. 1934),[20] but may also relate to other works that Bacon destroyed in the period up to 1945.

In 1952 Pulham broadcast a talk on photography for BBC Radio, which was published in *The Listener*;[21] the text was placed by Bacon among the finest writing on the subject, and Sylvester used it in his teaching. In an unpublished passage of the manuscript Pulham revealed: 'Latterly I have been most charmed by really bad Press photographs reproduced through a coarse screen on bad paper; they seem, making an unintentional selection, suppression of detail, much more convincing than the "see every pore" school.'[22] Pulham, together with Rodrigo Moynihan, the

Peter Rose Pulham: *Grisaille Figure*, 1947 (no. 85)

photographer Douglas Glass, and the critics Michael Middleton and John Davenport, took part in a 'Points of View' debate on photography at the Institute of Contemporary Arts (ICA) in March 1952, chaired by the architectural historian John Summerson. The discussion was scheduled for shortly after the closing of the first British exhibition of Henri Cartier-Bresson's photographs and coincided with a less-enthusiastically received retrospective of *Life* magazine photojournalism, opened the previous week by Cornell Capa. Pulham evidently enjoyed himself – 'Moynihan and I had things pretty well our own way', he wrote to Isabel Lambert[23] – and he delivered an even more extreme statement in favour of artless, automatist photography:

> Emotional and haphazard chance are the best conditions for good photography. The perfect photo is of a national calamity, when the camera is knocked out of the photographer's hand, develops itself in the gutter and is immediately published in the newspapers, where its impact as a smudged image is immeciate. Afterwards, the negative is stored in the police archives.[24]

Rodrigo Moynihan concurred: 'The *Life* exhibition is hideous because it is trying to be artistic. Photos are admirable when accidental, as are the photographic records in the *Daily Express* ... their smudged effect retains only the absolute essentials of information and eliminates irrelevant

Rodrigo Moynihan: *The Teaching Staff of the Painting School, Royal College of Art 1949–50*, 1951. Oil on canvas, 213.4 × 334.6 cm. Tate, London

Eric Stanley: Photograph used by Moynihan as the basis for his portrait group, 1950.
Collection of Mrs Mary Spear

John Minton (far left in the painting) was not present when the photograph was taken, and was added later in Moynihan's composition. The other sitters are (left to right): Colin Hayes; Carel Weight; Rodney Burn; Robert Buhler; Charles Mahoney; Kenneth Rowntree; Ruskin Spear; and Moynihan himself.

detail.'[25] In his painting *The Teaching Staff of the Painting School, Royal College of Art, 1949–50* (1951) Moynihan had used a photograph (taken by Ruskin Spear's nephew, Eric Stanley) as the basis of the composition; for his other epic group arrangement, *After the Conference: The Editors of Penguin Books 1951* (1951), he 'wanted to get all these figures as if they were just being dropped by accident into this pool' and shot 'quite a long film ... of them walking about completely aimlessly ... people not doing anything, just moving'.[26]

Concurrently, and particularly at the ICA and the RCA, a different kind of respect was emerging for the high professionalism and technical resourcefulness of photography in the American glossies. David Sylvester testified to the admiration in his circle for the work of Irving Penn in American *Vogue*,[27] and the British counterparts of the American magazines, though less well financed, were endeavouring to catch up. For Reyner Banham, 'the average Playtex or Maidenform ad in American *Vogue* was an instant deflater of the reputations of most artists then in Arts Council vogue'.[28] Len Deighton's introduction of a photographic element on the cover of the RCA's student magazine, *Ark 10*, in 1954, was a pivotal moment when the college – or rather its students – rejected the traditions of fine book illustration and ushered in Modernism; the RCA became a training ground for the graphic designers and art directors who led the magazine and advertising explosion in London in the 1960s.[29]

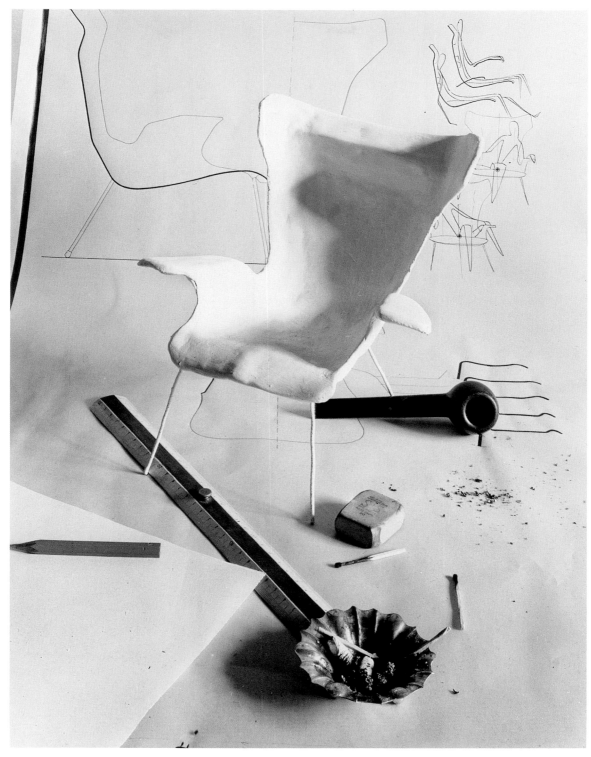

Irving Penn: *Architectural Still Life, Milan*, 1948. Vintage gelatin silver print, 34 × 26 cm.
© 1949 (renewed 1977) by Condé Nast Publications, Inc.

The first genre of photography that Penn mastered was the still-life. This unusual image was reproduced in a feature on the 'Design Renaissance in Italy' in the British edition of *House and Garden*, February–March 1950. In Milan, Penn had spent time with, and photographed, many of the young Italian architects and designers who were influential in Britain in the Fifties. The papier-mâché maquette of a chair that Penn incorporated was only three inches high and was designed by Begiojoso, Peressutti & Rogers.

Graham Sutherland: *Men Walking*, 1950. Oil on canvas, 145.4 × 98.4 cm. The Beaverbrook Foundation, The Beaverbrook Art Gallery, Fredericton, New Brunswick

Although this painting, and a closely related version without the dog, are traditionally dated to 1950, they probably, in the present author's opinion, date from 1952. This suggestion is based on comparisons with securely dated works and on the evidence of Richard Lannoy. Sutherland had asked Lannoy, in the first half of 1952, for advice about photography; Sutherland was particularly interested to learn about phenomena such as selective focus and 'random' cropping, and about images seen from the corner of the eye.

Barbara Braithwaite: *Umbrellas in the Street*, 1951. Watercolour and ink on paper, 32.9 × 40 cm. Arts Council Collection, Hayward Gallery, London

Moynihan, who was Professor of Painting at the RCA from 1948 to 1957, believed that 'Photography is interesting to the painter irrespective of what it may amount to in its own right';[30] the implication that its claims to be considered an independent art form were of dubious merit was aligned, paradoxically, with the Slade view, for the RCA's painters and graphic designers were generally more receptive to mass media and advertising photography 'in its own right'. David Sylvester taught at both schools, and compared Royal College students at this time ('rockers') with those at the Slade ('mods');[31] he planned to launch a magazine that would bridge the rivalry between the two establishments, believing that 'there were students unusually full of ideas and talent and energy at both schools'.[32]

Nigel Henderson, who left the Slade in 1949, remarked that photography was considered 'the devil's domain' at the school. But by the beginning of the Fifties the lectures of David Sylvester were making an impact, and a group of students including Michael Andrews, Barbara Braithwaite, Myles Murphy and Victor Willing participated in debates on photography. Andrews and Willing each produced a diploma work that reverberated in London, and that was interpreted in relation both to existentialism and to the photograph's isolation of a violent or anxious instant: as Myles Murphy commented: 'Slade students at that time could be divided into two camps – those who walked around with a Camus paperback in their pocket and those who didn't.'[33] In 1949 a film department was opened at the Slade, run by the documentary film-maker Thorold Dickinson. It was apparently little used, save by Lorenza Mazzetti, who arrived from Italy in 1950. Mazzetti was closest to the students interested in photography, and they were often prevailed upon to act in the short films she made at the Slade, such as Kafka's *Metamorphosis* (c. 1951), in which Lucian Freud, Claude Rogers and Michael Andrews also appeared. After leaving the Slade in 1954 Mazzetti joined the English 'Free Cinema' group. *Together* (1955) was filmed in London's Dockland; Mazzetti, who 'did not want anything happening in the story',[34] was helped with editing by Lindsay Anderson, and Walter Lassally shot some additional footage; the principal actors were Michael Andrews and Eduardo Paolozzi, who rose impressively to the difficult task of playing deaf mutes. Potentially the most interesting of her Slade projects (it has not yet re-emerged), for its documentary, *cinéma-vérité* connotations, was her film of prostitutes' shoes, made with a hand-held camera on location in Soho.

Lorenza Mazzetti: Still from the film *Together* (1955), as reproduced in *Ark* 17.
Private collection

Michael Andrews: *A Man who Suddenly Fell Over*, 1952 (no. 1)

A Man who Suddenly Fell Over, one of Michael Andrews's diploma-examination paintings in 1952, was triggered by an incident he witnessed on Gower Street while returning to the Slade from Soho, in which a middle-aged man lost his balance and his dignity and toppled painfully on to the pavement. The addition of the shocked woman was Andrews's invention, her anguished scream based on a newspaper photograph. Robert Melville described the painting as 'one of the boldest and most intransigent contributions to post-war realism'.[35] Andrews's interest in 'mysterious conventionality' was first demonstrated in the equally ambitious *August for the People* (1951), which is similarly dominated by a forlorn, bloated, awkward male figure, his dislocation emphasized through juxtaposition with the indifference and relaxed unconcern of the surrounding children on the beach. Andrews interpreted his observation of events in terms of a psychological reading of the participants. This, and the building of an image from disparate sources (which, particularly in the 1960s, usually meant a form of photography), would remain an essential part of his art for most of his career.

From 1949 to 1953 Victor Willing was Andrews's exact contemporary at the Slade. Although the proposed inter-college magazine – Willing had christened it *Gemini* – failed to materialize, Sylvester preserved an essay, 'Travel by Bus', that Willing had written for it.[36] Sylvester described Willing as influenced 'in equal measure' by Bacon and William Coldstream, Slade Professor of Fine Art from 1949 until 1975.[37] For most of the Fifties the Coldstream-derived 'sense of the

Victor Willing: *Act of Violence*, 1952 (no. 111)

potency and mystery of the gestural painter's marks on the canvas'[38] was paramount in Willing's work, but *Act of Violence*, his diploma piece at the Slade in 1952, is the riskiest, most Bacon-esque of his paintings. The nominal subject was Eliot's *The Waste Land*, but this 'flickering event', the 'unpremeditated form' (to adopt Willing's own phraseology), is one of the most extreme expositions of the influence of photography and of existentialism on British art, an extended solo improvisation on the theme of figurative, edgily gestural action painting. Although Willing virtually ceased to paint for a long period after 1962, in their subsequent careers both he and Andrews continued, with almost monastic devotion, the lone and eminently serious paths that these student paintings portended, amply justifying their elevation to the School of London pantheon.

Lucian Freud: *Juliet Moore Asleep*, 1943 (no. 41)

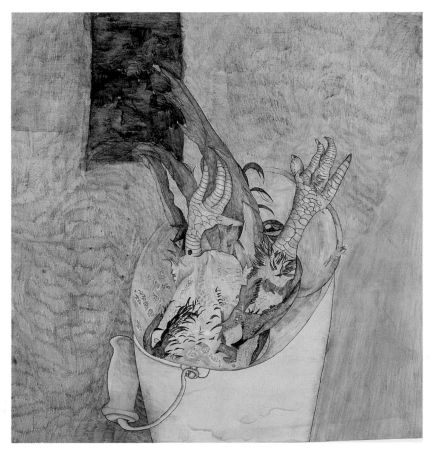

Lucian Freud: *Chicken in a Bucket*, 1944 (no. 42)

Lucian Freud: *Interior at Paddington*, 1951. Oil on canvas, 152.4 × 114.3 cm. Board of Trustees of the National Museums and Galleries on Merseyside, Liverpool (Walker Art Gallery)

Robert Medley: *Bicyclists Against a Blue Background*, 1951 (no. 74)

Carel Weight: *Anger*, 1955 (no. 107)

In 1949 Coldstream invited Robert Medley to teach theatre design at the Slade. Then in his mid-forties, Medley still 'suffered from an instability of style'.[39] The four paintings of *Bicyclists* that he made in 1950–51 were regarded by Medley as the 'most significant ... the largest and most ambitious'[40] he had done. He acknowledged the influence of Delacroix and Matisse, but the contemporary painter with whom he aligned himself was his friend Ceri Richards. Medley pronounced his own work 'diffuse, decorative and lyrical', concerned with 'integration' rather than the 'disruption' and 'isolation' of his Hanover Gallery stablemate Bacon. The idea for the *Bicyclists* originated from 'lounging about on a hot Saturday afternoon and watching the local youth on their "bikes" ... The boys combed their hair and the girls lay on the paper-strewn patch of grass waiting for attention'. Medley seldom painted from nature and, 'having no camera', he used for a model 'Ramsay MacClure, a student at Central School who was a close friend of Keith Vaughan'.[41] Despite his disavowals, in *Bicyclists Against a Blue Background* (1951) Medley, who admitted to the attraction of 'the actuality of violence and alienation',[42] approached, at the moment of his closest connection to Bacon and to Slade existentialism, a dramatization of contemporary tensions, expressed in the otiose youths and the abrupt diagonal division between the males and females. *Bicyclists Against a Blue Background* was another of the prize-winning paintings shown in *60 Paintings for '51*, a distinction shared by the festival's other mildly transgressive painting, Lucian Freud's *Interior at Paddington* (1951). Arguably Freud's most significant achievement up to that date, it was his first identifiably London painting. The incongruously raincoated figure (Harry Diamond, an itinerant scene painter, and later a notable photographer of London street life) stands on a crumpled red carpet, fist clenched, tense and ungainly, in an interior dominated by an aggressively spiky and meticulously painted potted plant – an archetypical Fifties motif.

Kenneth Armitage: *Figure Lying on its Side No. 5*, 1957 (no. 4)

Until the late 1970s Kenneth Armitage's sculpture was invariably concerned with the human form. Alan Bowness and others sought to distance his work of the Fifties from 'some of his *angst-ridden* fellow sculptors', and emphasized instead the 'playfulness and affection of Armitage's figures and groups'.[43] But the toppled, helpless *Figure Lying on its Side*, notwithstanding its wittiness, describes in terms of contemporary anxieties a human predicament that is closely related to Andrews's *A Man who Suddenly Fell Over*. In Armitage's early bronzes *People in a Wind* (1950) and *Family Going for a Walk* (1951), the figures are tilted, unstable, vaguely threatened; in the battle with gravity the up-ended figure *Roly-Poly 1* (1955) is equally vulnerable and exhausted, perhaps even extinguished.

Another stream of sculpture that developed simultaneously in the Fifties emerged out of Social Realism, and was most clearly exemplified in the work of George Fullard. Fullard was, in fact, closely associated with several of the Social Realist painters, including former RCA colleague Leslie Duxbury and the slightly later graduates Derrick Greaves and Jack Smith: John Berger included Fullard's drawings in the 1955 *Looking Forward* exhibition. What he achieved in his sculpture in the mid-Fifties was a kind of anti-monumental snapshot realism. *Goalkeeper* (1953), *Girl Skipping* (1955) and *Angry Woman* (1958) are all figures in motion – caught, that is, in the middle of an action, transitory, as opposed to adopting an exaggeratedly baroque attitude that is frozen and then modelled. Anthony Caro's fleshy, weighty figures are the most corporeal sculptures of the Fifties: *Woman Waking Up* (1956) seems to be struggling against gravity in an attempt to rouse herself. Although Caro ceased to make figurative sculpture after 1959, he, too, briefly experimented with figures in motion: *Man Taking off his Shirt* (1955–56), the Cigarette Smokers series (1957–58), and *Pulling on a Girdle* (1958–59) were all cast in bronze, their lumpy surfaces accentuating the rendering of restless movement, the stirrings of the heavy forms.

Anthony Caro: *Woman Waking Up*, 1956 (no. 20)

Kenneth Armitage: *People in the Wind*, 1950 (no. 3)

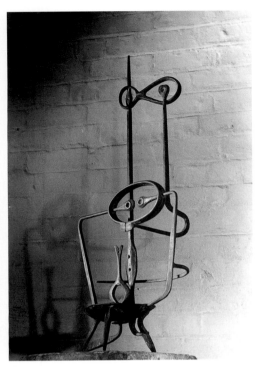

Reg Butler: *Family Group*, 1948–49.
Forged and welded iron, height 91.4 cm.
Hirshhorn Museum and Sculpture Garden,
Smithsonian Institution, Washington, D.C.

Reg Butler: *The Box*, 1951.
Iron, height 66 cm. Museum of Modern Art, New York

The Festival of Britain was conceived in a spirit of optimism, even levity, and the first exhibition of Reg Butler's sculpture, at the Hanover Gallery in 1949, revealed a talent that could superficially be co-opted to this cause. Although Butler became disenchanted by the problems associated with commissions for public sculpture, some of his most important projects in the period 1948–53 were both for public places and distinctly utopian in intent. The first to be executed was *Birdcage* (1951; see illus. p. 36), in forged and welded iron, the attenuated forms of which towered above the garden area outside the festival's Thames-side restaurant. However, an alternative reading identified such constructions not as light and linear, but as sinister and alien. Butler was one of eight young sculptors, including Kenneth Armitage, William Turnbull and Eduardo Paolozzi, who represented modern British sculpture at the 1952 Venice Biennale. In his introductory essay to the exhibition, Herbert Read borrowed from T.S. Eliot to describe the new work, in phrases that have often been repeated, as reflecting 'the iconography of despair ... the geometry of fear';[44] elsewhere, Patrick Heron remarked that, 'in Butler's case the *Angst* is real'.[45]

Read's support was instrumental in perpetuating the high international reputation of British sculpture, but he maintained his attachment to the work of his close friends Henry Moore and Barbara Hepworth. Moore himself appears to have responded to the new sculpture, and produced lighter, more open forms such as the various versions of *Standing Figure* (1950).[46] But the younger critics believed Moore's work had become heavy and repetitive – Reyner Banham, for example, held Detroit car styling to be above 'Moore-ish yokelry'[47] – and Butler's exploration of space through line and movement established him as a challenger. Greeting the first British sculptor to work in 'rods of steel' since Picasso and Julio Gonzales, Patrick Heron emphasized that Butler differed from his antecedents in achieving an organic cohesion by 'insisting that every limb of the figure – every bar, finger, prong or cross-piece – must be beaten out at the forge, or so arrived at, by means of the electro-welder or oxy-acetylene flame, that it no longer has the quality of *rods assembled*'.[48]

The device of the central 'platform' in *Birdcage* was first developed by Butler in 1948, in an unexecuted project, *Family Group* (1948–49), that he intended to site as a 'great towering fetish' on the Cornish coast. This in turn was closely related to those 'rather sinister machines', the radio and radar towers that Butler photographed in 1947 at Bawdsey, Suffolk. Butler had been carving in wood since the 1930s, but the impact of these gaunt, unsettling pieces of functional engineering provoked a decisive shift away from the influence of Henry Moore. The inspiration from industrial structures such as radar towers relates to Butler's polymathic engineering, manual, scientific and artistic skills. Trained as an architect, he qualified as an Associate of the Royal Institute of British Architects in 1937. He had built little before the War intervened, though in 1939 he was responsible for a flat-roofed house in the International Style at Great Munden, in his native Hertfordshire. A conscientious objector, during the war he worked as a blacksmith in the village of Iping, West Sussex, an experience manifested in his forging and welding skills. In 1946 he was appointed Technical Editor to the Architectural Press, remaining until 1950 when he became the first Gregory Fellow in Sculpture at Leeds University (his successor, in 1953, was Kenneth Armitage). The fellowship was the initiative of Eric C. Gregory, director of the publishers Lund Humphries, Honorary Treasurer of the ICA, and a friend as well as a benefactor of Butler. One of Gregory's aims was to combat metrocentrism, but although Butler took a flat in Leeds (furnished with his own Modernist designs) and fulfilled his teaching duties, he found himself unable to work there.

Reg Butler: *Woman*, 1949 (no. 18)

The expiration of the Gregory Fellowship coincided with Butler winning the international competition to design a monument to *The Unknown Political Prisoner*, for which he had been making small-scale wire studies since 1951. Butler appears to have elided the monument with a contemporaneous project, *The Box* (1951). Robert Melville reported in 1951[49] that Butler intended *The Box* to be placed on the cliffs at Dover, which by 1953 had become rumoured as a

Reg Butler: *Final Maquette for The Unknown Political Prisoner*, 1951–52 (no. 19)

possible location for Butler's monument; the proposal caused questions to be raised in Parliament, and newspapers satirized it in cartoons. The political implications of this controversial competition, which attracted 3500 entrants, have been uncovered by Robert Burstow: nominally sponsored by the ICA, its funding in fact originated with the CIA.[50] *The Box*, into which Butler enigmatically sealed small figures that only he had ever seen, was described by Robert Melville in science-fiction terms as a 'messenger from a world of obscure forces ... . The texture of the iron is rough and mottled by rust, and the whole contraption looks like an unearthed relic of the Industrial Revolution, an infernal machine on the point of exploding'.[51] Butler's figures recall Picasso's skeletal iron-wire sculptures of 1928–30, but they also suggest the metal armatures on which sculptures had been formed for centuries: in a reversal of the traditional procedures of figure sculpture, Butler stripped his bodies of flesh and sinew to expose a frame, a skeleton, a minimal representation of the human form.

Reg Butler: *Figure in Space*, 1957–58. Bronze, height 91.4 cm. Private collection

Though the majority of Butler's schemes in the period 1948–53 remained unexecuted beyond the wire-maquette stage, they were usually imagined as large-scale structures. An adept engineer, he built two cameras with which he skilfully photographed his own work. The photographs were frequently taken from a low viewpoint to increase the impression of height, a device employed by Henry Moore, who began photographing his own sculptures with a plate camera in the 1930s. According to Roger Berthoud, 'Moore was also, from the start, interested in certain photographic effects: by taking a close-up of a small carving only a few inches long against the sky or a distant landscape, it could be made to seem monumental, thus demonstrating that scale is not just a matter of size'.[52]

Reg Butler: *Japanese Girl*, 1979–81.
Painted bronze with hair on velvet-covered foam base, length 42 cm. Private collection

In 1953 Butler, who believed his linear wire structures were becoming mannered, began the 'process of defeating the linear'[53] and, working in bronze, engaged again with fully volumetric figures. Elegance and movement were retained, and the sense of unease took on sexual overtones. After 1957 Butler's sculptures frequently incorporated a Bacon-like external space-frame. If Lawrence Alloway was correct in hinting that Bacon's palette was modified by the burgeoning of colour reproduction in magazines,[54] the final development in the sculpture of Reg Butler may have stemmed from the same source. After thirty years of working in monochrome wood, iron or bronze, Butler's painted bronzes appeared as a dramatic evolution in the 1960s. In 1962 he warned students against 'the received image' and advocated 'the struggle with objective reality'; but into a string of art-education basics he inserted 'The news-value of colour'.[55]

NEW REALISMS

'James was a painter of pictures in oil-colours. The paintings were large, perhaps ugly, vigorous, and brutal. He was a success and made money from his so-called "awful" giant creations on canvas or hardboard ... Angry brush-strokes covered the canvas in front of him. He picked up on his brush some Prussian blue, and drew with it into the sticky wet mass of paint intended to be a door.' – *John Bratby (from his novel* Breakdown*)*

'There was something Derrick Greaves had said at a Young Contemporaries meeting that made me laugh: he confessed to the audience, "I was a teenage social realist".' – *Patrick Procktor*

'Realism is not a method but an attitude of mind. Roberts and Spear, Edward Middleditch and Alfred Daniels, paint in very different ways, but I believe that ... they share a similar attitude ... The realist always starts from the particular and from this beginning tries to deduce a typical truth.' – *John Berger*

Jack Smith: *Interior with Child*, 1953 (no. 89)

One of the more problematical terms in art discourse, realism has tended to be applied to British art of the Fifties as though it were synoymous with the Social Realism postulated by the critic John Berger. Even within Berger's realism, his Marxist criterion – that art should 'help men know and claim their social rights'[1] – was not exclusively fulfilled by John Bratby, Derrick Greaves, Edward Middleditch and Jack Smith, though they did receive his firm support. All four were given one-man shows at Helen Lessore's Beaux-Arts Gallery in 1953 and 1954, and hence became linked as the 'Beaux-Arts Quartet'; but following David Sylvester's article 'The Kitchen Sink' in *Encounter*, December 1954,[2] 'The Kitchen Sink School' was the epithet that stuck with the public, to the dismay of the artists in question. Soon the style became conflated by the press with the Angry Young Men of literature, the novelists John Wain, Kingsley Amis and Colin Wilson, and the playwright John Osborne, all of whom similarly disputed both their collective title and generic identity. Beyond the historical synchronicity, however, there was no significant connection between the painters and the undirected 'anger' of the writers, any more than with the left-leaning directors – Lindsay Anderson, Lorenza Mazzetti, Karel Reisz and Tony Richardson – of the poetic documentaries of the Free Cinema group, first screened in 1956.

In September 1952 the exhibition *Looking Forward*, organized by John Berger, opened at the Whitechapel Art Gallery. (Berger selected a touring version of *Looking Forward* in 1953 and another in 1955–57; he also wrote the catalogue introduction for *Looking at People*, organized by the sculptor Betty Rea and the illustrator Paul Hogarth, which opened in 1955 at the Whitworth Art Gallery, Manchester, and after touring England was sent in 1957 to the Pushkin Museum, Moscow, accompanied by Hogarth, Derrick Greaves and Ruskin Spear). In the catalogue of the Whitechapel's recent centenary review, the essay 'John Berger and Looking Forward' describes David Sylvester as Berger's 'arch-enemy'. While this may not be far from the truth, the writer also claims that Sylvester intended his Kitchen Sink remark 'disparagingly' and compares this with Sylvester's advocacy of 'American modernism and the existentially melodramatic work of Bacon and late Giacometti, which for Berger were essentially tasteless'. But neither Sylvester nor even Berger was as polarized or narrow in his tastes as this over-simplified opposition implies. Furthermore, the reference to Sylvester's support for American Modernism confuses chronology. Artists from the USA, the home of capitalism, were unlikely to meet with Berger's approbation, but neither, in 1952, had their importance been recognized by Sylvester. A residual anti-Americanism had conspired to keep American painting away from London: Jackson Pollock's paintings, for example, had not been seen in Britain before the *Opposing Forces* exhibition at the Institute of Contemporary Arts (ICA) in 1953. Another five years elapsed before Sylvester 'woke up to the value of American Abstract Expressionism',[3] by which time Social Realism was an issue that concerned neither him nor Berger.

The timing of the exhibition *Recent Trends in Realist Painting*, which opened at the ICA in July 1952, just two months in advance of *Looking Forward*, was probably not coincidental. The selectors of *Realist Painting* were Peter Watson, Robert Melville and David Sylvester, who admitted that it was 'eclectic to the point of absurdity'. Sylvester, however, wished to keep the debate over realism open, and not decided by doctrinaire politics: 'Is this moment', he enquired rhetorically, 'to be dogmatic about what is the "authentic" realism of the day?' The ICA exhibition encompassed Giacometti, Buffet, Gruber, André Minaux, Balthus and Paul Rebeyrolle, Bacon, Coldstream, Freud, Lambert, Minton, Pulham and Sutherland. This was evidently a broader realism than the one Berger proposed, and the inclusion of William Coldstream is a reminder that 'Euston Road Realism' was a term still in use at that time. The confrontation

John Bratby: *The Toilet*, 1956 (no. 17)

between Berger and Sylvester in fact centred on a larger issue than Social Realism – it was about the future direction of British art. Both, it should be remembered, were still in their twenties, brilliant and articulate, but ambitious and prickly. Their battle was publicly conjoined by January 1952, when Bacon and Balthus were fiercely debated in 'Points of View' at the ICA. The *Art News and Review* reported that when Berger said 'we look at Bacon instead of going to Belsen, and this is not a "constructive attitude"', the 'chairman, David Sylvester, could not but leave his strict office to combat Berger on this point: he pointed out that mere indignation is chaotic and he praised Bacon for presenting suffering without indignation'.[4]

The dualism is over-simplistic, but essentially Berger was arguing for the primacy of content, Sylvester urged the centrality of form. For Berger art was inextricable from ideology, whereas Sylvester believed, like Maurice Denis, that 'a picture – before it is a picture of a battle-horse, nude woman, or some anecdote – is essentially a plane surface covered by paints arranged in a certain order'.[5] Both as an artist and a critic Berger's terms of reference were rooted in Marxism. In 1950 his work was exhibited at the Lisle Street gallery of the Artists International Association, an organization with which the economist and Marxist historian Francis D. Klingender was closely involved. Klingender's book *Art and the Industrial Revolution*, published in 1947, was instrumental in many artists, Berger included, painting industrial themes. In the last years of his life the Marxist art historian Frederick Antal (he died in 1954) was frequently visited in London by Berger and Paul Hogarth. Antal was a follower of Riegl and Dvorak, an advocate of a balanced approach to 'art' and 'history' whose method embraced sociology, history and economics, as well as style. Berger evolved a third position, neither formalist nor historical, that the most valid response for an art critic was a purely personal one, albeit informed by his experience of life. Thus, although he tended to wear his ideology on his sleeve, his viewpoint – though not his judgments – did not differ markedly from Sylvester's.

None of the Kitchen Sink School (all of whom were still students in 1952) was included by Sylvester in *Recent Trends in Realist Painting*. But before writing the *Encounter* article he had already applauded the 'large canvasses' in Middleditch's first one-man show for their 'boldy dramatic decorative effect with an agreeably contemporary flavour of post-war, post-Yalta, disillusionment',[6] and spoken of Bratby as 'the most vigorous of our youngest painters but also the most complete master of his style'.[7] His praise for these artists was not unqualified; neither was he blinkered or partisan. Sylvester's *Encounter* article dwelt only on Bratby and Smith, and although he compared them unfavourably with Van Gogh (whom he recognized as a major influence on Bratby) and even with Bernard Buffet, he was not exclusively antipathetic, praising, for instance, Smith's 'handsome aesthetic arrangements' and the 'life and exultation in Bratby's work'.

Berger withdrew his support for the Social Realists when they changed their styles after 1955, and, in deserting the 'deliberate acceptance of the importance of the everyday and the ordinary',[8] failed to conform to his political agenda. In *Permanent Red* (1960), for example, he curiously suggested one reason Bratby had not fulfilled his expectations was that he 'became successful'.[9] Berger was right, nevertheless, to regret Bratby's self-referential and self-aggrandizing tendency to include his own hands in the foregrounds of his paintings, and the interminable repetition of his self-portrait. But while the timely connection may not have harmed their early careers, the painters themselves did not participate in Berger's political stance: Jack Smith wrote to *The Listener* to distance himself from Social Realism and from the notion of an art of protest,[10] and as Derrick Greaves comments, though he himself was 'a good

Edward Middleditch: *Pigeons in Trafalgar Square*, 1954 (no. 75)

John Berger: *Scaffolding: Festival of Britain*, 1950 (no. 11)

Prunella Clough: *Man with a Blowlamp*, 1950 (no. 22)

left-winger ... what we were most interested in was becoming the *Courbets de nos jours'*. Of the four, only Bratby maintained the vigorous application of paint, unprepossessing subject-matter and uncompromisingly confrontational approach beyond 1956. Somewhat disingenuously, the others dissociated themselves from their earlier quotidian themes; Jack Smith, for example, claimed that 'I just painted the objects around me. I lived in that kind of house ... . If one had lived in a palace, one might have painted chandeliers'.[11]

Social Realism was not confined to the Beaux-Arts Quartet, nor did it necessarily originate with them. Berger himself was a more-than-competent artist, who painted and drew urban scenes and industrial toil in a gritty, direct style that qualifies as a kind of realism; *Scaffolding: Festival of Britain* (1950) also demonstrates his grasp of formal structural values. Prunella Clough's extended involvement with paintings of workmen and industrial machinery in the Fifties falls into the same category, though her portrayals were humanist and non-judgmental, and her concerns, as evidenced in *Man with a Blowlamp* (1950), were with 'the nature and structure of an object' – that and seeing it as if it were 'strange and unfamiliar' – rather than political. Similarly, Joan Eardley's paintings of tenement children in Glasgow, a theme that preoccupied her from 1949, are distinguished by her free rendering and bright colours. Her affection for the children's uninhibited characters is obvious, and in *Street Kids* (*c.* 1949–51; see illus. p. 81) Eardley crystallizes a moment of intimacy between the three children, a convincing observation that outweighs any social message about the arguably 'sordid' environment in which the children lived and played.

The incipient realisms, social and otherwise, for which the Royal College of Art (RCA) was an important breeding ground were evolving immediately after the War – before, that is, the advent of the Beaux-Arts Quartet: Jack Smith did not enter the college until 1950, and Bratby followed in 1951. A major factor in this was the college's more socially mixed intake: the student population was now augmented by many ex-servicemen, often from different – that is, less exclusively middle-class – social backgrounds. Two exhibitions in London in 1950 were strongly influential on these RCA students, and they represented, in a sense, opposite poles of contemporary realism. Renato Guttuso, a member of the Italian Communist party and painter of robust, vivid images of Sicilian peasantry and other contemporary themes – subjects with a popular appeal in Italy – had his first British one-man show at the Hanover Gallery and became a hero of the radical Left. The ICA exhibition *Symbolic Realism in American Painting 1940–1950* included Andrew Wyeth, the Mexican Julio Castellanos, Honoré Sharrer, Pavel Tchelitchew and Bernard Perlin: their precisionist realism had a correlation with the modern French 'primitives', particularly Camille Bombois, who may also have influenced some of the RCA students.

Perlin's painting *Orthodox Boys* appealed particularly to those RCA students who had been inspired by the Mexican Muralists and by Ben Shahn, but who had hitherto encountered their works only in magazine reproductions. Among those strongly impressed by *Orthodox Boys* – thinly and meticulously painted in tempera, but with an urban immediacy that contrasted with its Renaissance method – were Alfred Daniels and John Titchell; the young Peter Blake, who did not enter the college until 1953, was another great admirer of the painting, which hung for many years in the Tate Gallery. But Alfred Daniels, for example, also had great respect for Guttuso, even if his own paintings, which were less vigorously painted and less politically directed than the Italian's, scarcely suggest a close correspondence. Like his contemporary London street scenes, *Sunday in the Grass* (1951) was inspired partly by Perlin, and also, especially in its colour, by the Indian miniature paintings Daniels was then studying. In common with many artists who

Alfred Daniels: *Sunday on the Grass*, 1951 (no. 28)

Bernard Perlin: *Orthodox Boys*, 1948 (no. 84)

Albert Herbert: *Children Playing*, 1952 (no. 51)

began in the mid-twentieth century, Daniels has continued to pursue a successful career outside the evolving mainstreams of contemporary art; in his case, besides his paintings, which have a staunch following, this involved a respected rôle as an author and lecturer on art technique. The laconic, leisurely mood of *Sunday on the Grass*, painted from a scene Daniels witnessed in Hyde Park, connects to realist ideas of the commonplace, and, littered with discarded everyday artefacts of consumerism, presages a prevailing theme in British Pop Art a decade later.

Albert Herbert is among RCA alumni who testify to the importance of David Sylvester's 1951 lecture at the college, 'Towards a New Realism', which argued that art 'must show that experiences are fleeting, that every experience dissolves into the next ... must be images in which the observer participates', an existentialist thesis that he illustrated with slides of the work of Giacometti and Bacon. Herbert, who 'instinctively wanted to make figurative, emotive, symbolic paintings',[12] felt liberated from the imperative to engage in 'Euston Road realism or some sort of formalism'.[13] Bacon, at the invitation of John Minton, had taken a studio at the college for a term in 1950, accepting on condition that he was not prepared to give any formal

Joan Eardley: *Street Kids*, *c.* 1949–51 (no. 40)

lessons. Herbert was one of those who slipped into the studio during his long lunchbreaks to see what Bacon was up to; later to paint mostly religious subjects in a neo-primitive style, Herbert was impressed by Bacon's paintings and briefly integrated his influence (noticeable in the painting of movement and overlapping of the central figures in *Children Playing*; 1952) into a realism that dealt with anxious, urban themes.

Sylvester's identification of existentialism as a cultural force central to the work of certain British artists in the early Fifties carried an added authority in that he had spent much of his time in Paris since 1947; the second of two important articles he wrote about Paul Klee, was

Francis Gruber: *Job*, 1944.
Oil on canvas, 161.9 × 129.2 cm. Tate, London

Magazine cutting used by Ruskin Spear as
a reference for *Haute Couture*, c. 1950s.
Collection of Mrs Mary Spear

published in Sartre and Merleau-Ponty's *Les Temps modernes* in January 1951. Two artists identified simultaneously with wartime Parisian Resistance, existentialism and realism were Francis Gruber, who died in 1948, and Bernard Buffet, and both were included in *Recent Trends in Realist Painting*. Their emaciated, angular figures occupied lifeless interiors, solitary and tense, and exerted a powerful influence in London that informed both the Kitchen Sink School and the wider realist movement. The subsequent eclipse of Buffet, in both France and Britain, may have led to an underestimation of the effect his paintings had in the Fifties: as Jacqueline Stanley (who entered the RCA in 1949) relates, 'he was extremely influential at the college for a while, though eventually his repetitiveness caused us to reconsider – we thought he had become too slick, rather flashy'.[14]

When Robin Darwin became Principal of the RCA in 1948 he immediately set out, like William Johnstone at the Central School and William Coldstream at the Slade, to engage tutors who might raise the Painting School into a prominent position once again. Only Carel Weight survived Darwin's ejection of painting staff from the previous era, in spite of having been an appointee of Gilbert Spencer, whom Darwin had summarily dismissed. The new instructors included Rodrigo Moynihan, John Minton and Robert Buhler, who were joined in the following year by Colin Hayes. Their contribution was considerable, and all enjoyed separate and distinguished careers outside of teaching, but the painter who probably did most to encourage a Social Realism among his students was Ruskin Spear.

The influence of Ruskin Spear has been undervalued. First, he was from a working-class background and the most actively left-wing among his colleagues. His rôle in the Artists International Association (AIA) – still an effective force in the early Fifties – underlined his credentials in this respect, even though the organization was in the process of becoming de-politicized. Born in Hammersmith, he won a scholarship to the local art school at the age of fifteen and another to the RCA in 1930. Although he became an Associate of the Royal Academy in 1944, and enjoyed a successful career as a portrait painter, he maintained a parallel commitment to wry and witty social observation that placed him in a narrative tradition stretching back to his erstwhile west London neighbour and artistic precursor, Hogarth.

Spear's post-war landscapes of his Hammersmith neighbourhood are affectionate portrayals of modern life in an urban environment, but increasingly in the Fifties his paintings incorporated a satirical commentary on contemporary *mores*, directed mostly at public figures in the burgeoning age of television. During the War – when he was exempt from service owing to lameness from polio and sold *Peace News* along Hammersmith Broadway – Spear made fashion drawings for *Vogue* to supplement his meagre income. Both his resentment at this employment and the first-hand knowledge he acquired of the fashion business inform his sardonic *Haute Couture* (1954). The bitter-sweet, *épater-les-bourgeois* compositions that Spear sent to the Royal Academy throughout the Fifties and Sixties were invariably based on photographs or half-tone reproductions in magazines or newspapers. The ecstatically twirling mannequin in *Haute Couture* was inspired by a torn-out page from an Italian magazine, and in *Catching the Night Train* (1959; see illus. p. 84), which the academy refused to hang, Spear skilfully replicates the ethereal glare of a *Daily Express* news photograph in which Princess Margaret and her dogs, on their way to Balmoral Castle, were caught in mid-stride by a pressman's flashgun.

Ruskin Spear: *Haute Couture*, 1954 (no. 95)

Ruskin Spear: *36 × 24 × 38 in. and Reads Books*, 1955.
Oil on board, 122 × 61 cm. Location unknown

Ruskin Spear: *Catching the Night Train*, 1959 (no. 96)

Photographer unknown: *Ruskin Spear in Hammersmith, c.* 1955. Collection of Mrs Mary Spear

Spear's use of photographs was seldom referred to in the Fifties, and the critics who did mention it generally related it to the practice of Walter Sickert. Those who admitted that Spear was an evocative artist with a coherent vision usually added that he was 'old-fashioned' or 'post-Sickertian'. Spear, a technically confident and highly accomplished artist, had indeed admired and studied Sickert's work, but must have resented the insistent comparison. In 1944 he painted a homage to *Ennui*, an atypical work in which a faithful rendition of Sickert's evocation of domestic boredom was re-set within bomb-shattered walls, the room opening out on to Hammersmith's partly derelict, depopulated Victorian terraces. It was an unusual and effective protest against the tedium and futility of an apparently interminable war, but it may have been the direct reference to Sickert that caused Spear eventually to destroy this picture.

Spear is credited with influencing RCA students towards such Sickertian devices as using a coloured ground to unify a composition, working with a limited palette, and a kind of tonal painting that retained elements of a Euston Road School linearity. He was undoubtedly the conduit for Sickert's famous dictum (written in the context of the dominance of the bourgeois Edwardianism of Sargent and Orpen) that 'The more our art is serious, the more will it tend to avoid the drawing-room and stick to the kitchen'.[15] The aspect of Spear's paintings most deprecated by the Kitchen Sink School was itself an Edwardian residue – a tendency towards flashiness, the bravura touches in his painting technique that were factors in provoking his students to forge a rawer, earthier style: 'We had intense conversations about the need for a lustier language than that', says Derrick Greaves; 'we resented the way Spear would use a hogshair brush to bop in the highlights as a *coup de grace*; we felt the need to start again and find a more direct way to paint.'[16] Nonetheless, if the Kitchen Sink School – or at least Bratby's product-orientated still lifes – contributed to the breakdown of cultural hierarchies and helped to pave the way for Pop Art, then Spear's iconography has equal claims to prescience. His subject-matter in the Fifties – ironic representations of newly affluent suburbia and modish celebrity – documents the invasion of the mass media and the onset of consumerism in a way that few of his contemporaries attempted.

Newspaper cutting used by Ruskin Spear as a reference for *Catching the Night Train*, 1959. Collection of Mrs Mary Spear

In retrospect Edward Middleditch and Derrick Greaves seem scarcely to qualify as Kitchen Sink painters. Middleditch painted a butcher and a baby in 1952, and a few industrial landscapes when he accompanied Greaves on visits to his native Sheffield in the following year; in addition to these 'everyday' subjects he was influenced by Spear's restricted palette – often dominated by cool grey-blue tones. But soon the abiding themes of his paintings became landscape and nature: their atmosphere of foreboding is presaged in the precocious *Pigeons in Trafalgar Square* (1954), a painting whose downbeat subject and tinge of menace helped to provoke John Minton's comment about 'Hope being out, and Doom being in ...'.[17] Minton was another RCA tutor to have a perceptible influence on Middleditch (as he did for a while on Jack Smith), who interpreted his teacher's Mediterraneanism with a disquieting and sensuous Romanticism.

Like Middleditch, Derrick Greaves painted very few Social Realist works, and then only for a limited period. His first visit to Italy, on an Abbey Major Scholarship in 1953, accelerated the end of his involvement with the style: he had arranged for his RCA portfolio to be sent from London to await his arrival in Rome, with the intention of working up his studies into paintings, but instead he burnt them all in a stove. Greaves's experience of fresco painting suggested parallels with his early experience as an apprentice sign-writer in Sheffield – the workshop, master-and-apprentice organization, painting *in situ* and the life-size human figure – that had a strong personal resonance for him. He responded by painting Italy in a manner he also subsequently rejected as 'too literal – a dusty road equals dry, dusty paint'. Returning to England after two years he 'took apart the language and syntax of painting and started again'. His painting *Dog* (1955), of Bob, an ebullient and mischievous cross-bred Airedale terrier that belonged to his first wife, has a direct charm and pathos, but was not aimed at becoming Holman-Hunt's *Scapegoat* reprised for cold-war Britain. Shortly after this Greaves's paintings were to be seen again in Italy, for, like the others from the Beaux-Arts Quartet he represented Britain (together with Ivon Hitchens and Lynn Chadwick) in the 1956 Venice Biennale, a prestigious event that heralded, paradoxically, the demise of Social Realism.

The Social Realist label was attached to other painters at the time. Leslie Duxbury, who had shared a house at 44 Pembroke Road since 1948 with George Fullard, Arthur Berry and Ernest Adsetts, and later Derrick Greaves and Jack Smith, was another alumnus of the RCA who briefly painted in the style. Peter Coker, later well known for his landscapes, attended the college from 1950 to 1954, and painted a butcher's shop near his home in Leytonstone in thick impasto and Van Gogh-like dark outlines, sufficient to be identified as a Social Realist in his first one-man show at the Zwemmer Gallery in 1956. But it was John Bratby who attracted the media attention. Even for those who found British painting polite, over-literary, stiff-upper-lipped and compromised, Bratby was uncouth, insouciant and raw. In appearance he resembled the character he described in his novels – an only-partly engaging slob, a proto-beatnik with his thinning, unkempt hair, cigarette hanging from his lip, and sloppy jumper. His paintings invited the inevitable comparisons with jazz and with Angry Young Men; he was the public face of Social Realism.

Bratby's dense impasto was rapidly and coarsely applied, its very brutality helping to impart a 'contemporary' urgency and authenticity. Van Gogh was his most obvious model – both as an artist and for his technique – but Soutine's writhing, violent paint and the restlessly vivid Expressionism of Kokoschka (whose presence in London between 1938 and 1953 was significant) were scarcely less important. Bratby also attested to the influence of two English painters,

Derrick Greaves: *Dog*, 1955 (no. 44)

Edward Burra and Stanley Spencer. Bratby doubtless included himself when he wistfully declared that 'A whole generation of student-painters (many of them ex-servicemen) was oppressed by the mighty talent of Stanley Spencer ...',[18] and many ex-RCA students confirm that Spencer was held up as an ideal in the Fifties.

The bespectacled Bratby was short-sighted, but if this might be put forward as an explanation for his thickly laid-on paint, he himself called it 'the natural result of vigour and energy in a painting'.[19] Alan Clutton-Brock related how Bratby, in Rome on an Abbey Minor Scholarship in 1954, contracted jaundice, which he blamed on unhygenic food. His answer was to buy three packets of Quaker Oats in a grocery where 'the sight of good English food made his eyes shine'.[20] The table-top cornucopias that he painted in England, piled to overflowing with foodstuffs, were the honest outpouring of a 'hungry', ambitious artist. It is tempting to see such paintings as *Jean and Still Life in Front of Window* (1954) in the context of the last year of food rationing in post-war austerity-era London, but in Bratby's case they appear to be, rather than a lament over deprivation, a celebration of the immediate onset of a more materially affluent society. The most overt Van Gogh reference in Bratby's work was perhaps to be found in *The Toilet*, the lavatory of which he painted two versions, in 1955 and 1956. *Vincent's Chair* (1888) is transmuted in Bratby's characteristically in-your-face way, though it was painted against warm, opulent, yellow walls that Derrick Greaves, on re-acquaintance with the painting after more than forty years, called 'with hindsight, curiously exotic'.

It fell to Jack Smith to provide the eponymous kitchen sink, and his large, dun-coloured and starkly quotidian monochromes quickly established his reputation. But the thematic consistency of the domestic interiors that he painted between 1952 and 1954 suggests that his agenda at this time exceeded the nominal representation of semi-poverty. In the basement of 44 Pembroke Road, with its Ascot geyser and Belfast sink, he painted his sister-in-law Barbara Smith and sundry children in a series of skewed compositions that sought to arrest an instant in time and were a psychological exploration of the teetering vulnerability of small children. In certain paintings, such as *After the Meal* (1952) and *Child Walking with Check Tablecloth* (1953) Smith experimented with asymmetrical spatial relationships, assigning key pictorial incidents to the periphery of the paintings in order to heighten the tension of the sombre, ostensibly mundane scenes. Similarly, in these de-centred compositions, the subsidiary elements, less precisely delineated, carve up the rectangle into passages that crowd against one another expressionistically, an apposite, unsettling foil for the tentative motion of a child.

The dislocation engendered by Smith's formal devices was exaggerated by his raised viewpoint and by areas of floorboarding or tablecloths that ran off the edge of the frame in deep perspective. After 1956 Smith totally rejected Social Realist subjects and began to paint evanescent, semi-abstract still lifes. The summation of the brief early stage of his career was the large, enigmatic *Creation and Crucifixion* (1956), which, irrespective of Smith's formal concerns, was surely conceived in part as a valedictory gesture, as the end of a phase that he had come to see as a cul-de-sac. Shirts hang from a washing-line, stiff or crumpled; chairs stand motionless, inanimate except for one that has been knocked over and leaps diagonally off the edge of the picture; cutlery slips off the tablecloths; tumblers literally tumble. Smith's new concern with light and incandescence is pre-eminent, and the creation and crucifixion metaphors are deftly integrated, but *Creation and Crucifixion* ultimately forms a disquieting climax, an apotheosis, to four years of work. The crucifixion analogy was suggested to Smith by his

John Bratby: *Jean and Still Life in Front of Window*, 1954 (no. 16)

Jack Smith: *Mother Bathing Child*, 1953.
Oil on board, 182.9 × 121.9 cm. Tate, London

observation of the series of shirts he painted immediately prior to this: *Shirt in Sunlight* (1956) is one of this series, and its radically simplified, almost abstract forms and engagement with light sources presage the direction he would take after completing *Creation and Crucifixion*.

Shirts had often figured in the backgrounds of Smith's interiors, a favoured element in the dense clutter of kitchen and laundry paraphernalia. But this was 1956, the year of Abstract Expressionism at the Tate Gallery, of the New Vision Centre Gallery and of the Tachiste invasion. Jack Smith's renouncement of figurative or political content is a paradigm for a major shift in British art. In the battle of the realisms, Social Realism had been all but eliminated.

Jack Smith: *Shirt in Sunlight*, 1956 (no. 90)

OPPOSING FORCES

'At the time, we were more united by what we opposed than by what we supported. "Antagonistic co-operation" ... constitutes the most accurate description of the Group.' – *Toni del Renzio*

'Group members such as del Renzio, Alloway, Reyner Banham and myself were bound together by our enthusiasm for the iconography of the New World. The American magazine represented a catalogue of an exotic society, bountiful and generous, where the event of selling tinned pears was transformed into multi-coloured dreams ... .' – *Eduardo Paolozzi*

'How pompous, formal and antiquated the art establishment was. The Independent Group was for practising artists and critics and no one else. They even talked tough, in a certain way – the linguistic equivalent of Brutalism.' – *Richard Lannoy*

'An image is cut out of a newspaper; shall we say a blurred news photo, flashlight taken in the rain, of a crashed aeroplane. A battered wheel rises sharply in the foreground near a happy face, a cowling like an eye waits in the vegetation.' – *Eduardo Paolozzi*

Nigel Henderson:
Eduardo Paolozzi's studio, Paris, 1949.
Private collection

MINISTER OF FOOD
LONDON 1946
PRODUCE OF CEYLON
265.47
PAOLOZZI

Independent Group: The Theorists

The Institute of Contemporary Arts (ICA) opened in 1948 and moved into its own premises at 17–18 Dover Street, London, in 1950. Under the presidency of Herbert Read and the chairmanship of Roland Penrose, the ICA's commitment to Modernism reflected their respective interests in a social, libertarian art and in Surrealism. But among the artists and critics who began to attend the ICA's programme of lectures and debates, and to frequent its bar and members' room, were some who disputed the received conventions of modern art theory and who regarded London's art establishment, even at the ICA, as 'pompous, formal and antiquated'.[1] From 1952 to 1955 these subversives, though they remained under the ICA umbrella, coalesced under the title of the Independent Group. This dissident clique formed around the critics Lawrence Alloway, Peter Reyner Banham and Toni del Renzio, and the artists Richard Hamilton, Nigel Henderson, Eduardo Paolozzi and William Turnbull. There is scant contemporary documentation of the Independent Group, which was virtually a closed discussion forum. The group's revisions of art theory and analytical and socio-anthropological readings of the mass media had only an indirect bearing on art practice, and little connection with *painting*, though its influence on debate about the urban environment is more readily discerned.

Toni del Renzio, though no longer a practising artist at the time of his involvement with the Independent Group, was the most polymathic of its members. A poet and critic, he had been a Surrealist painter, edited the Surrealist magazine *Arson* (only one volume of which was published, in March 1942) and in 1944 married the Surrealist painter Ithell Colquhoun (they were divorced four years later). He taught design at Camberwell School of Arts and Crafts from 1944 to 1946, redesigned another short-lived periodical, *Polemic,* in 1946, and in the Fifties worked as a graphic designer and as an art editor for numerous magazines. Through the wartime Surrealist connection, del Renzio had met Robert Melville (a contributor to *Arson*), likewise a leading art critic in the Fifties, and other Birmingham Surrealists such as Melville's artist brother, John Melville, Conroy Maddox and Emmy Bridgwater. Melville became an assistant to E.L.T. Mesens when the London Gallery re-opened in 1947, and moved two years later to work for Erica Brausen and Arthur Jeffress at the Hanover Gallery; Francis Bacon's first one-man show there prompted Melville's seminal article for *Horizon.* Melville, who moved freely between the ICA's Advisory Council and the Independent Group, became the art critic for the *Architectural Review* in 1952, the same year that Reyner Banham joined the magazine.

Reyner Banham trained with the Bristol Aeroplane Company, but from 1949 until 1952 studied art history at the Courtauld Institute: from these two disciplines he evolved his position that 'technology has outstripped art'.[2] Many Independent Group members had a common interest in Hollywood cinema, American comics and science fiction, and if Lawrence Alloway was most active in the analysis of these popular art forms then Banham was the most solidly demotic in his expressions of support for American product styling and technology. He recognized, however, the political contradiction inherent in this: 'how to maintain this discriminating admiration in the face of the conditioned-reflex atomic sabre-rattling of the Eisenhower regime?'[3]

During the war Lawrence Alloway, who had intended to be a poet, joined a University of London extra-mural evening class in art history at the National Gallery, where David Sylvester was a fellow student. Already a book reviewer for *The Sunday Times* and *The Observer,* his rejection as a contributor by the *New Statesman* was apparently a decisive factor in his detestation of class consciousness.[4] It may also explain his campaign to undermine not only the established hierarchies of art but also of art criticism. Charles Johnson, the Official Lecturer at the National

Gallery, had taught Alloway art history: he began to feed him lecturing jobs at the gallery, and in 1950 introduced him to Dr Richard Gainsborough, owner of the *Art News and Review*. Founded in 1949, the fortnightly *Art News and Review* was an outlet for the art criticism of Alloway, Reyner Banham, Robert Melville and, to a lesser extent, Toni del Renzio. When he joined the Independent Group, at the end of 1952, Alloway had a wide knowledge of art history and an acute critical perception that he delivered with an equally sharp thrust. Ambitious to operate on a broad cultural front, he devoured David Riesman's study of urban American society, *The Lonely Crowd* (1950), and 'frequently used its catch-phrases, such as "inner-directed" and "other-directed"'.[5] *The Mechanical Bride*, Marshall McLuhan's pioneering analysis of advertising and mass-media communications as symptoms of modern society, was not published in Britain until 1962, but Alloway had sent for a copy, which he had seen advertised in *View* magazine, immediately on its US publication in 1951. McLuhan's rejection of simplistic readings of 'highbrow' and 'lowbrow' as useful indicators of intellectual activity – 'the alert and detached mind ignores such categories'[6] – underpinned Alloway's 'Pop' theories in the Fifties, and resonated in his most often-quoted formulations, such as 'The Long Front of Culture'.[7]

According to Richard Hamilton, 'If there was one binding spirit amongst the people at the Independent Group, it was a distaste for Herbert Read's attitudes'.[8] Read's humanist absolutes

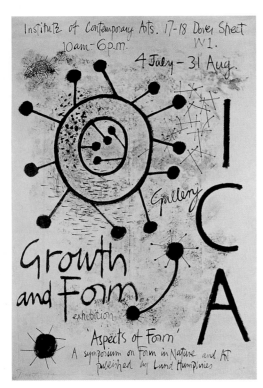

William Turnbull: Poster for *Growth and Form*, 1951.
75.5 × 50 cm. Private collection

Geoffrey Ashburner: Experimental *Vogue* cover, 1950.
Carbro-colour print, 35.2 × 27.2 cm. Collection of
Michael Ashburner

Geoffrey Ashburner (1920–1966) experimented with
colour photograms in 1949–51, using a version of the
defunct Vivex process.

were rejected, along with those of Roger Fry and Clive Bell that consigned art into a rarefied cultural vacuum: 'Significant form, design, vision, order, composition etc. were seen as high level abstractions, floating above the pictures like ill-fitting haloes.'[9] Although, as Mary Banham noted, there was an element of 'kicking Daddy'[10] in this, the group was serious in its hostility to Read's notion of art as transcendent and ahistorical. In *Nine Abstract Artists* (1954), Alloway attacked Read for his support of the 'transcendental quality' expressed in the work of Ben Nicholson, which 'must of necessity be far removed from the mundane world of actual appearances': 'There', commented Alloway acidly, 'the platonic drift of abstract aesthetics is summed up: geometry is the means to a high world.'[11] Within the Independent Group's factions there was concordance with Alloway's mission to free art from the 'iron curtain of traditional aesthetics which separate absolutely art from non-art'.[12]

In 1948 the first ICA exhibition, *40 Years of Modern Art 1907–1947*, included a drawing by Eduardo Paolozzi, and he was again represented, along with Richard Hamilton and William Turnbull, in *Aspects of British Art* in December 1950. The first ICA exhibition to be organized by a future Independent Group member was *Growth and Form* in July 1951, although its curator, Richard Hamilton, had designed the James Joyce exhibition and catalogue in June 1950. The original *On Growth and Form*, by D'Arcy Wentworth Thompson, was published in 1917 and was a touchstone for the proto-Independent Group nucleus. Thompson had aimed to demonstrate 'a certain mathematical aspect of morphology' and disputed Aristotle's 'teleological concept of end, of purpose or of "design"'.[13] This philosophical platform, which effectively sanctioned the group's iconoclasm, was augmented by A.C. Korzybski's *Science and Sanity: An Introduction to Non-Aristotelean Systems and General Semantics* (1933), in which he prised the signified from the signifier. Originally, Paolozzi and Henderson were involved with what became the *Growth and Form* project. Henderson had suggested seed dispersal as a theme, but it was Paolozzi who, in 1949, supplied the decisive push towards its ultimate form when he wrote to Henderson from Paris to report 'how keen his American friends were on D'Arcy Wentworth Thompson's book'.[14] The exhibition was scheduled as one of the ICA's contributions to the Festival of Britain, and it was Hamilton who energetically pursued the project through nervous committees; Paolozzi and Henderson eventually withdrew from the project, realizing it was 'Hamilton's drop'.[15]

The concept for *Growth and Form* may have drawn on the Modernist exhibition installations of Herbert Bayer and Moholy-Nagy, but it was an unfamiliar one in London at that time, a prototype multimedia or environmental art event that included film-loop projections and the stroboscopic lighting of water droplets. Assembled largely from non-fine-art materials, it anticipated the presentation of later Independent Group exhibitions, such as *Parallel of Life and Art* (1953). Hamilton researched recent scientific imagery to augment and update Thompson's illustrations, and the exhibits included radiographs, electron micrographs and film stills. Henderson contributed two photograms, and three models of skeletal structures were provided by the painter Martin Froy, Hamilton's contemporary at the Slade. *Growth and Form* was accompanied by a new book, *Aspects of Form*, edited by Lancelot Law Whyte. Whyte was responsible for the book's chronology and bibliography, and ensured the project's intellectual rigour. The scientists J.D. Bernal and C.H. Waddington were originally enlisted as consultants to the exhibition's management committee; in the event Bernal dropped out, but Waddington contributed an essay on 'The Character of Biological Form' to *Aspects of Form*. Director of the Institute of Animal Genetics, Edinburgh, and married to the architect Justin Blanco White,

Nigel Henderson: Installation photograph, *Parallel of Life and Art*, 1953. The Estate of Nigel Henderson

Professor Waddington's closest friends in the 1930s were John and Myfanwy Piper; he assembled a considerable art collection of his own, and in 1968 published *Beyond Appearance*, a study of the relations between painting and the natural sciences. Waddington's book was, regrettably, an exception, and the 'pooling of ideas' about art and science that Whyte had proposed was an initiative that barely survived the Fifties.

Large claims have been made for the alliance of art and science in *Growth and Form*, but it was by no means an isolated instance of the association of the disciplines. Since *Growth and Form* was a contribution to the Festival of Britain, it should be noted that the Festival Pattern Group, formed in 1949 by Mark Hartland Thomas of the Council for Industrial Design (and based on the researches of Professor Kathleen Lonsdale and Dr Helen Megaw) was responsible for disseminating the crystal, molecular and biological forms that were the basis of a high proportion of the distinctive mainstream pattern designs of the Fifties. It is possible, therefore, that the designs marketed by Paolozzi and Henderson after 1956 did not fail because they were too advanced or innovatory, but because they were dated and over-familiar.

Another key essay in *Aspects of Form* was E.H. Gombrich's 'Meditations on a Hobby Horse, or The Roots of Artistic Form'. In their discussions of the 'age-old problem of universals',[16] this, and a contemporary ICA lecture by S. Giedion, further corroborated the non-Aristotelean view of art. It is doubtful that non-Aristotelean logic was studied in depth by the Independent Group – Alloway, for example, first encountered it in a science-fiction novel, A.E. Van Vogt's *The World of Null-A* (1948) – but they distilled from it what was germane to their evolving theories. For Richard Hamilton the elimination of value judgments meant that 'we were able to say everything we can think of is right and can be used'.[17] Intense debates centred on Alloway's

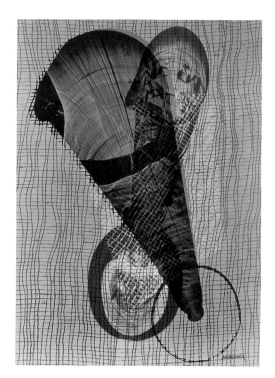

Geoffrey Ashburner: *Variations 3*, 1950. Carbro-colour print, 35 × 24.6 cm. Collection of Michael Ashburner

A version of this print was published in *Vogue*, July 1950. In 1951 Ashburner also made colour prints for displays in the Festival of Britain.

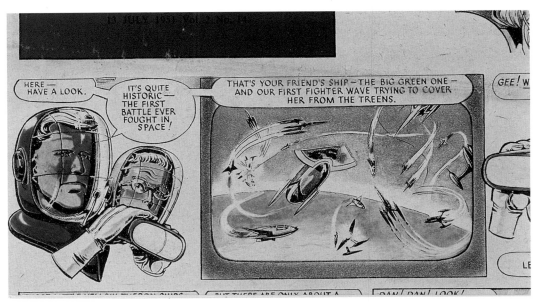

Frank Hampson: Detail of Dan Dare cartoon strip, 'Pilot of the Future', *Eagle*, 13 July 1951. Private collection

The Roberto Matta exhibition at the ICA preceded this comic strip by six months, and the cartoon illustrator's looping spacecraft may have been directly indebted to Matta's whirling cosmoses; both Matta's paintings and the Dan Dare series reflected Cold War anxieties, expressed in the comic strip in terms of potential alien invasion.

pluralism, on his investigation of 'low' as well 'high' art, and on the multidisciplinary elisions of art, science and technology; these were the basis of the 'machine aesthetic' developed by Reyner Banham.

Sigfried Giedion's *Space, Time and Architecture* (1941) and *Mechanization Takes Command* (1948) were already considered seminal texts in 1950, when he gave what was the first public lecture at the Dover Street premises of the ICA on 'Palaeolithic Art and Modernism'. An early exposition of the ideas he developed into *The Eternal Present: The Beginnings of Art* (published seventeen years later), Giedion's concepts of transparency, simultaneity and interpenetration had important ramifications for the rendering of pictorial space. In order to stress their unique spatial sense, Giedion had directed a photographer to re-photograph cave paintings to emphasize how the prehistoric imagery, unlike the verticals of Egyptian art or the rectangular picture plane, floated and drifted around multiple viewpoints. In January 1951 the ICA exhibition of Roberto Matta's hallucinatory paintings of vertiginous cosmic spaces, of a cataclysmic universe in flux, helped to refocus attention on the question of non-Euclidean space. David Sylvester, though never formally an Independent Group member, frequented their meetings and chaired many of the ICA's 'Points of View' debates. He had returned from Paris with a clear formulation of the significance of the multiple viewpoints in the late Berne-period work of Paul Klee, a concept he termed 'afocalism'. He coined another phrase, the 'multi-evocative sign', which was immediately absorbed into Independent Group parlance; he later regretted his inability to see, at this point, the correspondence between Klee's 'afocalism' and the 'all-over' viewpoints of Jackson Pollock. Versions of his lecture 'Cubism, Klee and Architecture', given at the ICA in October 1951, were delivered, resoundingly, at the Royal College of Art (RCA) and the Slade School of Fine Art, and published in the *Architectural Review*, December 1951, as 'Architecture in Modern Painting'.

The Catalyst: Nigel Henderson

The Independent Group was, as John McHale observed, a 'small, cohesive, quarrelsome, abrasive group',[18] and its heterogeneity is underlined in the opposition to Alloway's and Banham's Americanism that came from Toni del Renzio and Nigel Henderson, who located their own interests within the continuity of European culture. Henderson, only fitfully productive and an unusually unambitious artist, has remained the most opaque member of the Independent Group.[19] His extant collages mostly post-date the group, and his corpus is dominated by images that resist classification as either photography or art. Yet his role in the group was crucial: he was the catalyst who alerted his colleagues to sources of visual imagery that uncovered innumerable areas of inquiry. It was Henderson, for example, who introduced Richard Hamilton (whom he had befriended at the Slade) to Roland Penrose in order to propose *Growth and Form*, and who loaned Hamilton his copy of Duchamp's *Green Box* (1934); in Paris he took Eduardo Paolozzi to meet Peggy Guggenheim, and was, as Paolozzi acknowledged, 'my introduction to another world'.[20] Most significantly, Henderson was a link across the trajectory of the war years, re-establishing connections within British culture that had been severed in 1939.

Nigel Henderson: *Untitled*, c. 1956 (no. 50)

The basis for this image was a photograph Henderson had taken of Paris walls in 1949.

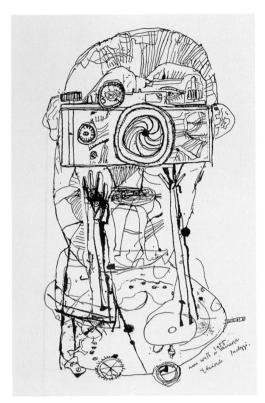

Eduardo Paolozzi: *Man with a Camera*, 1955
(reproduced in *Architectural Design*, April 1956).
Private collection

Unlike the other members of the Independent Group, the slightly older Henderson had already made significant forays into the avant-garde art world in the 1930s. He was directly acquainted with Surrealism, Dada and collage, frequented Bloomsbury Group activities, danced with Rupert Doone's 'Group Theatre' (he also helped Robert Medley with the sets for Louis MacNiece's *Agamemnon*), and, like many of his contemporaries, was briefly a member of the Communist party. His mother, Wyn Henderson, had been involved with Nancy Cunard's Hours Press and with the Aquila Press from 1927 to 1930, and ran the London gallery Guggenheim Jeune for Peggy Guggenheim from 1938 until the War intervened. Through his mother he met Tanguy, Ernst and Duchamp, Auden, Brecht and Dylan Thomas, Julian Trevelyan, Graham Bell and Humphrey Jennings. More significant in its implications for the Independent Group was his love affair with Vera Meynell (co-founder of the Nonesuch Press), who introduced him to scientists such as N.W. Pirie and J.D. Bernal. To his contemporaries, Desmond Bernal, atheist, Marxist and Professor of Physics at Birkbeck College, was 'The Sage'. He told Henderson 'about Chevreul and the Rods and Cones and Seurat'[21] and 'held him spellbound with talk of spaceships'.[22] Bernal's work on x-ray crystallography and cybernetics, his predictions of the future shape of man and his sweeping convergence of the ancient past and distant future anticipated a good segment of the Independent Group agenda. Encouraged by Vera Meynell, Henderson studied biology at Chelsea Polytechnic, became fascinated with microscopy and considered taking up marine biology. Mostly, though, he assimilated non-art sources in terms of their potential as visual stimuli: ultimately the scientist was, for Henderson, someone who 'disintegrates the commonplace'.[23]

A bomber pilot with Coastal Command, Henderson was exhilarated by aerial views of the landscape, the macrocosmic foil to his earlier microcosms. He was invalided out of the RAF in 1943 and in the same year married Judith Stephen, daughter of Adrian and Karen Stephen and niece of Virginia Woolf. Two years later the couple moved to Bethnal Green, in London's East End. Judith Henderson, an economist and anthropologist, was conducting a survey, 'Discover Your Neighbour', organized by the sociologist J.L. Peterson, that required its tutors to live on site. Judith's detailed recording of a neighbouring working-class family was another bridge with the 1930s, a return to the aims of the pre-war Mass-Observation scheme, and indeed her work had the continuing interest and support of Mass-Observation founder Tom Harrisson.

Henderson's friendships in the late 1930s with Julian Trevelyan and Graham Bell coincided with their involvement in Mass-Observation's 'Worktown' project in Bolton, when Trevelyan was making photo-montages and Bell used news photographs in his paintings. In the 'Worktown' photographs of Humphrey Spender and others, signs of popular culture – fairground slogans, advertising hoardings – form a backdrop to street life. Henderson's photographic agenda was neither sociological nor political, but his work was ineluctably informed by his connections to pre-war socialism, Surrealism, Euston Road Realism and documentary photography. The Mass-Observation experiment was effectively ended by the War, and Bell, an RAF navigator, died in action in 1943. A former photojournalist for *Picture Post*, Humphrey Spender taught textile design at the RCA from 1953, and his 'Worktown' photographs remained largely unpublished until the 1980s. And Humphrey Jennings's tragic death in 1950 appeared to seal the post-war eclipse of the poetic-Surrealist-documentary axis. In the catalogue of a memorial exhibition at the ICA in February 1951 Kathleen Raine placed Jennings within the school of '"scientific" literary criticism that produced Empson's conception of the ambiguity (more properly the multiplicity) of the poetic statement',[24] a reading that resonated with Henderson and the Independent Group.

Nigel Henderson: *Leicester Square*, 1949. Private collection

(Within the labyrinth of contemporary social contexts it may be mentioned that on his marriage to Freda Elliott in 1951 Paolozzi took a flat in Kathleen Raine's house in Paulton's Square, Chelsea; Raine had translated Paul Foulquie's *L'Existentialisme* into English in 1948.)

Henderson was, then, a transmitter and developer of many contexts through into the Fifties. An ex-serviceman's grant allowed him to enrol at the Slade in 1945, where he worked assiduously in the life room. His drawing skills were, however, perfunctory: he failed to finish a painting there and in any case found the academic curriculum unconducive. He met kindred spirits at the Slade in Eduardo Paolozzi and William Turnbull, but this was before the advent of William Coldstream as Principal, and all three rebelled against the conventional teaching: they began to work outside the Slade and to crash other courses at the university, especially in the Department of Anatomy. Paolozzi soon left for Paris, eager to live and work at the main source of their inspirations. Henderson stayed in London, though he made several extended visits to Paris during Paolozzi's two-year stay. In 1948 he borrowed a Leica camera from Humphrey Swingler (the documentary film-maker and brother of the Communist poet Randall Swingler) with the intention of documenting life at the Slade. Uncomfortable with the miniature camera's rangefinder, he soon changed to a 120 roll-film Rolleicord, preferring the larger image on its ground-glass screen. At first he did not print his own negatives, but Paolozzi, on returning to London in October 1949, brought from Paris the gift of a small enlarger. Henderson set up the equipment in the family's bathroom, where he and Paolozzi experimented at night. They made photograms 'using debris from bomb-sites'[25] and would 'cram all sorts of things into the slot conventionally

Nigel Henderson: Newsagent's, Bethnal Green, c. 1950–52. Private collection

With the renewed interest in Henderson's photographs in the 1970s, such urban vernacular images as this were described as 'Pop'; Henderson, however, resented being pigeon-holed as a 'sweet shop photographer'.

Nigel Henderson: Cecil Collins, 1951 (no. 48)

In this out-take from a portrait sitting commissioned by *Vogue*, Henderson placed Collins, a Neo-Romantic artist established in the 1930s, in a hieratic pose based on ecclesiastical sculpture of the late thirteenth century.

allocated to the negative'.[26] Henderson projected light through torn fabrics on to sensitized paper, and the 'fractured cells' reminded him of 'botanical micro sections'.[27] Henderson affirmed his admiration for the work of the artist and film-maker Len Lye, who had designed collage book covers for Wyn Henderson at the Hours Press, and he was almost certainly familiar with Lye's experimental films, such as the biomorphic *Tusalava* (1929).

The Hendersons' home from 1945 until 1954 was at 46 Chisenhale Road, an 1860s terrace on the borders of Bow and Bethnal Green. Today well kept and almost genteel, the area was soot-blackened, bomb-damaged and impoverished in the 1940s. Under a looming, red-brick London County Council Board School, Chisenhale Road terminated with a pub in one direction and a fur factory in the other. It was one block north of Roman Road, which, lined with shops and shoppers, provided many of Henderson's subjects. The solidly working-class surroundings, perversely exotic in their unfamiliarity, exerted a strong fascination on this privileged, upper-middle-class couple. The ceremonial of East End street life – 'I just walked and walked and stared at everything'[28] – was a form of auto-therapy in the treatment of the nervous breakdown he had suffered during the War. At first he was an observant outsider – it was some years before he considered photographing this 'sort of stage set against which people were more or less unconsciously acting'.[29] Dating from 1950–52, these 'street photographs', especially the urban-vernacular shop windows, replete with advertising slogans, are the images appropriated in recent accounts of 'proto-Pop'. Contrary to Pop claims, none of the photographs was taken for publication, and they remained virtually unknown and unpublished outside the immediate circle of the Independent Group.[30]

Henderson's absorption of Surrealist concepts such as automatism and the found object was, from 1949, manifest in his encounters with both the textures – 'the cracks and slicks and erosive marks on pavement slabs'[31] – and street life of urban London. He photographed fugitive situations, exposing film that, once developed, he could later 'scrutinise'.[32] Photography was not, for him, a means for making definitive statements but a medium for *revelation*. The camera was an apparatus for making open-ended – *latent* – images. The darkroom was an extender of the potentialities: he regarded the enlarger as 'a kind of drawing instrument',[33] a means of further altering perceptions and releasing 'an energy of image from trivial data'.[34]

In 1951 Henderson began to teach an evening class at the Central School of Arts and Crafts. William Johnstone left Camberwell School of Arts and Crafts to become Principal of the Central School in 1947, determined to 'shake it out of its "arty-crafty" standards and to bring it in line with modern thinking'.[35] He introduced a basic design class on the Bauhaus model, but with a less rigid aspect that reflected his own experience studying in the Paris studio of André L'Hôte. Individual teachers were allowed considerable freedom in framing their courses, and the experiences of progressive schools such as the Central evolved into what is now termed a foundation course. Henderson's colleagues included Paolozzi, Turnbull, Hamilton, Wright, Victor Pasmore, Louis Le Brocquy, Cecil Collins, Paul Hogarth, Mervyn Peake, Keith Vaughan and Patrick Heron. Their classes were not in fine art but were part of the post-war initiative to raise the standards of industrial design: when Alan Davie joined the staff in 1953 it was to teach basic design in the jewellery department, and only later did he teach experimental painting. Henderson's class was in 'creative photography', and it is consistent with the uncertain status of photography at that time that it was conducted 'out of harm's way in the basement, where few students even found it'.[36] The more persistent were rewarded, however, as Ken Garland attests: 'Not only did Nigel open you up to all kinds of experimentation with the photographic process, he was also completely at home with the European modernism that had by-passed Britain. We had a lot of catching up to do, and it was Nigel and not our main tutors that introduced us to key texts like Kepes' *Language of Vision* and Mcholy-Nagy's *Vision in Motion*.'[37]

Parallel of Life and Art, an exhibition organized by Henderson, Paolozzi, and Alison and Peter Smithson, opened at the ICA in September 1953. It extended many of the ideas essayed in *Growth and Form*. Its 'all-over', apparently random, non-consecutive arrangement – its collage of images – invited viewers to create their own associations, to become active participants. If the 'strong visual experience' Henderson hoped to achieve met with incomprehension in many quarters, others benefited from its stimulus. Ron Herron, designer of the 'Walking City' in 1964 but then a trainee architect, recalled: 'it had just amazing images ... the juxtaposition of all those images! I was just knocked out by it.'[38] In 1953 Denise Scott Brown was a student at the Architectural Association. Later a partner of Robert Venturi (they co-authored *Learning from Las Vegas* in 1972) and an important link in transatlantic architectural thinking, her testimony to the impact of Brutalism, and specific citation of Henderson's photographs in *Parallel of Life and Art*, is especially significant.[39]

The images in *Parallel of Life and Art* were deliberately un-pretty, raw and grainy. A conscious democratization of visual information juxtaposed work by Klee, Dubuffet and Alberto Burri with non-art material such as huge, commercially produced blow-ups of micro-photographs, fossils or news photographs. Reyner Banham located the origins of New Brutalism in this display,[40] but the non-hierarchical disposition of the objects was central to the concept of 'image' – of an image, that is, as the conveyor of meaning irrespective of its status as high or low art. Most of the exhibits were mediated through photography, and Henderson's experience as a photographer stands, therefore, at the intersection of these experiments in perception and the lateral association of images.

Nigel Henderson: Eduardo Paolozzi, 1949. Private collection

Eduardo Paolozzi: Renewing Surrealism

Recalling his time at the Slade, Paolozzi described himself, Henderson and Turnbull as being among 'a small minority sharing an enthusiasm for the world of Picasso and Matisse and a disregard for the staff and our fellow students'.[41] Paolozzi responded by working not in the school's sculpture studio but in the basement of the student house at 28 Cartwright Gardens. Here he mined a rich vein of precocious inspiration. In January 1947, aged twenty-three and still a student, he was given his first one-man show at the Mayor Gallery. To Paolozzi, raw materials equated with raw objects. The spontaneous and ebullient barbarism and the coarsely scored but dynamic textures of his early sculpture were unlike anything that had been seen before from a British sculptor; the antithesis of Henry Moore's sophistication, they were the first visual evidence in London of what was later identified as New Brutalism. They evoke Paolozzi's later definition of collage, in which he exhorts: 'damage, erase, destroy, deface and transform – all parts of a metaphor for the creative act itself':[42] Robert Melville's perceptive account of the Mayor Gallery show in *Horizon* referred to 'endlessly transformable objects with an immutable fetishistic significance'.[43]

The exhibition was a near sell-out and its success enabled Paolozzi to quit the Slade and move to Paris in the summer of 1947. In the previous year the sculptor Raymond Mason, described by Paolozzi as 'a leader and a giant among his fellow students at the Slade',[44] had moved to Paris (where he has since remained), and he passed on his room on the Ile St-Louis to Paolozzi in October 1947. Paolozzi's Paris-period sculptures – *Forms on a Bow* and *Growth (Table Sculpture)* (both 1949) – were made in plaster and later cast in bronze in London. He was introduced to Giacometti by Isabel Lambert (who had modelled for, and briefly lived with, Giacometti); his sculptures were indebted not to Giacometti's contemporary attenuated figures-in-space, however, but to his earlier, Surrealist, table-top tableaux, such as *Man and Woman* (1928–29). It has been suggested that *Growth (Table Sculpture)* derives from the bone structure of a fish,[45] which is convincing in that it alludes to both Giacometti's search for 'a kind

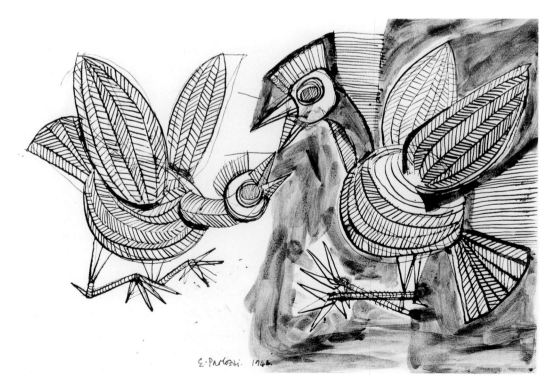

Eduardo Paolozzi: *Cocks Fighting*, 1948 (no. 77)

Eduardo Paolozzi: *Two Forms on a Rod*, 1948–49 (no. 78)

of skeleton in space'[46] and Paolozzi's own collage-drawing, *Fish* (1946). Paolozzi's gift to Lambert of the skeleton of a bat may also be significant in this context. His pen-and-ink drawings, such as *Cocks Fighting* (1948), continued a style he had begun in London in 1946, and in which Robert Melville astutely detected the influence of Robert Colquhoun. Indebted also to Picasso, their close hatching suggests, in addition, Paolozzi's familiarity with the drawings of Dubuffet, whose 'Foyer de l'Art Brut', opened in 1947, he visited with Turnbull.

On returning to London in October 1949, Paolozzi resumed the rough, hand-moulded surfaces that had distinguished the Picasso-esque sculptures he modelled from obdurate concrete while at the Slade. The drawings he made after he started to teach in the textile department at the Central School of Arts and Crafts in 1949, such as *Untitled* (1951; see illus. p. 107), have stronger affinities with Paul Klee. The Klee retrospective at the National Gallery in 1945 was evidently an important event in this respect, and Nigel Henderson acknowledged the currency of Klee in their Slade circle. Conversations with David Sylvester in both Paris and London reinforced the connection with Klee's 'afocalism' and with existentialism, and Paolozzi's silkscreens of the early Fifties, Henderson's photograms and Turnbull's drawings all reflect Klee's extemporized drawing and random asymmetry.

At the first meeting of the newly formed Independent Group, in April 1952, Eduardo Paolozzi gave a now-famous projection, through 'a rather hot epidiascope',[47] of illustrations gathered from popular magazine pages and American mass-media exotica in Paris and London since 1947. Although some of his *Time* magazine collages and scrapbook pages were exhibited at the ICA in 1954, these interests remained virtually unknown outside his Independent Group

Eduardo Paolozzi: *Growth (Table Sculpture)*, 1949 (no. 80)

Eduardo Paolozzi: *Forms on a Bow*, 1949 (no. 79)

intimates until he made the Bunk series of screen prints in 1972. It was not until long after the demise of the Independent Group that the epidiascope presentation of 1952 began to sediment into its mythical status as the first exposition of Pop Art, or indeed that the title 'Bunk' was retrospectively appended to it. An avid cinema-goer and collector of pulp imagery since childhood, Paolozzi resisted any limitations on his voracious appetite for images. But the identification with Pop Art is based on a misconception of Paolozzi's, and the Independent Group's, engagement with the popular arts. The stimulation they found in images from 'alternative culture' was not intended to be regurgitated in an unmediated form, but, having been assimilated into their open-ended visual vocabulary, integrated into art that was independent of, albeit enriched by, these sources. In Paolozzi's case the most overt debt, apart from the collages themselves, was visible in the mechanical debris that he began to incorporate in his sculpture.

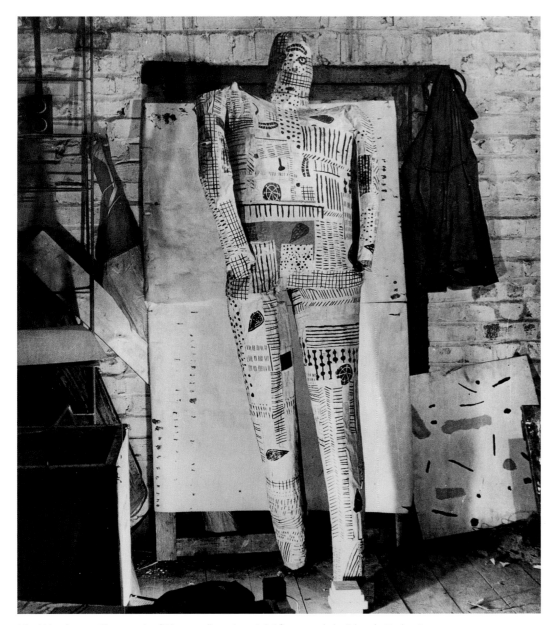

Nigel Henderson: Photograph of (destroyed) papier-mâché figure made by Eduardo Paolozzi, 1953.
The Estate of Nigel Henderson

Installation photograph including modern 'Judas' figures in the exhibition *Mexican Art*, Tate Gallery, 1953. Private collection

Paolozzi, who complained that artists were insufficiently receptive to unusual exhibitions such as *Mexican Art*, made an immediate creative response himself.

Partly owing, no doubt, to his teaching commitments, together with his designs for fabrics, tiles and wallpaper and his involvement with the Independent Group, Paolozzi's output of sculpture dwindled until 1954. He did, however, in the intervening period, collaborate with architects in several public sculptural projects that presaged one of the main aims of the exhibition *This is Tomorrow* in 1956. In the ICA's new Dover Street premises in 1950, the gallery, bar and members' club room were remodelled by the architect Jane Drew (the partner of Maxwell Fry in Fry, Drew). Paolozzi decorated the bar and made a table in conjunction with a young Central School student of his, Terence Conran. Both the bronze *Cage*, which Jane Drew commissioned for the Festival of Britain, and the large, outdoor, festival wall fountain, were in an 'open' linear style Paolozzi abandoned after designing three further welded-steel fountains for the International Horticulture Exhibition in Hamburg in 1953;[48] they may have been a concession to festival levity, for, as William Feaver remarked, they 'succeeded in hinting simultaneously at Giacometti and Heath Robinson'.[49] Many smaller-scale decorative works followed, such as the ceiling canopy he designed for *Tomorrow's Furniture*, an ICA exhibition in June 1953 for which Toni del Renzio was the consultant. Hammer Prints, the applied-arts venture he formed in 1954

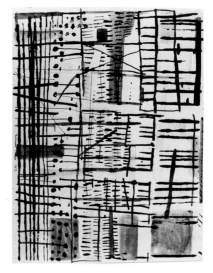

Eduardo Paolozzi: *Untitled*, 1951 (no. 81)

Eduardo Paolozzi: *Man in a Motor Car*, 1955.
Wax (presumed not to be extant, dimensions unknown)

in partnership with Nigel and Judith Henderson, was based near Thorpe-le-Soken, Essex, where Paolozzi and his family took a cottage adjacent to the Hendersons. Their tiles and fabrics, in particular, were incorporated into many contemporary decorative schemes, but it was difficult to compete with larger firms, and the failing business was formally wound up in 1964.

Paolozzi emerged from this relatively fallow period for autonomous sculpture by reverting to direct, tactile methods of representing the human image. Like much of his early output, many of these sculptures are now lost – for example, the wax figurines *Man Looking Up* and *Man in a Motor Car* (both 1955). The demi-figures exhibited at the Hanover Gallery in 1956, such as *Head and Arm* (c. 1954) and *Damaged Warrior* (1956), contained residual elements of the brief influence of Marino Marini, while the device of the upraised arm was foreshadowed in collages Paolozzi made in Hamburg in 1953, in which he superimposed machine elements on to engraved illustrations of antique sculpture. The robotic figures that followed, however diagrammatic or mechanistic, were invariably male (unusually for contemporary figure sculpture) and simultaneously heroic and tragic: hard and tough but oddly touching. Paolozzi made at least twenty such sculptures between 1956 and 1959, among which the most moving of the man-machines was *St Sebastian* (1957).[50] Paolozzi, who clearly identified with these metal men, called the semi-autobiographical Sebastian 'a sort of God I made out of my own necessity: a very beautiful young man being killed by arrows, which has a great deal of symbolism in it'.[51] In their isolation and pathos, the robots stand alongside Giacometti's stick figures as the ultimate existential sculptures, functionless technomorphs devised by Paolozzi for cold-war society.

Eduardo Paolozzi: *Robot*, c. 1956 (no. 82)

Eduardo Paolozzi: *St Sebastian* 1, 1957 (no. 83)

William Turnbull: In Space

Like Paolozzi, William Turnbull was familiar from childhood with popular imagery. Paolozzi collected cigarette cards and comics, but Turnbull, whose cousins had sent him magazines from America, hailed from Dundee, where, as a teenager, he worked as an illustrator for D.C. Thompson comics.[52] He read *Astounding Science Fiction*, paying special attention to articles by Isaac Asimov, and as an aficionado of American movies was at one time Lawrence Alloway's main film-going companion. But although this background facilitated Turnbull's participation in Independent Group debates, it is a mistake to infer that these sources played a direct part in his sculpture or painting, about which he was eminently serious and which never strayed towards Pop. Indeed, his sculpture, without being portentous, has a dignity and severity that is almost the antithesis of Pop.

Turnbull's sculpture incorporates the most sophisticated translation of the Independent Group debates about space. His reading of Giedion's theories of Palaeolithic art, for example, laid particular stress on the concept of *movement*, the fluidity of overlapping forms in constant motion: 'This', Turnbull observes, 'is what you would expect from a nomadic society, for Art is governed by Man's position – his orientation – in the universe.'[53] Serving in the RAF during the War, Turnbull flew aircraft at night: 'There were no lights – we were flying through blackness: the world never looked the same after that, it was never like a Dutch landscape.' Referring to the interpenetration of space, he remarks on the exhilaration gained from the aerobatics of a Tiger Moth slicing through space; 'skating', he adds, 'is the nearest activity to this.' Turnbull's sculpture in the early Fifties explored the representation of space and time in terms of implied movement. Even the hieratic, totemic *Idols* that he began in 1956, though ostensibly static, have an internal motion, an active surface and an inner dynamic. The primitivistic, monolithic *Idol 2* (1956) has an energy that reverberates to claim the space around it: it is an object of veneration, a mute presence. But Turnbull's chief preoccupation, from the outset, has been with scale: 'In Paris I carried with me this image, this dream, of my sculptures being so large that you could walk through them, but I soon realized that the whole thing was about scale, not about size.' He recalls two further incidents in France in the late 1940s, both formative: 'I was lying in a garden one summer in the French countryside reading Kafka's *The Metamorphosis* and insects were moving and buzzing around in the sunlight – they were Kafka's insects in space.' On another occasion he visited the Louvre to study Assyrian sculpture: 'I read in the pamphlet about a certain figure that seemed potentially very interesting, but I couldn't find it. Eventually I saw the reason it had eluded me – it was only about two inches high.'

If it is understood that Turnbull seldom had the opportunity to realise the sculptures he made between 1948 and 1954 beyond the plaster maquette stage, his dream of large-scale casting is easier to understand. Indeed, considering the quality of his work, Turnbull's lack of commercial success until the late Fifties is difficult to comprehend. Only one piece was sold from his first one-man show at the Hanover Gallery in 1950, and this was in plaster. He conceived these attenuated, slightly unstable forms 'as if they had a magnetic rod in them, sending out a vibration'. In their inexhaustible invention they cumulatively present an extension of Giacometti's exploration of linear forms in space, their energy and movement (sometimes actual as well as implied) the chief points of divergence from Giacometti's preoccupations with distance and perspective. In the bronze *Acrobat* (1951; he had made a similarly reductive drawing of a monocyclist on a highwire in 1947), Turnbull added a playful element to the implication of teetering motion. The *Acrobat* recalls the small bronze tableau *Playground (Game)* (1949), a sophisticated essay in the delineation and organization of vertical forms in

William Turnbull: *Idol 2*, 1956 (no. 104)

(opposite) **Nigel Henderson:** William Turnbull exhibition, Hanover Gallery, London, 1950. Private collection

William Turnbull: *Mobile Stabile*, 1949.
Bronze, 38.4 × 68.9 × 50.8 cm. Tate, London

space that refers to prehistoric sites of ritual, like those at Avebury, Wiltshire. Connecting through contemporary interest in the ludic (*Playground (Game)* is exactly contemporaneous with Huizinga's *Homo Ludens*) these works look forward to another sadly unrealized project of Turnbull's for a playground, an 'open' arena for human activity.[54]

In the making of his sculpture Turnbull is open to an element of chance. This he relates partly to Zen influences, which assumed a major importance in his work after 1955, and partly back to the RAF, where, literally, 'things were very chancy'. Working in plaster, 'you moved it about until you got what you wanted'. Sticking corrugated cardboard on to the surfaces of the standing female figures he embarked upon in 1954 was itself a risk, and partly an exercise in seeing what came out: 'In this process there was something I was searching for, and the ultimate form the work took was a matter of *recognition* of the point at which the answer came to me.' For this reason he has never been able to work with assistants: 'I tried an assistant once, but I had to send the guy out to a café because I simply couldn't work. How can I discover something when someone else is handling the material – you can't control the change.' By 1955 the female figures had evolved into the *Idols*. Hieratic, like Cycladic or Romanesque sculpture, these figures were conceived holistically, as 'absolutely one piece – not with bits added piecemeal like Baroque or Rococo sculpture'.

William Turnbull: *Acrobat*, 1951 (no. 101)

William Turnbull: *Head-form, c.* 1955 (no. 102)

William Turnbull: *Mask*, 1955–56 (no. 103)

Throughout his career Turnbull has painted and drawn at the same time as making sculpture, although either discipline might dominate for short periods. In the same way that his pre-Paris sculpture *Horse* (1946) achieved a convincing representation with an economy of means, Turnbull's drawings and paintings of heads eschew conventional anatomy, their marks emblematic of a human head rather than descriptive. Like the sculptures of heads, the techniques used in the paintings are diverse, but always depend partly on chance. *Mask* (1955-56) is assembled from thick, short lines and dabs of oil paint; other heads are more calligraphic, while the untitled *Head-form* (*c.* 1955) is spattered in layers of radiant colour.

Richard Hamilton: *Reaper (o)*, 1949 (no. 46)

Richard Hamilton: *$he*, 1958–61.
Oil, cellulose paint and collage on wood, 121.9 × 81.3 cm. Tate, London

Richard Hamilton: Mechanical Brides

From his astringent *Reaper* drypoint etchings of 1949 to *$he*, the painting begun in 1958 but not finished until 1961, Richard Hamilton was one of the most thoughtful, intellectual, but unprolific of artists. A slow, cautious worker, his output was further limited by teaching commitments, from which he was not entirely free until 1966. And although his paintings were exhibited at the Hanover Gallery in 1955, it was not until his next one-man show there in 1964 that they gained significant public visibility and began to make a wider impact.

By 1949 reapers were becoming redundant, standing obsolescent in the corners of fields, replaced by the combine harvester. The departure points for Hamilton's *Reaper* etchings, those austere and rigorously factual observations, probably included the illustration in Giedion's *Mechanization Takes Command* (1948) of the first mechanized reaper of 1831, and the 'Water Mill', 'Chocolate Grinder' and 'Oculist Witnesses' passages of Duchamp's *Large Glass* (1915–23). The exhibition *Man, Machine and Motion*, organized by Hamilton and Reyner Banham, opened in 1955 at the Hatton Gallery, Newcastle-upon-Tyne, before travelling to the ICA. Presented, like *Growth and Form*, mostly in the form of photographs, the exhibition was conceived as an examination of the fusion of man and machines, and of the formulation of a new mythology around the dynamized technological superman. The technological themes of *Man, Machine and*

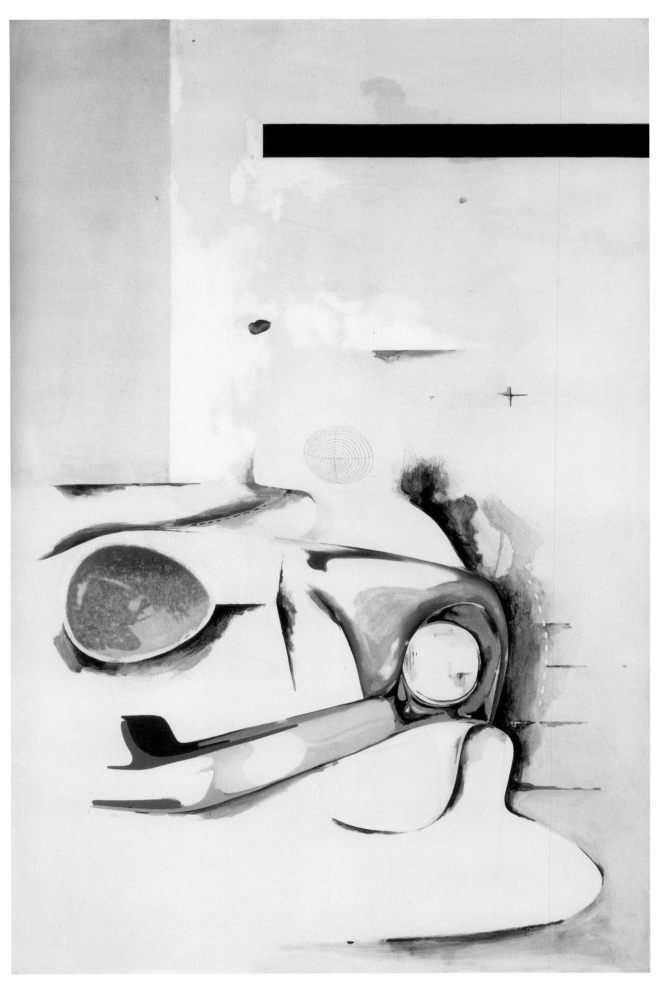

Richard Hamilton: *Hommage à Chrysler Corp.*, 1957 (no. 47)

Richard Hamilton: *Just what is it that makes today's homes so different, so appealing?* 1956.
Collage, 26 × 25 cm. Kunsthalle Tübingen. Collection of G.F. Zundel

Motion again coincided with those of Hamilton's paintings in the mid-Fifties. Lawrence Alloway's review of Hamilton's exhibition at the Hanover Gallery in 1955 interpreted his strategies of motion analysis in terms of the influence of the cinema: thus *Trainsition IIII* (1954) 'recalls the train and car races of Hollywood', *Carapace* (1954) 'the ever-loving view through the windscreen' and (mischievously) *re Nude* (1954) 'is a kind of dolly shot'.[55]

The Detroit auto-styling researches of Reyner Banham informed both *Man, Machine and Motion* and the painting *Hommage à Chrysler Corp.* (1957). The first of Hamilton's major paintings to deal with mass-media imagery, *Hommage à Chrysler Corp.* inaugurated a series of related investigations that he continued until *Towards a definitive statement on the coming trends in menswear* (1962). Cool, analytical, but with a strange majesty, *Hommage à Chrysler Corp.* is assembled in what Hamilton called 'tabular' form, of discrete components, an 'anthology of presentation techniques'[56] compiled from magazine sources. At the same time Hamilton began his typographical rendering of Duchamp's *Green Box* (1934): the ambiguity towards Pop imagery – celebrated but simultaneously critiqued in *Hommage à Chrysler Corp.* – is expressed in its Duchampian detachment. The cumulative effect of a 'Bug Eyed Monster was encouraged', commented Hamilton, 'in a patronising sort of way':[57] his engagement, therefore, with mass-media imagery was conducted from an intellectual distance that differentiates it from the first Pop paintings of 1960.

Richard Lannoy: Visitor, *This is Tomorrow* exhibition, Whitechapel Art Gallery, London, 1956.
Collection of the artist

Alison and Peter Smithson: Dressing Room, House of the Future, 1956. Collection of Alison and Peter Smithson, Architects

Shortly before painting *Hommage à Chrysler Corp.*, at a defining 'proto-Pop' moment, Hamilton had set out his famous definition of Pop in a letter to Alison and Peter Smithson.[58] The Smithsons themselves had flirted with a Pop aesthetic of expendability in their 'House of the Future' designs, in which the lavatory, with its spatially distinct presentation of the fittings, is comparable to Hamilton's 'tabular' paintings. At the same time the Smithsons' 'But Today We Collect Ads' was published as a 'Personal Statement' in the RCA magazine *Ark*.[59] During the War Alison Smithson saw fashion magazines sent from America to her grandmother, 'cultural parcels' that included photographs of a 'technical virtuosity' that the Smithsons now placed above the 'fine art' architecture that, they believed, must come to terms with 'the piece of paper blowing about the street, the throw-away object, the pop package'.[60] Their 'House of the Future' was intended as a prediction of domestic life in 1981; its fibreglass, plastic and tubular steel furniture was unveiled at the *Daily Mail* Ideal Home Exhibition at Olympia in March 1956, five months before the 'Fun House' installation conceived by Hamilton, John McHale and the architect John Voelcker for *This is Tomorrow*.

John McHale: *Transistor*, 1954 (no. 70)

John McHale

A Scot, like William Turnbull and Eduardo Paolozzi, John McHale is described by Magda Cordell (later Cordell McHale) as having been a Glasgow streetfighter in his youth and a featherweight boxer in the Navy: sufficient preparation to equip him to break into the Independent Group, undaunted by its 'tough-talking'. By 1951 he had begun to make constructivist assemblages and sculptures. Although the interactive construction kits that he attempted to market were a commercial failure, they have a significance in that McHale conceived them in Duchampian terms as empowering the spectator in a creative interaction. But the body of work that McHale produced between 1954 and 1962 consisted mainly of collages whose themes were related entirely to his and the Independent Group's monitoring of the mass media and communications technology. With Lawrence Alloway, McHale became convenor of the group's 'second session' in 1955, devoted to popular culture and the fine arts. Among the lectures they arranged was a conversation between Reyner Banham and Gillo Dorfles on 'Aesthetics and Italian Product Design'. Dorfles's book *Kitsch*, published in 1968, reprinted McHale's article 'The Plastic Parthenon', which examined the increasing globalization of culture and

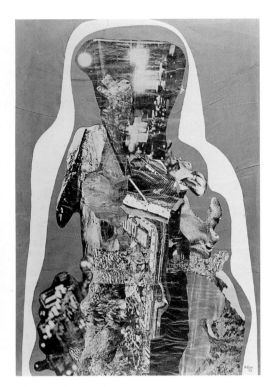

John McHale: *Suited Figure*, 1956 (no. 71)

John McHale: *Virginia Imported*, 1956 (no. 72)

communications, and the nature and expendability of sacred and secular symbols. McHale's engagement with the Independent Group also resulted in less predictable involvements with wider ICA activities – he was, for example, the designer of the Bacon and the Picasso exhibitions in 1955.

Between 1956 and 1959 McHale was the former Independent Group member most consistently involved in producing work that was sourced in popular imagery. Before that his experiments were inspired principally by developments in technology, such as the Transistor series, in 1955, which was based on the radio and computer transistor (invented in 1948) and the Shannon diagram. In 1955 he was awarded a visiting scholarship to attend Yale University, where he intended to study colour theory with Josef Albers. This was his first visit to America, however, and contact with the signs and symbols of the urban environment immediately altered his priorities. McHale, who became 'obsessed with the American scene and the throwaway civilization',[61] photographed neon signs and diners, and collected magazines. When Magda Cordell visited him in New York, McHale met her in a taxi at Idlewild Airport and they drove directly to Times Square: 'We were fascinated by the huge Camel advert, puffing smoke.'[62] They rummaged in the second-hand shops on 42nd Street, which remained open until 2 am, buying up American magazines – *Vogue, MAD, Colliers, Look* – as source material. These had been coveted as scarce imports into Britain: 'Under government rationing, food still seemed like a luxury, and we were amazed at American ads that would spread a fried egg, larger than life, across two pages of a glossy magazine.'[63]

McHale was still in the United States during most of the preparation of the Voelcker–Hamilton–McHale group 'Fun House' for *This is Tomorrow*, but shipped back a huge trunk full of glossy magazines, the raw material for the group's 'Pop' collages. As Hamilton recounted, the package contained 'the first Elvis Presley records to land on these shores ... protectively interleaved with copies of MAD magazine so that no one knew what was ballast and what was cargo'.[64] Of the twelve stands in *This is Tomorrow* only the 'Fun House' installation, for which Frank Cordell's film-world contacts were instrumental in securing the loan of Robbie the Robot from the film *The Forbidden Planet* (1956), captured the public's imagination. On his return to London in July 1956, McHale began to construct the Telemath collages, reassembling mass-media materials into new technological automata. *First Contact* (1958) is McHale's major work. It presents a pair of robotic semi-humans, 'out of Frankenstein by IBM',[65] that appear to be accompanied by a child – a mutant nuclear family? On a painted ground, this dense, multilayered collage of signs is a masterly combination of elements of photograms and photographs, as well as recycled magazine cuts. The 'adults' are symbolically if ambiguously gendered, the male composed of hydrogen-bomb clouds, the female with a web-like womb and a phallic piece of machine art doubling as mouth and lipstick; the TV monitor with its diminutive operator returns the viewer to McHale's prevailing theme: communications.

By 1959 he felt he had exhausted the potential of collage and began to paint hard-edged, near-abstract, reductive figures that Reyner Banham called 'iron men, square-heads in drainpipe trousers, Ned Kellys of the poison ivy league':[66] they were to be the last series he produced before emigrating. He had been responsible for the first British article on Buckminster Fuller (*Architectural Review*, July 1956), on whom he published a book in the USA in 1962. McHale, whose doctorate was in sociology, had met Lawrence Alloway at art-history lectures at the Courtauld Institute, probably before 1951, when he contributed an article on art education to *Athene*, of which Alloway was then editor. Richard Hamilton credits McHale and Alloway with

John McHale: *First Contact*, 1958 (no. 73)

having introduced to the Independent Group such key texts as Norbert Wiener on cybernetics, Claude Shannon on information theory and von Neumann and Morgenstern's *Theory of Games and Economic Behaviour*.[67] After 1962, when he and Magda Cordell emigrated to the USA, McHale's interests took him in the direction of information theory, and he decided that henceforth he would make art only for his private consumption. McHale's career as an educator was subsequently in futurology, a subject that can be understood as a logical outcome of Independent Group theory and on which he published widely and with distinction.

CITIES/BODIES

'The fifties were a time of ... punitive conventions, of a grey uniformity ... . Soho was perhaps the only area in London where the rules didn't apply. It was a Bohemian no-go area ... .' – *George Melly*

'Roger Mayne caught the poverty and the children's games all right, but he also caught the elusive whiff of the new abundance.'
– *Theo Crosby*

'The concept of Britain as the fertile breeding-place and deserving object of attacks by passionate young men has given way to the concept of Britain as the dynamic leader of popular culture.' – *D.E. Cooper*

Roger Mayne: Queue for *The Fly*, West End, London, 1958 (no. 67)

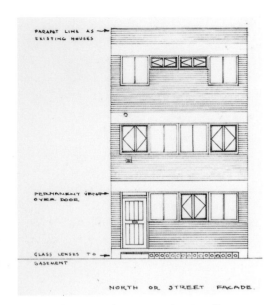

Alison and Peter Smithson: *Front elevation of house in Soho*, 1953.
Collection of Alison and Peter Smithson, Architects

The Smithsons' unexecuted design for their house in Soho would have been the most overt expression of New Brutalism in architecture.

Reg Butler: *The Oracle*, 1952.
Shell bronze, length 172.7 cm. Hatfield College of Technology

Dissemination

Toni del Renzio observed of the hermetic core of 'eighteen to twenty people' who constituted the Independent Group that 'it was very hard for anybody else to get in, even if they wanted to'.[1] The dissemination of the ideas that emerged from Dover Street depended on the involvement of members in teaching and writing on a broader cultural front. Outside the original nine or ten members of the Independent Group, the fringe membership was comprised almost entirely of architects: Alison and Peter Smithson, Colin St John Wilson, James Stirling, Sam Stevens, Cedric Price and Theo Crosby. The students most interested in the group's debates and exhibitions were predominantly those who attended the Architectural Association rather than London's art schools. Compared to the dearth of contemporary references to the group's activities in art magazines (a few notices in the *Art News and Review* are the main exception), it is at least slightly more conspicuous in the *Architectural Review* and *Architectural Design*. From 1952 to 1964 Reyner Banham was a writer and editor at the *Architectural Review,* and from 1953 to 1961 Theo Crosby was Technical Editor of *Architectural Design*. It was on Crosby's advice that in 1954 Monica Pidgeon, editor of *Architectural Design*, invited Lawrence Alloway to contribute art reviews to the magazine, and Crosby was also responsible for important contributions by Paolozzi, McHale and Hamilton.[2]

According to Mary Banham, at the *Architectural Review* Reyner Banham 'met most of the world's best-known architects, who would not pass through London without visiting the Bride of Denmark'.[3] The Bride of Denmark, a pub installed in the basement of the Architectural Press building in Queen Anne's Gate, was designed partly by Reg Butler, who worked three days a week as Technical Editor to the Architectural Press from 1946 to 1950. It was probably Banham, with his background in aeronautical engineering, who suggested that the second talk in the original Independent Group programme, convened by Richard Lannoy, should be given by a member of the De Havilland design team responsible for the development of the Comet, the first commercial jet aeroplane. Butler, six of whose works had recently been included in *Young Sculptors* at the Institute of Contemporary Arts (ICA), was then living at Hatfield, Hertfordshire, near the De Havilland headquarters. The three 'watchers' in Butler's *The Unknown Political Prisoner* were, Richard Calvocoressi suggested, based on his habit of straining skywards to view the test runs of De Havilland delta-wing aircraft. Butler's sculpture *The Oracle* (1952), commissioned by the architect Howard Robertson for the foyer of Hatfield College of Technology, elides prehistory and modern engineering. His aim to combine 'the earliest flying creatures, the pterodactyls, and the biomorphic aspect of the latest jet aircraft'[4] recalls the chronological span of the ICA exhibition *40000 Years of Art* in 1948; in *The Oracle*, Banham's and Butler's interests coincide in a symbiosis of art and technology.

Theo Crosby's editorial role at *Architectural Design* also included responsibility for the layout of the magazine. Since he had no special training for this he sought the advice of Edward Wright, an occasional participant in Independent Group activities and the designer of several ICA exhibition catalogues. Many of the students in Edward Wright's evening class in typography at the Central School, from 1952 to 1955, figured prominently in design and architecture in the 1960s and later. Among distinguished alumni, in addition to Theo Crosby, were the architectural historian Joseph Rykwert, the architect Pat Crooke, the American photographer Don Hunstein and the graphic designers Germano Facetti and Ken Garland. Wright had been invited by Anthony Froshaug to devise a class in what Lawrence Gowing called 'extempore typography': Froshaug had helped to introduce into Britain the Modernist typography of Jan Tschichold, and Wright was equally interested in the Continental designers. Wright brought to the course his wide

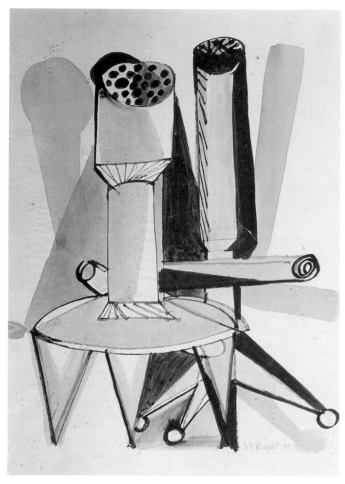

Edward Wright: *Bunsen Burners*, 1948 (no. 113)   Edward Wright: *Letter Collage*, 1947 (no. 112)

learning and an open-minded approach to seeking new ways of graphic communication: he and his students worked with wood type, using an ancient Albion hand press, and what they produced was often closer to concrete poetry than conventional graphics.

In the 1930s Wright had trained at the Bartlett School as an architect, which also allowed him to attend life classes at the Slade School of Fine Art, and after the War he worked on film titling and animation for MGM's documentary unit 'Metro-News' and in Paris for 'Metro-Journal'. In London, from 1946 Wright frequented the Anglo-French Art Centre, where Tristan Tzara, Oscar Dominguez and Fernand Léger were among the visiting lecturers. His first one-man exhibition, *Useful and Metaphorical Objects* at the Mayor Gallery in 1948, was comprised of ink-and-gouache drawings of everyday domestic objects, such as *Bunsen Burners* (1948). From this mundane and unprepossessing subject-matter he managed, as Joseph Rykwert commented, 'to wrest an epic dignity by giving it a rhythmic, sculptural energy'.[5] The choice of banal objects was deliberate, a witty but serious gesture towards a democratized, non-hierarchical art that did not depend on 'attractive' raw material. Wright's innovatory typography became sought after for inscriptions on buildings, beginning in 1956 with the appropriately futuristic typeface he designed for the Smithsons' 'House of the Future'. In the same year he designed the catalogue for *This is Tomorrow*, its most enduring artefact and one of the most satisfactory contributions to the exhibition. At the same time Wright began to teach graphic design at the Royal College of Art (RCA), and here, and later at Chelsea School of Art, he attracted another generation of loyal followers who continued to spread his ideas.

Edward Wright: Joseph Rykwert and David Russell, 1955. Collection of Anna Yandell

Charles Loupot's *St Raphael* posters – this example was photographed in France – were much admired by British graphic designers in the Fifties; Loupot re-worked styles of vernacular graffiti with great sophistication.

Ken Garland became art editor of *Design* magazine in 1958, and his distinguished career in graphics has included the design of many exhibition catalogues, as well as an important rôle as an educator. Germano Facetti, who moved to London in 1950, designed in many media (including the Wishbone rocking chair, in partnership with John Ollis, in 1954) and was also a conduit for the influence of Italian design in Britain in the Fifties. He is best known in this country for his complete redesign of Penguin Books, for whom he was art editor from 1960 to 1973. Terence Conran, a major popularizer and disseminator of 'modern' design, cites as the two main influences on his career Eduardo Paolozzi (with whom he studied textile design at the Central School) and Michael Wickham.[6] It was Michael Wickham who introduced Conran to France, but in *House and Garden* in the Fifties his photographs, and the articles written by Cynthia Blackburn, whom he married, were also instrumental in publicizing the work of many young architects and designers. *House and Garden* was edited from 1947 to 1955 by Anthony Hunt, who was succeeded by Michael Middleton, and, from 1957, by Robert Harling. For the non-specialist public the magazine was the medium through which they might first encounter not only the designs of Conran but also the architecture of Colin St John Wilson, as well as features on the studio homes of Alan Davie or Reg Butler.

In the three years before they attended the ninth Congrès Internationaux d'Architecture Moderne (CIAM), held at Aix-en-Provence in July 1953, Alison and Peter Smithson had been visiting Nigel and Judith Henderson at their home in Bethnal Green. Their presentation at the CIAM, in the form of a table-top grille, incorporated eleven of Henderson's photographs of East End street life. His photographs had, as the Smithsons acknowledged, informed their themes of 'Association and Identity'. Henderson had helped to identify 'the element missing in the new towns',[7] outlined in the Smithsons' proposals for the Golden Lane project in 1952. Their designs for a 'multi-level city with residential streets-in-the-air' sought to reclaim for the modern

Nigel Henderson: Gillian Alexander skipping, Chisenhale Road, *c*. 1950–52. The Estate of Nigel Henderson

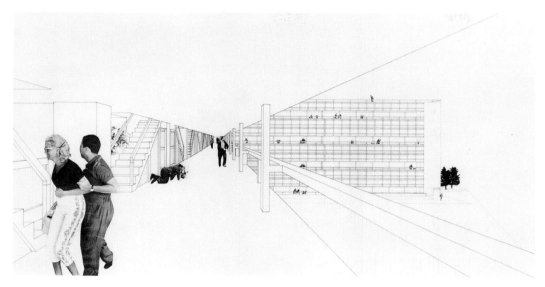

Alison and Peter Smithson: *Golden Lane, Street Deck*, 1952–53.
Collage: rapidograph and magazine cut-outs, 52 × 97.8 cm. Collection of Alison and Peter Smithson, Architects

urban environment the potential for human association that was documented and celebrated in Henderson's photographs. The Smithsons became the most influential theorists among British architects in the Fifties, and their ideas were soon dispersed internationally.

The Smithsons, with Henderson and Paolozzi the team responsible for *Parallel of Life and Art*, re-formed to make the environment 'Patio and Pavilion' as their contribution to the exhibition *This is Tomorrow*. Staged at the Whitechapel Art Gallery (it was too large for the ICA), *This is Tomorrow* opened in August 1956. The project had been mooted in 1954, and it is ironic that the most publicly visible event involving the Independent Group did not materialize until after its dissolution. It originated in a proposal to hold a co-operative 'art in architecture' exhibition on the lines of *La Groupe éspace* in Paris, whose English representative was the artist Paule Vezelay. The English artists and architects, however, refused to submit to the 'orthodox integration' and 'dogmatic ideas of synthesis'[8] advocated by the French. The twelve 'stands' that comprised *This is Tomorrow* were dominated, nevertheless, by scarcely unorthodox architectural installations of Constructivist painting and sculpture. There were some good things, but no radical solutions. Adrian Heath, Victor Pasmore, Robert Adams, Anthony Hill, and Kenneth and Mary Martin had been included in Alloway's first book, *Nine Abstract Artists*, published in 1954. In the same year John Weekes (the architect who collaborated with Adrian Heath on *This is Tomorrow*) had organized, with Robert Adams, Kenneth Martin and Victor Pasmore, an exhibition with similar objectives at the Building Centre. The laudable ambition of *This is Tomorrow*, to promote new levels of collaboration between architects and artists, must be counted as a failure. James Stirling, who became the most renowned of the architect exhibitors in *This is Tomorrow*, frankly disowned the co-operative principle in his catalogue text. Confirming a megalomania in architects that has undermined most collaborations of this kind, his biographer Mark Girouard comments that, after *This is Tomorrow*, Stirling 'was never again to show the slightest desire to collaborate with artists or sculptors'.[9] Subsequent to the International Union of Architects (IUA) Congress, in 1961, it is difficult to identify more than a handful of buildings in the last forty years that incorporated an artwork as more than an aesthetic fig-leaf. The IUA exhibition involved former Independent Group members Theo Crosby, William Turnbull, John McHale, Richard

Richard Lannoy: Installation photograph of 'Patio and Pavilion', *This is Tomorrow*, 1956. Collection of the artist

Brian Wall: *Landscape Sculpture*, 1958 (no. 106)

Anthony Caro: *Twenty-Four Hours*, 1960 (no. 21)

Hamilton, Eduardo Paolozzi and many others, including the Constructivists Anthony Hill and Kenneth and Mary Martin. The sculptors who contributed included Robert Adams, Bryan Kneale, Brian Wall and Anthony Caro, whose 'abstract' welded-steel forms eschewed the direct representation of the body and represented a new and soon dominant direction in British sculpture.

The most striking aspect of the downbeat 'Patio and Pavilion' – Reyner Banham invoked the insistent 'atomic holocaust' metaphor[10] and Colin St John Wilson called the objects 'ludicrously antediluvian'[11] – was Nigel Henderson's collage *Head of a Man* (1956). Its dimensions, 168 × 120 cm (63 × 48 in.), exceptional in Henderson's œuvre, were dictated by the environment, and he seldom worked on this scale again until renewing his interest in collage in the 1970s. By 1956 the Independent Group had disbanded, and Henderson, living at Thorpe-le-Soken, had ceased to

Nigel Henderson: Installation photograph of 'Patio and Pavilion', *This is Tomorrow*, 1956 (showing *Head of a Man*). The Estate of Nigel Henderson

teach at the Central School and lost regular contact with the metropolitan milieu. *Head of a Man* was his contribution to the tradition of isolated, paternalistic human heads that had preoccupied many artists, including Turnbull and Paolozzi, since the ICA exhibition *The Wonder and Horror of the Human Head* in 1953. While indebted, in its random linearity, to the drawings of Turnbull and Paolozzi, Henderson's *Man* differs in its psychological connotations. Where Turnbull and Paolozzi were concerned with the totemic, *Head of a Man* is more sinister, a golem or Übermensch. Henderson possibly recalled J.D. Bernal's chilling vision of humans evolved into disembodied brains serviced by machines. His parents divorced when he was a child, and 'vivid memories of the tensions between an aloof, emotionally inflexible father and a vibrant, phenomenal mother'[12] may also have informed this haunting image, a parallel to Francis Bacon's disquieting 'father-figures'. Henderson's excoriated golem is matched in prose by his own terse evocation of 'An astringent man, steeled and sealed in pince-nez, regards with loathing a house he is intent on igniting with his lenses of hate ...'.[13]

In addition to the Smithsons, many of the future leaders of the British architectural profession had been closely connected to the Independent Group in their formative years. From 1951 to 1955 Colin St John Wilson worked for the Housing Department of the London County Council (LCC), where, with Alan Colquhoun and Peter Carter, he was responsible for some boldly Corbusian schemes, tough and uncompromising enough to be categorized as New Brutalism. James Stirling, another rugged Scot, only very briefly at the LCC, was equally influenced by Le Corbusier, though like the others this was the post-Unité d'Habitation Corbusier of raw, shuttered concrete – béton brut. Stirling regularly attended Mary and Reyner Banham's Sunday coffee mornings at their flat in Oppidans Road, close to William and Cathy Turnbull and next door to Colin St John Wilson; these informal gatherings at the Banhams' were an unofficial Independent Group outpost with an architectural bias. Stirling exhibited in *Tomorrow's Furniture* at the ICA (1952), but like his young contemporaries he found it hard to win a major architectural commission; the Engineering Block at Leicester University, which he designed in partnership with James Gowan, was not begun until 1959.

In the Fifties Jon Catleugh was also with the LCC Architecture Department, working on London schools; though not a member of the Independent Group's inner circle, he was an exhibitor in both *Tomorrow's Furniture* and *This is Tomorrow*. He was also a painter who, having admired Jackson Pollock's work at Peggy Guggenheim's Venice pavilion in 1949, worked in a manner directly influenced by him: Colin St John Wilson's notes for Catleugh's exhibition at the Gimpel Fils Gallery in 1952 referred to the chance aspect of his dripped and trickled industrial paints.[14] In 1951 he designed the sets for Picasso's play *Desire Caught by the Tail*, which Roland Penrose had translated, at the Watergate Theatre. Light was projected on to sheets of crumpled aluminium by a light-and-sound collective, London Mobilux, that included John Hoppe, an Australian who gave a demonstration of kinetic light and musique concrète at the third of the original series of Independent Group meetings.

Richard Lannoy, who arranged Hoppe's performance, had been introduced to him by Harley Usill, whom he met by chance in the ICA gallery. Shortly afterwards Usill founded Argo Records, a company that pioneered 'alternative' recordings in Britain, including poetry readings by T.S. Eliot and Dylan Thomas. The majority of Independent Group members were aficionados of jazz: Steve Race led a discussion on jazz at the ICA, George Melly's Trio performed there, and Humphrey Lyttleton's 100 Club, nearby on Oxford Street (the subject of a Slade School painting

J.D.H. Catleugh: Set for *Desire Caught by the Tail*, 1951

by Michael Andrews, 1950–51) was a favourite venue. The improvisational aspect of jazz had parallels in Independent Group theory, and in 1954 Paolozzi cited 'bop by [Dizzy] Gillespie' as well as 'symphonies by Bartok' as influences.[15] Nigel Henderson, a jazz enthusiast, was introduced by the artist Sam Kaner, formerly a drummer with a US Air Force dance band, to Ronnie Scott, and Kaner and Henderson designed posters for Ronnie Scott's Orchestra. The crossing of disciplines was not always accomplished smoothly: Henderson lamented that Ronnie Scott (whom he described as 'musically very hip ... but visually square to the point of cuboid') rejected his more unusual ideas and preferred his musicians 'lined up in rows like circus ponies and dressed like doormen outside the Dominion Cinema'.[16]

Jazz was also the favoured music of London's art students, as links between art and music assumed a much greater significance after the War. Humphrey Lyttleton (born 1920) studied at Camberwell School of Arts and Crafts in 1946–47, and his tutors, John Minton and Susan Einzig, attended his jazz performances. The architect of the Brutalist house that Lyttleton built at Arkley, Hertfordshire, in 1958 was John Voelcker, and John McHale made a photo-collage mural for the interior. Around 1950 both Lyttleton and George Melly, then still working in E.L.T. Mesens's London Gallery, played at RCA dances. The social and musical axis of the college provided the

Peter and Alison Smithson: 'Mobility' article for *Architectural Design*, November 1957, incorporating 'Play Brubeck' drawing.
Private collection

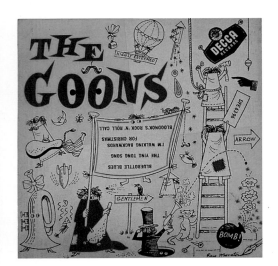

Rex Moreton: Record sleeve: *The Goons*, c. 1956.
Private collection

Rex Moreton (born 1928) was a graphic designer
responsible for several Decca-label EP and LP designs.
Shortly after designing this he became a photographer.

John McHale: Invitation to Independent Group talk
'Gold Pan Alley' by Frank Cordell, 1955.
Collage, 11.6 × 23.5 cm. Private collection

context for the development of several visual artists towards performance. From 1951 to 1954 Bruce Lacey (born 1927) studied painting at the RCA but spent much of his time performing and making films with fellow ex-Hornsey College student John Sewell.[17] Lacey was at the centre of a group of Dadaist subversives that included Len Deighton, Ted Dicks and John Sewell, who in 1954 founded the Dodo Society at the RCA. Lacey's 'magic-lantern' lectures at the college employed a satirical, Surreal, non-linear sequencing, a less earnest version of contemporary events at the ICA. He also made props for late-Fifties television series featuring former members of *The Goon Show*, whose zany humour he abundantly shared.

From the jazz and performance group The Alberts, formed by Lacey and the Grey brothers at the end of the 1950s and featuring Lacey's 'hominoid' robots, stemmed the tradition of 'art-school' bands that by the early 1960s had transmuted into art-school rock. The neo-Edwardianism of The Alberts stemmed from the Edwardian artefacts Lacey had collected since childhood, and that had characterized the Dodo Society. Other bands in this tradition, the Temperance Seven and, in the 1960s, the Bonzo Dog Doo-Dah Band, both included ex-RCA students. These developments foregrounded a specifically British trait, a native Dadaism that ran counter to the Americanism of the Independent Group. Ted Dicks wrote about bop in *Ark* 10, in which he was introduced as 'A leading rowdy in RCA social life, when he gets together with Bruce Lacey all hell breaks loose'. Dicks did not continue with painting after he left the RCA but became a musician, composer, and the author of many hit records. Magda Cordell's husband, Frank Cordell, was a musical director at EMI Records and thus at the centre of Britain's popular music of the mid-Fifties: 'Gold Pan Alley', the talk he gave to the final Independent Group meeting in July 1955, attracted only fourteen members, but its publication in *Ark* in 1956 ensured a wider audience.

The ICA's programme embraced many media, and in some disciplines complemented or expanded the Independent Group's avant-garde agenda. The ICA organized performances and discussions of Indian, African and West Indian music, and Berg, Britten, Schoenberg and Varèse, and in February 1953 Pierre Schaeffer demonstrated the musique concrète that he had been developing at Radiodiffusion Française. Schaeffer experimented with the manipulation of non-musical sources such as street noises, railway sounds and radio commercials, and his collaboration with Pierre Henry on the existentially titled *Symphonie pour un homme seul* in 1949–50 was one of the first publicly broadcast electronic works. The correlation between Schaeffer's taped collages of 'found sound' and the 'as found' element in the Independent Groups's visual language does not, however, appear to have been creatively exploited by the group.

In the early Fifties Henderson and Paolozzi collaborated on two short films made from found footage that they spliced together in random sequence, prefiguring Paolozzi's *The History of Nothing* in 1962. John McHale and Magda Cordell began to film TV commercials about 1956, principally as a way to finance their paintings and collages, activities that limited gallery sales could not support. Clients at their 'small but high-powered design studio'[18] included Revlon, Frigidaire and EMI Records. They also made a more serious film in connection with Alison and Peter Smithson's Berlin-Haupstadt competition project in 1958; for reasons of cost, filming was entirely undertaken in London rather than Berlin, though as Cordell comments: 'since the subject was urbanism, where it was shot was immaterial to the essence of the film. After all, a city is a city'.[19]

Julian Trevelyan: *Hyde Park*, 1956 (no. 99)

Nigel Henderson: Colony Room (including Isabel Lambert, right), 1951.
Private collection

The Metropolitan Experience

Although many of the artists featured in *Transition* painted London, few, apart from Auerbach and Kossoff, made the city their subject in a sustained way. In the second half of the Fifties, however, Julian Trevelyan made many impressively evocative studies of London that encapsulate the life and pace of the city. Among a body of freely and vigorously painted urban episodes that deserves to be better known are the nocturnes *Hyde Park* (1956) and *Piccadilly Circus at Night* (1957). In 1951, shortly before leaving London for the country, Michael Ayrton painted *The Sweep and Others* (1951) in an atypically urban setting, and David Tindle's *Shell Site: South Bank* (1959) is an early work that treats an architectural subject with the same interests in balanced composition, surface texture and delicacy of colour that distinguish his rural landscapes. Compared to the confident rise of a new office block, Michael Andrews imagines his *Flats* (1959) as forlorn, the Modernist 1930s optimism of their conception faded: it is an adroit psychological rendering of the inanimate.

David Tindle: *Shell Site: South Bank*, 1959 (no. 98)

In the disparate assembly of urban villages that is London, artists have gravitated to different areas, often attracted by low-priced accommodation. By 1960 a large contingent of the city's avant-garde was living within a mile of Notting Hill Gate, but in the immediate post-war period the pubs, clubs and cafés of Soho remained a magnet for those stricken by what Julian Maclaren-Ross called 'Sohoitis'. Memorably chronicled and photographed by Daniel Farson, Soho's drinking haunts and its homosexual underworld attracted many of London's leading painters, including Bacon, Minton, Wilde, Colquhoun, MacBryde, Freud, Auerbach and Andrews. A favourite drinking club, the Colony Room, was opened by Muriel Belcher in 1948, with Bacon as a subsidized attraction. Belcher herself was the subject of major paintings by Bacon, beginning with the atypical but penetrating portrait of 1959. Michael Andrews painted a (still extant) mural after Bonnard at the Colony Room in 1957; when he returned to London in 1961 he began two major paintings completed the following year, *Colony Room I* and *Colony Room II*, the former including Bacon, Freud, John Deakin, Bruce and Jeffrey Bernard, and Henrietta Moraes.

Michael Andrews: *Flats*, 1959 (no. 2)

Michael Ayrton: *The Sweep and Others*, 1951 (no. 8)

Julian Trevelyan: *Piccadilly Circus at Night*, 1957 (no. 100)

Colony Room membership was not restricted to artists; indeed, its appeal, according to Daniel Farson, lay in its 'marvellous mix of people'. Other meeting places offered different mixes. The Café Torino, for example, housed separate expatriate groups of Hungarians, Poles and Italians, as well as architects, designers and journalists. In 1956 David Archer opened a poetry bookshop in Greek Street, Soho, that enjoyed greater success as a meeting place than as a retail outlet, owing principally to Archer's reluctance to part with his stock. In the 1930s Archer's Parton Press had published Dylan Thomas, W.S. Graham and David Gascoyne, and during the War he had run the press from Glasgow, where he opened the Scott Street Arts Centre. Benjamin Creme and Robert Frame, who illustrated a book of Sidney Graham's poems, *Cage without Grievance*, published by Parton Press in 1942, joined the exodus from Glasgow to London shortly afterwards. Archer's new shop in Greek Street incorporated a gallery and coffee bar, and a ceiling photo-mural designed by Germano Facetti.

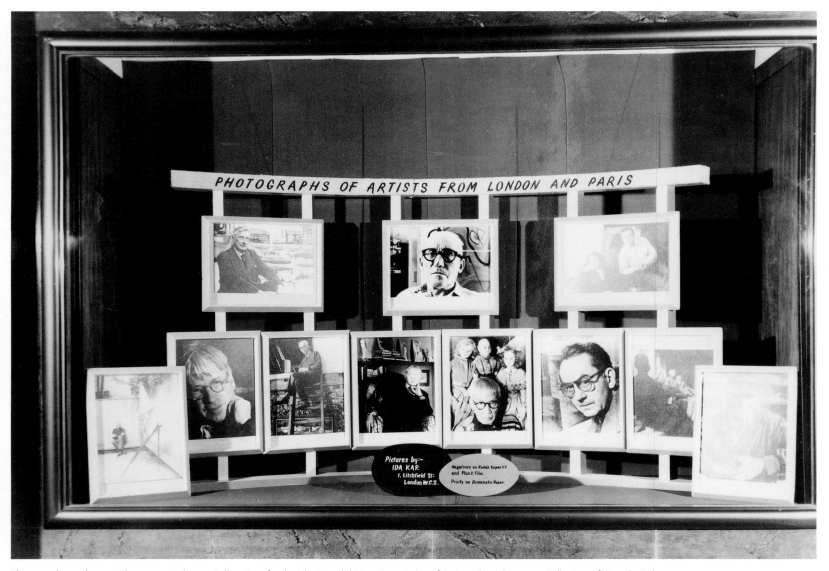

Photographer unknown: Showcase window at Gallery One for the Ida Kar exhibition *Forty Artists of Paris and London*, 1954. Collection of Dorothy Bohm

Photography exhibitions remained scarce throughout the Fifties. John Deakin had his first exhibition, of photographs of Paris, at David Archer's bookshop in 1956. A Soho habitué and soon an intimate of its artistic circles, Deakin arrived in London in the late 1940s. His engagement by *Vogue* as a fashion and portrait photographer afforded him the opportunity to be paid to photograph London's cultural life. His perceptive and 'brutal portraits', as Daniel Farson termed them, were admired by Bacon for their close scrutiny and lack of artifice; Bacon later commissioned Deakin to take the photographs that he used for his portraits of Lucian Freud, Isabel Rawsthorne, George Dyer and Henrietta Moraes. Ida Kar's portraits of *Forty Artists of Paris and London* were shown at Gallery One (run by her husband Victor Musgrave) in 1954, and she was given a major retrospective at the Whitechapel Art Gallery in 1960. The New Vision Centre Gallery staged a pioneering exhibition of photographs by Eric Locker and Lea Goodman, students at the London College of Printing, in 1956, but in general, apart from the ICA exhibitions referred to earlier, interest in exhibiting photography was still at the slow incubation stage.

By 1953 Italian-style espresso bars were opening up both inside and outside of Soho, partly in response to the independence and spending power of a new cultural phenomenon soon identified as 'teenagers'. The advent of American rock and roll in Britain in 1956 introduced an unforeseen element into the cultural equation, and some of Soho's coffee bars became polarized around the musical tastes of their clienteles: the left-wing Partisan Coffee House, for example,

Patrick Crooke: Christmas card for Café Torino, 1955. Collection of Germano Facetti

remained a home of acoustic folk and protest music, while the Two Is catered for the more hedonistic brand of amplified rock music. The 'cultured' middle classes were unprepared for this assault on traditional values, which threatened to explode to an extent where it could no longer be marginalized or simply ignored. The hysterical media reaction to the 'youthquake' demonstrated the extent to which the Independent Group's embracing of 'low' culture was a minority pursuit: even group members generally preferred to monitor it from a distance, although this second wave of Americanization was welcomed by, for example, the novelist Colin MacInnes and certain students at the RCA.

Edward Wright: Café Torino, c. 1955. Collection of Anna Yandell

Paradoxically, the Teddy Boys, the most extreme expression of youth power, associated with mob violence and codified by their dress, were not especially Americanized. First identified as a subcultural phenomenon in 1953, their long drape jackets and drainpipe trousers were based on the neo-Edwardian upper-class male fashion that enjoyed a brief flowering in Mayfair shortly after the War. Sociologists consistently read the working-class environment as one of drab uniformity, and the 'Teds' as posing a problem of delinquency.[20] In the Fifties the architect Roderick Gradidge (1928–2001), educated at Stowe and the Architectural Association, frequented the York Minster and many of the other Bacon-circle homosexual hang-outs of Soho. In 1955 he was one of the first non-sailors to wear an earring, and shortly afterwards began to tattoo his body. A fervent admirer of Lutyens and a pioneering conservationist of Victorian architecture, Gradidge proposed an English alternative to New Brutalist architecture, citing Teddy Boys, who 'produced an English style', as a useful analogy. He brought a unique and disarmingly original perspective to debates about Pop architecture with his rhetorical 'What has trad to do with rock? Just that has Corb to brute', and insisted that 'What is the point, is the necessity, is to produce architecture fit for Teds to live in'.[21]

Record sleeve: Beat Girl, 1960. Private collection

The British film industry, noting the popularity of imported American rock-and-roll films, launched a counter-initiative. Expresso Bongo (1959), a musical vehicle for the 'English Elvis', Cliff Richard, began strongly with compelling evocations of Soho, shot on location, before losing the plot in a bizarre religious apotheosis, strangely premonitory of the singer's career. Beat Girl (1960) – 'Mad about Beat – Living for Kicks' – introduced pop singer Adam Faith. Its storyline involved an architect who, preoccupied with his utopian plans, failed to comprehend his mildly errant daughter, who had become involved in street rivalry between Teddy Boys and 'the non-existent London version of the American Beats';[22] some unusual but trickily effective photography was credited by the film's former Free Cinema cameraman, Walter Lassally, to the director, Edmond T. Greville.

Roger Mayne: Leeds, 1958 (no. 66)

Bryan Ingham: *Landscape at Peckham*, c. 1959.
Oil on hardboard, 61 × 122 cm. Guildhall Art Gallery (Corporation of London)

Ingham's painting records a terrace of Victorian housing awaiting demolition; like many of
Mayne's London photographs, it was conceived as a valediction for an urban environment.

Roger Mayne's 'Southam Street' photographs also connect photography and architecture. They
were first published in the serial form that Mayne intended by Theo Crosby in *Uppercase* 5 in 1961.
Though Mayne was no promoter of Pop, his affection for the children at play in the theatre of a
decaying North Kensington neighbourhood was obvious. The photographs were influential on
architects, at a time when the ludic was paramount among London's architectural avant garde,
and on architectural photographers, who began to reject the sanitized and glamorized perfection
of images of modern buildings and to incorporate the humans who actually used them.
Conscious that the North Kensington environment he had photographed since 1955 was in
danger of being swept away (the Victorian terraces were demolished and the inhabitants
rehoused in 1968), Mayne's work became more politicized, as his ironic juxtaposition of a luxury
cruiser with slum clearance and urban decay in *Leeds* (1958) demonstrates. The Golden Lane
Estate competition, in which the Smithsons were unsuccessful in 1952, was won by Chamberlin,
Powell & Bon. The same firm was appointed as architects of the Barbican development in 1956,
and its revised plan accepted three years later. In 1961 Nikolaus Pevsner wrote that 'In 1954 ...
there was hardly an inkling of a new post-war London to be seen' but that seven years later new
building was progressing 'so fast that it was hard to keep pace'.[23] Since much London
architecture of that time failed to win wide approval, it is interesting that in 1961 Pevsner was
able to greet the 'thrilling ... results' of the Barbican's 'eighteen-storey towers'.[24]

John Chillingworth: *Teenagers*, 1959. Collection of John Chillingworth

In the process of making this marvellously evocative photograph, John Chillingworth (born 1928), on an assignment from *Queen* magazine, followed a young married couple in London over a period of a week. This image, which was not published in the magazine, was taken at the north London flat where the 'teenagers' lived.

The jacket of *Absolute Beginners* (1959), the last in a trilogy of London novels by Colin MacInnes, was photographed by Roger Mayne and featured a young London couple of MacInnes's acquaintance. *Absolute Beginners* explored the 'teenage world of coffee-bars, motor-scooters and jazz-clubs'. Adopted by the media as a spokesman for the 'teenage problem', MacInnes contributed an article, 'Reaching for Twenty', to *Queen* magazine.[25] The same London couple, Alex and Jean, acted out the rôles of the teenagers, and on this occasion the photographer was former *Picture Post* photojournalist John Chillingworth. In a review of MacInnes's book, Richard Wollheim described the 'hip' teenager as representing a limited social stratum, its effect in inverse proportion to its actual extent, 'in other words, an aristocracy'.[26] Wollheim compellingly related the *air froid* of this new aristocracy to the cult of 'coolness': he noted the heterogeneity of cool, which he located in 'the novels of Kerouac and Pasolini; in films from France and Poland and Japan; and in the cafés and bars of every American or Americanized city in the world'. Partly 'global village', his definition also suggests a factor in Britain's gradual climb, after Suez, out of its imperialist, isolationist mentality, and the adoption of a more international perspective that was gradually reflected in the art of the Fifties.

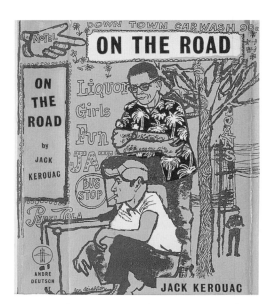

Len Deighton: Book jacket for first British edition of *On the Road* by Jack Kerouac, 1958.
Private collection

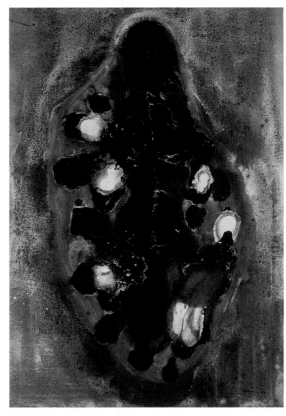

Magda Cordell: *Presence B*, c. 1958–60 (no. 27)

Bodies

Following the exhibition of her monotypes and collages at the ICA in 1955, Magda Cordell's one-woman show at the Hanover Gallery in January 1956 coincided with the Tate's showing of Abstract Expressionism and invited the inevitable comparisons. The closest affinities in her work are not, though, with the New York painters but with the Ecole de Paris, with Dubuffet's *Corps de Dames* and with Wols and Fautrier: Robert Melville specifically cited *Opposing Forces*, the 1953 ICA exhibition of French Action Painting, in calling Cordell 'the only artist of consequence whose work was directly influenced by the ICA show'.[27] Lawrence Alloway's appropriation of Cordell's paintings as a kind of British science-fiction art is misleading: the string of poetic adjectives he attached to her work (solar, galactic, far-out, hyperspace) applies only to the luscious surfaces and amorphous forms of a brief period in her work, begun around 1955 and soon discontinued, and characterized by paintings such as *Android* and *Super-Nova* (both 1955). But the question of influence begs the point, for by 1954 Cordell had discovered a personal iconography. None of her earlier grid paintings survive, but they were dense, dynamic and painterly rather than Constructivist. After 1956 she found her inspiration solely in the human figure: 'it was always the most exciting shape, then I realized it was living and breathing, too.'[28] Her subject-matter became exclusively the female body: over-scale, primitive earth mothers and boldly frontal forms – part embryos, part sexual organs – that were affirmations of renewal and metaphors for the body and for society in a constant state of flux.

Magda Cordell: *Grid Painting*, c. 1953

All of Cordell's grid paintings were destroyed, and this photograph is the only surviving record.

A Hungarian refugee, she had lost most of her family and friends in the War but managed herself to survive. Her paintings, which translate her personal experience into the universal, are about the pain and the strength of women. To express this, she developed a vocabulary of deeply sensuous surface textures, flicking dry pigment on to the canvas and fixing it with washes of glaze; the subtlety of her colours sets up a creative tension with the uncompromising forms and the vigorous, swirling application of paint. The wives of Independent Group members were all talented in their own right, yet were patronized and marginalized by the rest of the group, and

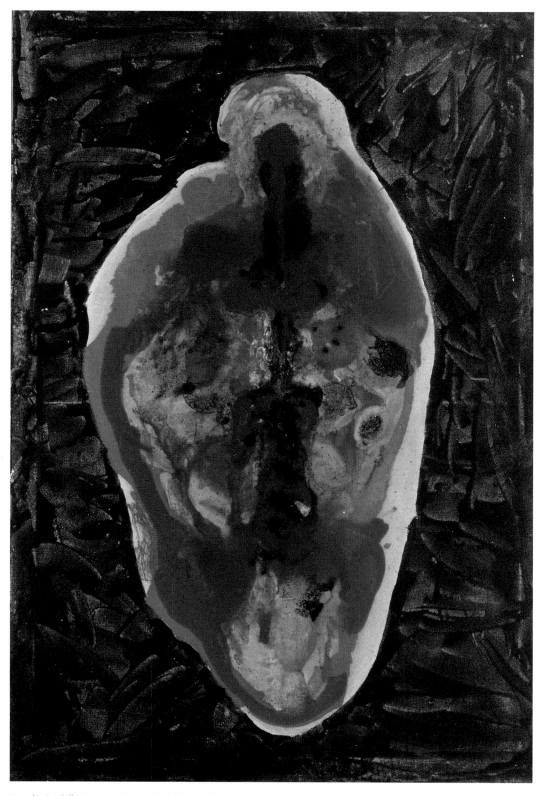

Magda Cordell: *Presence A, c.* 1958–60 (no. 26)

Cordell's battle for recognition was fought principally on this male-dominated territory. An artist more than a theorist, at least at this stage of her career, she seldom participated in Independent Group debates. Nevertheless, she pursued her proto-feminist agenda with conviction, amused when her male peers were intimidated by her larger-than-life female anatomies. She emigrated to the USA in 1962, before the feminist movement had coalesced, and before her work achieved the wider recognition in Britain that it warranted. Cordell is another artist whose extreme, courageous, isolated talent is long overdue a comprehensive retrospective reassessment.

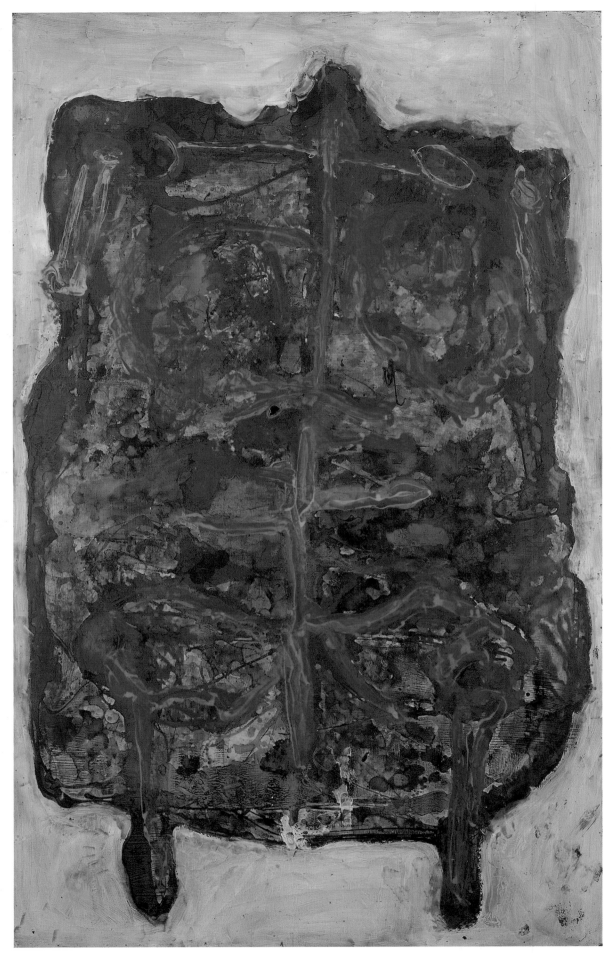

Magda Cordell (later Magda Cordell McHale): *Figure, 59, c.* 1958 (no. 25)

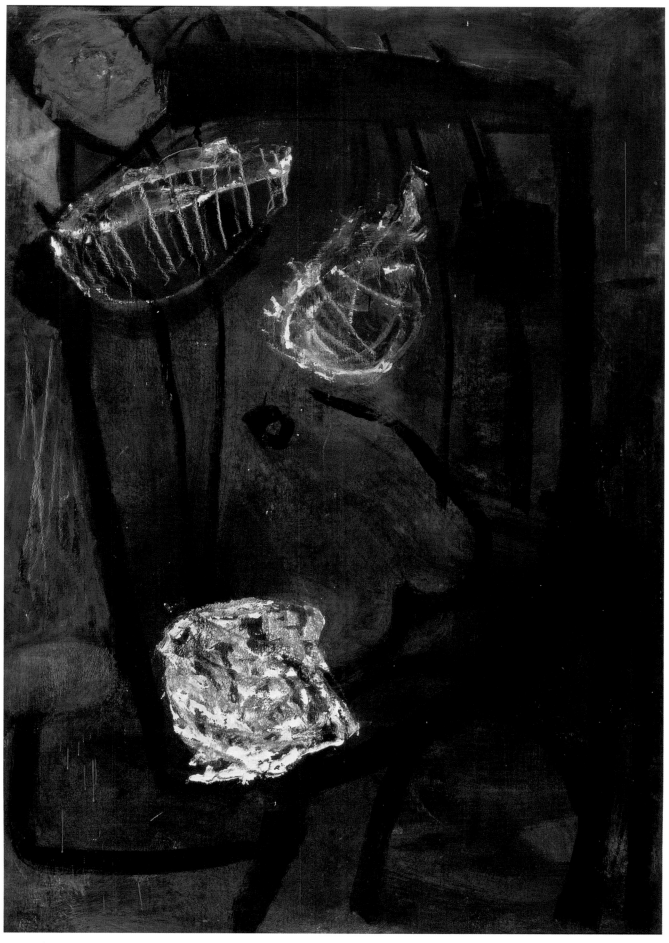

Roger Hilton: *Grey Figure*, 1957 (no. 54)

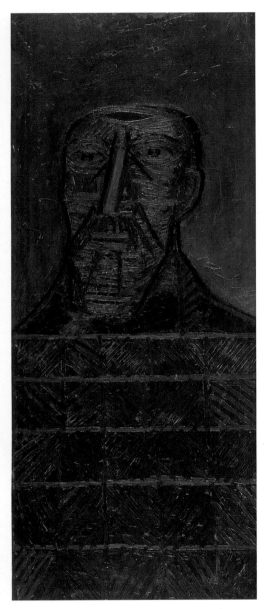

Francis Newton Souza: *Untitled, c.* 1952.
Oil on board, 47 × 112 cm. England & Co. Gallery, London

A different kind of prejudice attended the efforts of Afro-Asian artists to establish themselves in Britain. In 1949 one of the first to arrive in London was the Indian Francis Newton Souza, a notable painter of the body. After studying at the Central School, Souza struggled for several years to achieve recognition, and supported himself largely through writing. It was not until after he had shown in Paris that his work began to be accepted in Britain, when he was given the first of several one-man shows at Gallery One by Victor Musgrave in 1955. The exhibition sold out, John Berger wrote appreciatively about it in the *New Statesman* and Souza became successful. Souza's art is driven by the tension between opposites: if the contradictions between Hinduism and Catholicism (he was brought up a Catholic), narcissism and humanitarianism, and Eastern and Western art traditions are not completely resolved in his paintings, it is in the spaces between these disciplines that their power resides: *The Emperor* (1958; see illus. p. 16) is Souza at his boldest and most confident. From 1956 the New Vision Centre Gallery provided exhibition space for many Commonwealth artists, but the perception remained that black or Asian artists were denied opportunities on grounds of race. Racial discrimination has been cited (though there were also compelling personal reasons) as a factor in Souza's decision to emigrate to the USA in 1967, as it was in the case of the Guyanan Frank Bowling, who moved to New York in 1966. The work of Frank Bowling lies outside the scope of this study, since it did not come to prominence until the 1960s, but as an RCA contemporary of the British Pop painters from 1959 to 1962 his feeling of exclusion should be apprehended. Bowling was interested in painting Pop subjects relevant to his own culture, such as the death of Patrice Lumumba: 'So I was isolated. It was a racist thing anyway, the whole thing ... I did not paint Marilyn Monroe because she did not interest me ... .'[29]

Many artists usually associated with abstract or formal concerns have occasionally, or for limited periods, painted the body, although it was generally rendered in flattened, semi-abstract forms. Among the St Ives artists, Roger Hilton returned to the human form regularly throughout his career, and *Grey Figure* (1957) is a fine example, rapidly painted in what was, for him, a limited palette of subdued but subtly luminous colours. Neither the subject nor the Braque-like linearity of *Two Women in a Café* (1950; see illus. p. 19) by Patrick Heron hint at what was to come from this lyrical abstractionist, who after 1955 never painted the figure. Following a visit to Patrick and Della Heron at Zennor, Sandra Blow stayed for a year in Cornwall in 1957–58, 'where she learnt much from Roger Hilton'.[30] Involved with texture and process, she is another fine painter whose early work has received less recognition than it is due. Apart from the life drawings she made in the Fifties as a student at St Martin's School of Art, she has seldom painted the figure; *Oil Drawing* (1959) was an abstract composition that subsequently suggested to the artist a seated figure, an interpretation of the form that has sedimented for her as its dominant characteristic.

Franciszka Themerson, a multi-talented Polish refugee who arrived in London in 1940, was, like Adler and Herman, a foreign artist whose presence considerably enriched the London art scene. The daughter of the academic painter Jakub Weinles, she was trained at the Warsaw Academy of Fine Arts and married the writer Stefan Themerson in 1931. In Warsaw she collaborated with her husband in experimental photography and film-making, the first of many joint ventures, and set up Poland's pioneer film co-operative. In 1948 the Themersons founded Gaberbocchus Press in London, with Franciszka as art director. Among the many important and beautiful books they published over the next thirty-one years, the first, in 1948, was a hand-printed volume on Jankel Adler, which he also illustrated.

Sandra Blow: *Oil Drawing*, 1959 (no. 14)

In 1957, in the basement of their premises in Formosa Place, the Themersons opened the Gaberbocchus Common Room, a meeting place and lecture hall devoted to the closer integration of art and science. Although the initiative survived barely two years, its broadly based membership and range of speakers was a significant attempt to continue the breakdown of the philosophical barriers between the arts and sciences that had recommenced at the ICA at the beginning of the decade but, after a promising start, disintegrated. Stefan Themerson had read C.P. Snow's 'Two Cultures' essay in the *New Statesman* in 1956 and embarked on a protracted correspondence with Snow, who, before eventually deciding to expand the text into a book, had

Franciszka Themerson: *Comme la vie est lente, comme l'espérance est violente*, 1959 (no. 97)

wanted Gaberbocchus Press to print a version of the original article. The Common Room talks embraced psychology, cybernetics, poetry, sociology, experimental film, music and painting (among the speakers were F.N. Souza and William Crozier). A William Fry play, *The Foggy Day Dew*, was produced by William Jay, who had produced Alfred Jarry's *Ubu Roi* at the ICA in 1952 (for which Franciszka Themerson designed the masks), and the Watergate Theatre performance of *Desire Caught by the Tail* the previous year.

Simultaneously, Franciszka Themerson's intellectual struggle with her own pictorial language was reaching resolution. She gave a talk to the Common Room in November 1957 entitled 'Bi-Abstract Pictures', the name she used to describe the incorporation into her paintings of abstractions from nature and abstractions of emotions. As figures from her drawings invaded her abstract paintings she learned to reconcile abstraction and representation: 'Every new abstract picture of mine had its human inhabitants', she declared of her figures trapped in space.[31] Her mature style is expressed eloquently in *Comme la vie est lente, comme l'espérance est violente* (1959; the title is a quotation from Apollinaire), in which she drew her figures into the thick, chalk-white paint, the incisions suggesting to one critic 'white modern cave paintings'.[32] Propelled by a seriousness and a refined quietude, these unusual paintings do indeed attain an impressive and timeless dignity, a fulfilment of Klee's dictum that the hand should be an instrument of the distant past.

In the Barbican Gallery exhibition *The Sixties Art Scene in London* (1993) the curator, David Mellor, postulated a defining moment in the formation of a new sensibility in English art. The specific incident occurred in December 1956, when John Minton launched into a prolonged attack on

William Green: *Nude*, 1958 (no. 45)

American Action Painting in front of Sketch Club students at the RCA's Painting School. Rounding on a poured-bitumen painting by Robyn Denny and an abstract, gestural work by Richard Smith, he violently condemned their lack of finish and arbitrary markings, declaring of Denny's painting 'You could call it "Eden Come Home" if you wanted to'. Shortly afterwards Denny adopted Minton's random reference to the Prime Minister, scrawled 'Eden Come Home' on a large board painted in bitumen and scorched the surface; to compound the mischief Smith then signed the work. William Green, who was absent during Minton's diatribe, achieved notoriety in the following year when he was filmed by Ken Russell bicycling over a black-bitumen-and-enamel-painted board for the BBC TV arts programme *Monitor*. Green's *Nude* (1958), despite having been made under protest at the RCA to fulfil a requirement of the Rome and Abbey Scholarships, is perversely successful, and a rare figurative work: the paint is applied in drips, streaks and thin layered washes so that the obscured figure emerges, mysteriously, to resemble a Giacometti, another playful *provocateur* of the body realized in paint.

CONTINUUM

'Forms of pop imagery and pop culture were often enjoyed by avant-garde artists (unlike the middlebrow who see themselves as the guardians of high culture) long before Coke culture came in ... in 1917 the Cubist ballet Parade, on which Picasso worked with Cocteau, Matisse, and Satie, introduced "a little American girl" who (in Cocteau's words) "quivers like movies ... dances a rag-time ... buys a Kodak" by way of representing Coke culture in the bud.' – *David Sylvester*

'Richard Hamilton ... came and talked about the pictures, and they gave out little prizes of two or three pounds. He gave a prize to Ron [Kitaj] and a prize to me, and from that moment on the staff of the College never said a word to me about my work being awful. Before that they said it was junk.' – *David Hockney*

' ... large in scale, brilliant in colour and polished in finish.' – *Marco Livingstone*

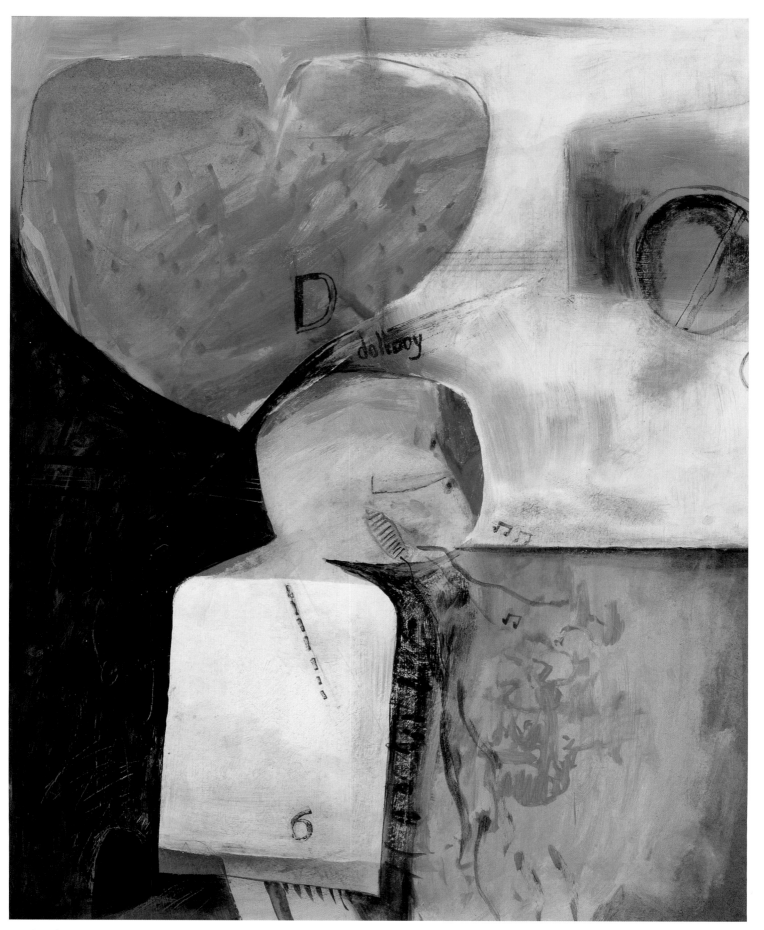

David Hockney: *Doll Boy* (study), 1960 (no. 55)

One of the transitions in British art in the last years of the Fifties was symbolized with tragic finality by John Minton's suicide in 1957. In January 1956 the exhibition *Modern Art in the United States* opened at the Tate Gallery. In the room devoted to Abstract Expressionism the gestural painting of Pollock, Kline and De Kooning acted as a trigger for the Royal College of Art (RCA) dissenters, precipitating the final push out of what they saw as English parochialism, the demise of Minton's pictorial, illustrational conventions and his compromised attempts to paint his sexuality. British artists had been painting in a gestural manner influenced by the Tachistes long before the Tate show, but the scale and confidence of the American paintings made the decisive impression. The New Vision Centre Gallery was opened in 1956 by the painters Denis Bowen, Frank Avray Wilson and Halima Nalecz with the timely boast that it was 'Fiercely non-figurative, violently tachiste, remarkably international'.[1] One of the gallery's early exhibitions, in December 1956, was of paintings by Ralph Rumney, whose *Untitled* (1956) is part Tachisme and part precocious indication of a British development of American Action Painting: within the clusters of dense, irradiant colour, Rumney's incorporation of circular encrustations of paint from the bottoms of cans is a typically wilful gesture. His work had a firm intellectual underpinning, but its element of playfulness was an important characteristic of much late-Fifties painting. In *Existentialism, Marxism and Anarchism* (1950), Herbert Read contended that the work ethic had made the Marxist 'a very dull boy' and that the existentialist inhabited an 'abyss of nothingness': he cited Huizinga's *Homo Ludens*, published in 1949, as confirmation of the vital creative rôle of play, which he equated with freedom. Rumney, who had travelled and worked in France and Italy since 1952, became a founder member of the *Internationale Situationniste* in 1957.[2] Although he was soon expelled by the Situationists, Rumney's 'psychogeography' (the investigation of perceptions of urban spaces)[3] was manifest two years later in the first London exposition of Situationist environmentalism, *Place*, at the Institute of Contemporary Arts (ICA). Having contributed to this transition in art practice, Rumney grew increasingly disillusioned with a rapidly changing art scene that marginalized Situationism: he ceased to make artworks in the early 1960s and did not resume until 1983.

The impact of Abstract Expressionism was reflected in London in three important group exhibitions in 1957, beginning in January with *Statements: A Review of British Abstract Art in 1956* at the ICA, organized by Lawrence Alloway, who had been since 1955 the institute's assistant director. In foregrounding gestural painting in *Statements*, Alloway can be seen trying to slough off his earlier connection with the Constructivists, while attempting, somewhat uncomfortably, to assimilate such makers of post-Dubuffet images as his ex-Independent Group colleagues Paolozzi, Turnbull and Cordell. Patrick Heron was mainly responsible for the selection of *Metavisual Tachiste Abstract* at the Redfern Gallery in April, and attempted (as he had with his earlier School of London) to be inclusive. In the catalogue preface Denys Sutton greeted Action Painting – which he defined as a hybrid of Dubuffet, Ernst and Pollock – as an 'international style susceptible of different interpretations': Heron included his fellow St Ives painters Peter Lanyon, Roger Hilton and Terry Frost, as well as Robyn Denny, Ralph Rumney, William Gear and Alan Davie. Ralph Rumney's *The Change* (1957) was reproduced on the cover of the catalogue, which was designed by Robyn Denny. *Dimensions*, at the O'Hana Gallery in December 1957, was, at the invitation of Frank Avray Wilson, jointly organized by Alloway and Toni del Renzio, who was responsible for compiling a 'table of events' in abstract art since 1945, a 'conscious effort to set down the links before they were forgotten' that 'caused people like David Sylvester great merriment'.[4] The bias of the exhibition in favour of painterly as opposed to geometric abstraction ultimately backfired, and *Dimensions* is characterized by Margaret Garlake as

Ralph Rumney: *Untitled*, 1956 (no. 88)

Harold Cohen: *Plan for a City*, 1958 (no. 23)

marking the beginning of a new recognition of Constructivism.[5] Among the gestural painters in *Dimensions* was Harold Cohen, who, like many young painters, passed through a period in the late Fifties of strong American influence, before emancipating himself from it. *Plan for a City* (1958) combines vigorously painted symbols – mark-making – with an urban inflection that doubtless appealed to Alloway. In the catalogue of *Abstract Expressionism*, an exhibition he co-organized with Harold Cohen at the Arts Council Gallery in 1958, Alloway might have been describing *Plan for a City* when he wrote that 'in abstract impressionism the free, sensual paint, liberated by action painting, turns into landscape all the time'.

Place, an exhibition of thirty-four paintings by Ralph Rumney, Robyn Denny and Richard Smith, was organized by Roger Coleman for the ICA in September 1959 as an environmental installation, a precursor of the *Situation* exhibitions in 1960 and 1961. The arrangement of the back-to-back floor-mounted canvases, in two standard sizes and limited to four colours, was intended to free viewers to determine their own relationships with the space. *Place* was, according to Smith, 'about making exhibitions ... we were conscious of the ICA tradition of "Form and Function", of huge blow-ups of photos and photostats',[6] and the generic link with

Richard Smith: *Yellow, Yellow*, 1957 (no. 92)

Parallel of Life and Art, for example, is evident. Coleman, who had been Smith's and Denny's contemporary at the RCA from 1954 to 1957, had become close to Alloway, and in March 1957 joined him on the ICA Exhibitions sub-committee. The three issues of *Ark* that Coleman edited at the RCA in 1956–57 continued the dissemination of ideas incubated at the Independent Group: they contained articles by Alloway, Frank Cordell, del Renzio, John McHale, Robert Melville, Alison and Peter Smithson, and Edward Wright, all of whom had been connected with the group. Alloway gained access through *Ark* to a larger constituency than the Independent Group, but the problems inherent in trying to reconcile Action Painting with the Independent Group's mass-media research beset much of his writing at this time. For him the difficulty would be magnified when art began to emerge from the RCA that appeared to have re-worked 'Pop' sources in an unmediated or insufficiently digested form.

Alloway had recognized that his low-art interests could be misapprehended, and set forth the limits of the consumption of mass-media images in a discussion of Paolozzi: 'The images he collects ... do not in themselves set his imagination working. Rather, when he draws or models, his experience of visual symbols (art and non-art) is part of his way of seeing.'[7] Ultimately, the paintings that became labelled as British Pop Art in 1961 bore little resemblance to what Alloway had foreseen as the manifestation of his theories. When Richard Hamilton asked Alloway his opinion of his first 'Pop inventory' paintings he provoked the 'outright answer "I think they're stupid"'; Hamilton realized that for Alloway 'The heresy was to pull things out from one point along the continuum and drop them in at another, then stir well – the fine/pop soup alternative'.[8]

That, in relation to the origins of British Pop Art, there was dichotomy between theory and practice was becoming clear. Even the RCA painters such as Smith and Denny who were stimulated by, and participated in, ICA debates remained completely uninterested in the art produced by former members of the Independent Group, and looked instead to the Americans. By the spring 1960 issue of *Ark* it was evident that the next intake of RCA students was in open revolt against Alloway's version of Pop, which to them was over-intellectual and irrelevant. The art editor of *Ark* 25, Terry Green, recalled, 'There was a very posey thing around at that time which had to do with artists being intellectuals. We didn't like that. That's why we put Brigitte Bardot on the cover'.[9] As a Slade student from 1958 to 1962 Patrick Procktor was relatively inured to the extremes of both painterly abstraction and proto-Pop. He attended ICA debates, however, and was aware of events elsewhere in London: 'We had rather a lot of Willem de Kooning stuffed down our throats, by Lawrence Alloway and Andrew Forge', and at an ICA 'session about Pop Art', led by Alloway, 'the utmost pretentious noises were coming from the stage'.[10] The reaction to these 'pretensions' from Procktor's contemporaries at the RCA, and a hitherto forbidden sense of humour, was further manifest in the same issue of *Ark,* in 'Only Sixteen', a pastiche of a *Teen Romance* comic strip, contributed by a former student, Peter Blake.[11]

Unlike Alloway, Roger Coleman admired Peter Blake's painting and was the first person to write about it, in *Ark* in 1956.[12] Blake's reappearance in the magazine in 1960, the year in which Derek Boshier, Pauline Boty, Patrick Caulfield, Allen Jones, David Hockney and Peter Phillips were all RCA students, was significant. Blake had left the college in 1956 to take up a Leverhulme Travelling Fellowship in Europe, and on his return the following year four of the drawings he made on the Continent were reproduced in *Ark*.[13] Subsequently Blake maintained friendships with many RCA students, even at the height of the interest in painterly abstraction. His example

R.B. Kitaj: *The Murder of Rosa Luxemburg*, 1960.
Oil and collage on canvas, 153 × 152.4 cm. Tate, London

was crucial in maintaining the continuity of non-academic figurative painting at the college; this, and the arrival at the college of R.B. Kitaj in 1958, was a key factor in the emergence of British Pop Art at the RCA in 1960.

The Pop Art trajectory described by Peter Blake begins in August 1951 with the Whitechapel Art Gallery exhibition *Black Eyes and Lemonade*, which Blake attended. The exhibition, devoted to the 'Popular and Traditional Arts', was the gallery's contribution to the Festival of Britain. *English Popular Art*, the second book on the subject by Enid Marx and Margaret Lambert, was published simultaneously. Enid Marx taught part-time at Gravesend School of Art, where Blake began his studies in 1946, aged fourteen. An author and illustrator of children's books, she also encouraged Blake's interest in the popular arts and in the graphic arts of the urban environment in which he lived; another of his tutors was Barnett Freedman, a distinguished illustrator and painter who also directed Blake towards graphic design. Blake took his portfolio to the RCA in 1950, hoping to be accepted on the graphic design course. His entry was delayed until 1953 by national service in the RAF, and he was then invited to join the Painting School. By about

John Deakin: Installation photograph, *Black Eyes and Lemonade*, Whitechapel Art Gallery, London, 1951. Private collection

1952 Blake, always a skilful and meticulous draughtsman, had begun to develop a personal iconography, and had adopted certain pictorial devices, such as frontal-figure compositions and the radical cropping of features, that characterized many of his paintings in the Fifties.

Blake readily acknowledges the influence, while at the RCA, of the American Symbolic Realists, in particular Bernard Perlin, Ben Shahn and Honoré Sharrer, and the British artists Alfred Daniels and Peter Gooding. His own work might have stuck within the confines of a finely painted but derivative realism had he not determined to paint only subjects with a strong personal resonance. Of *Children Reading Comics* (1954), which was based on a family snapshot of Blake and his sister, he says, 'I was calling on the person I was'.[14] Blake himself was only twenty-two at the time, but the theme of the painting was partly inspired by his younger brother Terry, who read comics such as the *Eagle*. The painting embodies many Blakeian hallmarks, such as the juxtaposition of areas painted with infinite precision and painterly, smudged or 'uncompleted' passages: this unconventional development of realism was an important aspect of Blake's modernity. *Children Reading Comics* is not an expression of Blake's feelings about specific children, it is about the world of children: its contemporaneity further depends on a

Peter Blake: *Children reading Comics*, 1954.
Oil on hardboard, 36.9 × 47 cm. Tullie House Museum and Art Services, Carlisle

slightly disturbing psychological acumen that distinguishes it from any other painting of that time. Since he only painted things he admired or loved, Blake was never satirical – if sometimes ironic – but there is in certain of his paintings, however affectionate, a wistful yearning, a sense of loss. Having begun art school at fourteen – 'I went straight from childhood to art' – Blake may have been compensating for, and imagining, those lost years.

The two most important and complex paintings Blake made at the RCA were *The Preparation for the Entry into Jerusalem* (1955–56) and *On the Balcony* (1955–57). Both subjects were set by the tutors, and were typical of the themes dictated by art colleges in the Fifties: *Yellow, Yellow* (1957; see illus. p. 153), for example, by Blake's friend Richard Smith, was his interpretation of *Susannah and the Elders*. Blake cunningly modified the set topic *The Entry into Jerusalem* into *The Preparation for the Entry into Jerusalem* as a means of introducing the figures of the children, who are shown together with the props for a Sunday School play that he imagined. The perspective shift – the ground is painted in the vertical dimension and appears like a geometrical abstract – is a device that gives the painting a disconcerting edge. The method of assembling discrete elements – from the Mobo Bronco (a popular toy) to the engraving of

Peter Blake: *Preparation for the Entry into Jerusalem*, 1955–56 (no. 12)

Peter Blake: *On the Balcony*, 1955–57. Oil on canvas, 121.3 × 90.8 cm. Tate, London

Some of the source images used for *On the Balcony*. Collection of Peter Blake

Jerusalem – foreshadows a characteristic of RCA Pop painting after 1960. *On the Balcony* extends this idea: a cornucopia of pictorial references (it incorporates twenty-seven balcony images – art pin-ups), it relates to the then-current device of the tack-board, the artist's or designer's memorandum of sources. *On the Balcony* contains four versions of the subject as it might have been interpreted and painted by RCA contemporaries of Blake, including a Kitchen Sink still-life and a 'Leon Kossoff'. The painting was not completed until after Blake's return from the Leverhulme Fellowship in 1957, when he added the 'Richard Smith' and the 'Robyn Denny'. The origin of the device of children holding paintings was Honoré Sharrer's *Workers and Paintings* (1943), which Blake had adopted in *Children Reading Comics*: 'I was interested in the way Sharrer's people presented themselves to the viewer. In *Comics* I used the idea to convey a sense of immediacy – "We've just read this" or "This is what we're reading".'

Peter Blake: *Got a Girl*, 1960–61 (no. 13)

Blake's iconography, previously exclusively British, first embraced American actors and pop stars in 1959 – Elvis Presley, Kim Novak, The Everly Brothers. In the catalogue of the mixed exhibition of Blake, Theo Crosby and John Latham at the ICA in 1960, Alloway was making reference to these subjects in his comment 'Blake works as a fan'. At this point Blake's modernity was signified in the allusions to Jasper Johns's emblematic paintings of objects and the American hard-edge abstractionists; he always retained, though, a figurative element in these paintings, the objects of his fandom incorporated usually by means of collage at the edges of his painted hardboard bases. In *Fine Art Bit* (1959) the inclusion of six postcards of famous paintings sets up a witty dialogue with the abstract painting underneath and with the painting's provocative title. *Fine Art Bit*, *Everly Wall* (1959) and *Girlie Door* (1959) exemplify a radical change in style for Blake, in which he aimed to invoke Pop subjects that would resonate with a wide audience; in 1959 they ushered in fully fledged British Pop.

Between 1957 and 1961 the paintings of Richard Smith were, for Lawrence Alloway, 'central to [the] development' of what he identified as the 'second phase' of British Pop Art.[15] Alloway defined this as the abstract phase, and the gestural abstract paintings Smith made at the RCA are exemplified by one of his last works there, the Prix de Rome painting *Yellow, Yellow* (1957; see illus. p. 153). The bold marks in *Yellow, Yellow* and the prominent brush strokes attest to the

Richard Smith: *Penny*, 1960 (no. 93)

importance for Britain's young painters of the Tate's showing of Abstract Expressionism in the previous year – although Smith's strongest and most specific response was to a Sam Francis exhibition he saw at the Galerie Rive Droite in Paris in 1956. He had always been fascinated by the popular arts. Like Alloway, Smith owned a copy of the American edition of McLuhan's *The Mechanical Bride*, brought back at his request by a cousin who worked in advertising and occasionally visited New York: the analyses of advertisements were, for him, 'a revelation'.[16] He wrote about film backgrounds and on ideograms for *Ark*, which also ran a feature with pull-out illustrations from a film project, *Ev'ry-which-way* by Smith and Denny, that 'aimed to connect our sense of art with a mid-century urban consciousness'.[17] Smith was making large and vigorous paintings influenced by Rothko and De Kooning, but he evolved an original style only after the relationship with Pop became implicit. By early 1959, when he was still living in London, paintings like *Valentine* (1959) and *MM* (1959) alluded to – without aiming to represent – popular imagery. The mass-media sources were deftly integrated into his formal, spatial and painterly concerns. The oblique references to product advertising in Smith's paintings, such as the sensuously shimmering *Penny* (1960), fulfilled Alloway's programme for a kind of painting that was informed by the popular arts 'but checked by puzzles and paradoxes about the play of signs at different levels of signification'.[18] Poised at the intersection of formal concerns with colour and form and alluding to the mass media, Smith's elegant but powerful paintings stand astride the edge of these two impulses, radiant, pulsating like vast blow-ups of fragments of high-key, soft-focus advertising photographs. The analogy with the numinous, blurred close-up returns us to a pervasive Fifties motif – flicker.

Smith was intrigued by the packaging of products, noting that the buyer seldom saw the product itself but only its outer cover – as in the cigarette or cosmetic packaging that were favourite sources. At no time were the commodity references in Smith's paintings explicit, however. When he arrived in New York in late 1959 the leap forward in his art was due to several external factors. First 'it was a question of supplies. You could get eight foot stretchers from Art Chassis, great rolls of canvas – cotton duck – and relatively cheap oil paints from Grandmacher'. With the financial independence afforded by the fellowship there came the liberation of working in a large loft studio, and he rented a space downtown in Howard Street, next door to Frank Stella: 'In London we mostly worked in the cramped front rooms of our flats, now I felt I could make these splashy, painted things.' Moreover, as Smith notes,

> the New York art world was so much smaller in scale then than it is now, and my milieu included Mike Goldberg, Ellsworth Kelly, Lee Krasner, Kenneth Noland, Agnes Martin, and David Smith. Dorothy Miller was very friendly, Ivan Karp would drop by, and so would Henry Geldzahler on his Sunday rounds of artists' studios: sometimes I had the encouragement of friends being impressed with what I was doing.[19]

Smith returned to London in 1961, having had his first one-man show at the Green Gallery, New York, and found his work identified with the 'third phase' of Pop Art.

The shared concerns of Smith and Robyn Denny while students at the RCA are revealed, in retrospect, as transitional stages in their development, and the paintings they made in the Fifties bear only a vestigial relationship with the mature – but distinct – styles they both evolved by 1960. Since 1960 Denny has continued to make paintings that address fundamental issues of space, scale and the interaction of the spectator with painting. Denny's *Baby is Three* (1960)

Robyn Denny: *Red Beat 6*, 1958 (no. 37)

may be considered as one of the first examples of his maturity, for it articulately explores all of these themes. Throughout the 1960s many of Denny's paintings employed the formal device of a rectilinear 'door frame', usually sited on the baseline of the composition, a portal that invited the viewer across the threshold of the picture surface into the space of the painting. His earlier work, however, engages at many points with aspects of the investigation of the relationship between viewer, art and the environment in its insistence on an active two-way participation and human-size scale. In the exhibition *Place*, for example, the seven-foot-high (210 cm) paintings were placed on the ground to occupy the floor plane on which the viewer stood, to break down the disjunction between the spectator and a picture hanging on a wall. At this point Denny became, in a sense, the apogee of Alloway's commitment to an art that grew out of urbanism, an art that sought to retrieve its once inextricable relationship with society. Ironically, when *Baby is Three* was included in the first *Situation* exhibition, Alloway read its denial of 'image' as a flaw, its 'brutal ... visual jumps' as having missed 'the threshold of comfort'.[20]

Even as a student Denny was concerned with public art, and his first article for *Ark*, published in 1956, advocated the medium of mosaic, in which Denny was then working, for its potential

Robyn Denny: *Abbey Wood No. 1*, 1958–59 (no. 38)

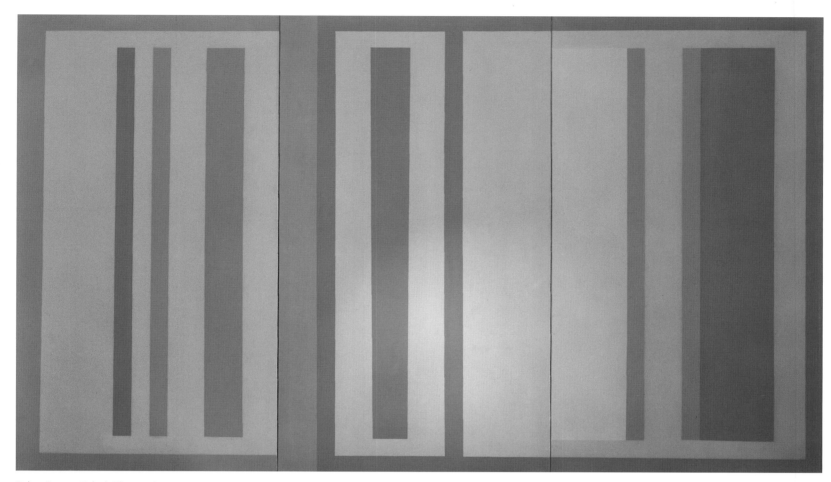

Robyn Denny: *Baby is Three*, 1960 (no. 39)

to achieve a 'reconciliation between architecture and the fine arts'.[21] At the RCA none of the tutors had alerted students to collage, and it was left to the writer and critic Jasia Reichardt to introduce Denny, Smith and Blake to the work of Kurt Schwitters. Denny's thesis in 1957 was entitled 'Language, Symbol, Image', and his interest in lettering and communication spilled over into paintings such as *Red Beat 6* (1958). The vestigial word-language 'Go Go Go' in *Red Beat 6* shows Denny investigating the perceptual, leaving a hint to the painting's mood that might help viewers to negotiate their dialogue with the painting. This phase culminated in 1959 with two works that were actually executed for public spaces, the *Austin Reed Mural* and a ten-foot-square mosaic mural for Abbey Wood Primary School. Both grew out of Denny's letter collages but cleverly exploited the perceptual disruption of the alternating dominance of field and symbol. As Robert Kudelka observed, Denny's mature painting may be seen as a constant refinement of the process foreshadowed in *Abbey Wood No. 1* (1958–59), in which the static painting activates the spectator.

Lawrence Alloway located the inception of what he called the 'third phase' of Pop Art in the opening of the *Young Contemporaries* exhibition in February 1961. Alloway was one of the selectors, and in the catalogue he noted how the RCA artists Boshier, Hockney, Kitaj, Jones and Phillips 'connected their art with the city ... using typical products and objects, including the techniques of graffiti and the imagery of mass communications'. The following year, however,

Allen Jones: *City*, 1961 (no. 58)

having left London and emigrated to the USA, Alloway sent a review to *The Listener* in which he expressed growing concerns over the art he had helped to initiate: 'happy in the playground of the opened-out situation', he complained, 'pop artists lack a grasp of the history their art belongs to, as well as a sense of the internal rigour necessary to art.'[22] In fact Allen Jones was expelled from the RCA in spring 1960, the scapegoat for what the college authorities believed was subversive behaviour among the students. The prize awarded to Jones in the *Young Contemporaries* exhibition resulted in a commission from Courtaulds Ltd for the vast, cinemascopic *City* (1961), which originally hung in the company's restaurant at their City of London headquarters. The main motif is a man fleeing with a bag of stolen loot, which Jones

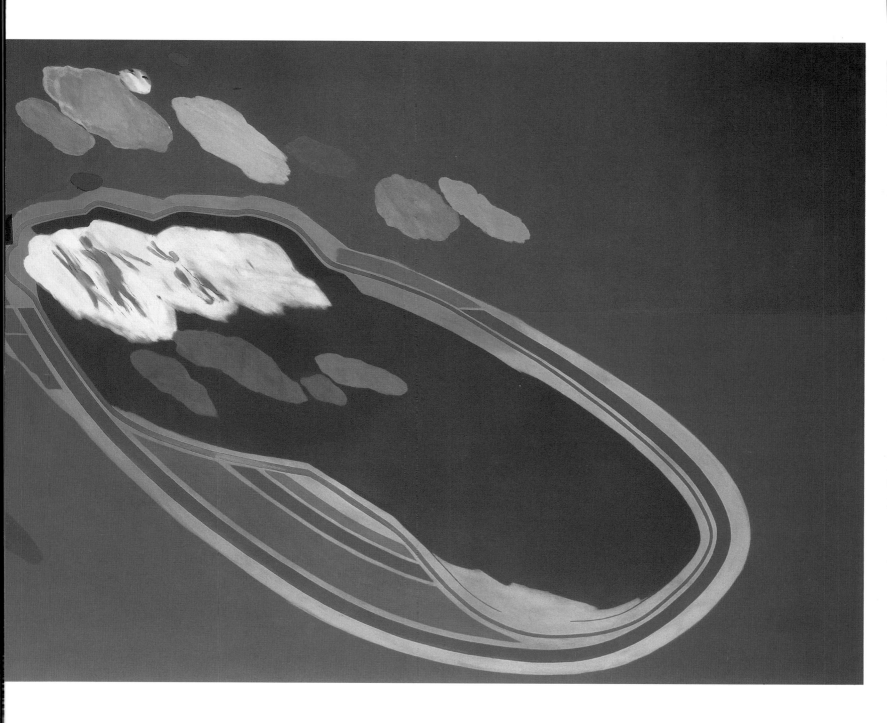

presented as 'a cautionary tale for big business'.[23] In the chronology of Jones's early paintings *City* falls between *The Artist Thinks* (1960) and the Bus paintings (1962), and shares their heraldic colour, flat field and economy of means. Replete with art-historical references drawn from various sources, it is typical of early British Pop. *City* is also, in some respects, a resumé of debates on art and perception in the early Fifties. For Jones, the floating figure was a specific reference to his admiration for Chagall, but the interest in non-gravity, of which Chagall provided a modern parallel, was a topic discussed in broader terms at Giedion's ICA lecture on cave paintings in 1950. Similarly, Jones's elliptical 'swag-bag', which he based on Kandinsky's early improvisations, also returns the Fifties art narrative to David Sylvester's talks on Klee and peripheral vision.

On leaving Bradford College of Art in 1957, David Hockney began national service as a conscientious objector. As a result, for two years prior to entering the RCA in autumn 1959, he had had little opportunity to paint. At the RCA he briefly forsook figurative painting and experimented with abstraction; he had been impressed in 1958 with Alan Davie's first retrospective, which he saw at Wakefield Art Gallery, where it was mounted by the gallery's influential director (and early Hockney patron), Helen Kapp. Of the few Hockney abstract works to survive, *Growing Discontent* (1959–60) possibly indicates his discomfort with non-referential, abstract concepts, and he soon reverted to subjects with a direct personal relevance. *Doll Boy* (1960; see illus. p. 149), one of several versions of this painting, was also one of the first of Hockney's paintings in which the subject-matter was motivated by, and incorporated references to, Hockney's homosexuality. As is now well known, the title refers to Cliff Richard's first number-one hit record, 'Living Doll' (1959), Hockney having transposed the gender of the object of adoration in the lyrics. In *Going to be a Queen for Tonight* (1960) Hockney boldly employs childlike graffiti that has been related to Dubuffet and to the scrawlings in men's lavatories; it may also indicate familiarity with Robyn Denny's incorporation of graffiti-like marks in his paintings. Another characteristic of Hockney's early paintings, the areas of raw, unpainted canvas, was, like the passages of smeared paint, derived from Francis Bacon, and is evident in both *Doll Boy* and *I'm in the Mood for Love* (1961; see illus. p. 172); these devices were employed for different reasons, however, by Hockney, who was by this time determined to make it clear that he was making paintings that were not literal representations of fact but whose meaning resided in the marks he made on the canvas.

Hockney assimilated the influences of Kitaj, Picasso, Dubuffet and Klee, integrating them into his own style. If Lawrence Alloway believed that the paintings Hockney and the other 'Young Contemporaries' exhibited in 1961 lacked 'intellectual rigour', then perhaps their work was better off without it. By 1962 British art was attracting a larger constituency than ever before, and in the firmament of new young artists Hockney was the brightest star. The story of how Hockney and his fellow students were about to be failed in their final diploma examinations at the RCA in 1962, and the last-minute reversal when Robin Darwin awarded Hockney a gold medal, is now legendary. The gold medal for 'outstanding distinction' accompanied further awards to Hockney of a first-class diploma and the college life-drawing prize. It was made in front of a distinguished audience that included, ironically, Sir Herbert Read (knighted in 1953 for services to literature rather than to art), who found Pop Art 'tedious'; he was a witness to the dissolution of many of his beliefs. Violating the accepted dress code, which required an academic gown, Hockney, his hair dyed blond, defiantly and provocatively overturned tradition by attending the ceremony wearing a gold-lamé jacket. The event that crystallized the transition in British art also proclaimed the imminent revolution in society – and was literally dazzling.

David Hockney: *Going to be a Queen for Tonight*, 1960 (no. 56)

Apart from the car and van, this view across London, with the polychrome Gothic of St Mary Magdalene, Paddington, in the distance, shows a London that seems scarcely to have changed since Taine wrote about the city in 1872. But this remarkable photograph was taken in 1960. At precisely that moment British Pop was evolving at the Royal College of Art; the young painters there were among the capital's tiny avant-garde, but soon the changes they presaged were reflected in both the urban environment and in society as a whole.

Roger Mayne: Harrow Road looking towards Clarendon Crescent with slum clearance in background, 1960 (no. 69)

David Hockney: *I'm in the Mood for Love*, 1961 (no. 57)

Notes

IN TRANSITION

1. J. Minton, 'Three Young Contemporaries', *Ark* 13, p. 12.

2. N. Barber, *Conversations with Painters*, London 1964, p. 111.

3. L.R. Lippard (ed.), *Pop Art*, London 1966, p. 50.

4. *The Expendable Ikon: Works by John McHale*, exhib. cat., Buffalo NY, Albright-Knox Art Gallery, 1984, p. 32.

5. J. Hopkins, *Michael Ayrton: A Biography*, London 1994, p. 176.

6. T. Crosby, 'Roger Mayne', *Creative Camera*, May 1986, p. 13.

7. H. Jennings, *Pandaemonium*, London 1987, p. xii.

8. G. Whitham, 'This is Tomorrow: Genesis of an Exhibition', in E. Leffingwell, K. Marta (eds.), *Modern Dreams*, New York 1988, p. 38.

9. R. Spencer (ed.), *Eduardo Paolozzi: Writings and Interviews*, Oxford 2000, pp. 76–77.

10. J. Trevelyan, *Indigo Days*, London 1957, p. 80.

11. F. Spalding, *Dance till the Stars Come Down: A Biography of John Minton*, London 1991, p. 216.

12. Bryan Robertson, article for *The Studio*, March 1946, quoted in *Studio International*, February 1969, p. 58.

13. Minton, *op. cit.* note 1, p. 14.

14. J. Bratby, *Painters on Painting: John Bratby ARA on Stanley Spencer's 'Early Self-Portrait'*, London 1969, p. 6.

SHADOWS AND UTOPIAS

1. In the collection of the Ashmolean Museum of Art and Archaeology, Oxford.

2. Letter from L. Bomberg, *Architectural Review*, April 1959, p. 228.

3. *Ibid.*

4. R. Cork, *David Bomberg*, New Haven CT and London 1987, p. 266.

5. *Ibid.*, p. 285.

6. *Ibid.*, p. 286.

7. R. Hughes, *Frank Auerbach*, London 1992, p. 84.

8. *Ibid.*, p. 83.

9. *Ibid.*

10. From the *Jewish Chronicle*, 8 May 1914, quoted in Cork, *op. cit.* note 4, p. 2.

11. L. Alloway, *Nine Abstract Artists*, London 1954, p. 2.

12. J. Piper, *British Romantic Artists*, London 1942, p. 46.

13. *Robert Colquhoun*, exhib. cat., ed. B. Robertson, London, Whitechapel Art Gallery, 1958, pp. 5–7.

14. *A Paradise Lost*, exhib. cat. by D. Mellor, London, Barbican Art Gallery, 1987, p. 25.

15. *Isabel Rawsthorne 1912–1992*, exhib. cat., Harrogate, The Mercer Art Gallery, 1997, p. 4.

16. T. del Renzio, 'Pioneers and Trendies', *Art and Artists*, February 1984, p. 25.

17. R. Landau, *New Directions in British Architecture*, London 1968, p. 25.

18. T. del Renzio, 'Redfern Gallery', *Art News and Review*, 13 December 1952, p. 4.

19. Josef Herman to Douglas Hall, 23 October 1972, Scottish National Gallery of Modern Art, Edinburgh.

20. R. Heller, *Josef Herman*, London 1998, p. 41.

21. M. Merchant, *Josef Herman: The Early Years in Scotland and Wales*, Llandybie 1984, p. 9.

22. Alan Davie interviewed by the author, May 2001.

23. *Alan Davie*, exhib. cat. by P. Elliott, Edinburgh, Scottish National Gallery of Modern Art, 2000–01, p. 23.

24. M. Garlake, *New Art New World*, New Haven CT and London 1998, p. 26.

25. R. Berthoud, *Graham Sutherland: A Biography*, London 1982, p. 70.

26. See *Gerald Wilde*, exhib. cat., ed. C. Hawes, London, October Gallery, 1988, pp. 49–50, and *Ark* 16, p. 24.

27. *Gerald Wilde*, *cit.* note 26, pp. 6–9.

28. L. Alloway, 'City Notes', *Architectural Design*, January 1959, pp. 34–35.

DISRUPTION

1. D. Sylvester, *Interviews with Francis Bacon*, London 1983, p. 30.

2. J. Russell, *Francis Bacon*, London 1979, p. 71.

3. Sylvester, *op. cit.* note 1, p. 57.

4. Richard Lannoy in conversation with the author, August 2000.

5. A. Brighton, *Francis Bacon*, London 2001, pp. 24–29.

6. M. Peppiatt, *Francis Bacon: Anatomy of an Enigma*, London 1996, p. 77.

7. Quoted in *ibid.*, p. 75.

8. *Francis Bacon*, exhib. cat. by L. Alloway, New York, Solomon R. Guggenheim Museum, 1963, p. 20.

9. See P. Cecil (ed.), *Flickers of the Dreamachine*, Hove 1998.

10. R. Melville, 'Francis Bacon', *Horizon* 120–21, December 1949 – January 1950, p. 419.

11. J. Rothenstein and R. Alley, *Francis Bacon*, London 1964, pp. 70–71.

12. A. Scharf, *Art and Photography*, Harmondsworth 1974, p. 220; Van Deren Coke, *The Painter and the Photograph*, New Mexico 1972, pp. 110 ff.

13. See G. Lista, *Futurism and Photography*, London 2001.

14. For Bernard Cohen's pejorative use of this phrase see *Paris Post War: Art and Existentialism 1945–55*, exhib. cat., ed. F. Morris, London, Tate Gallery, 1993, pp. 53–62.

15. Sutherland's biomorphs had initially influenced Bacon, but this process had been reversed, as Sutherland's *Man Walking Dog* (1952) demonstrates.

16. D. Sylvester, *About Modern Art*, London 1997, p. 23.

17. Undated holograph letter from Henderson to Mark Haworth-Booth, *c.* 1976.

18. Information from David Sylvester, who first met Pulham at Rodrigo Moynihan's home in 1946.

19. Pulham's photographs of Surrealist painters were reproduced in *Lilliput*, October 1943, pp. 319–30.

20. Rothenstein and Alley, *op. cit.* note 11, p. 13.

21. P.R. Pulham, 'The Camera and the Artist', *The Listener*, 24 January 1952, pp. 144–46.

22. P.R. Pulham, 1951 (unpublished typescript, private collection).

23. Tate Archive, holograph, P.R. Pulham to Isabel Lambert, undated (March 1952).

24. From transcript of proceedings of ICA debate recorded by Richard Lannoy, 11 March 1952.

25. *Ibid.*

26. Moynihan interviewed by David Sylvester on BBC Radio, *Third Programme*, 1962, printed in *Rodrigo Moynihan: A Retrospective Exhibition*, exhib. cat., London, Royal Academy of Arts, 1978, p. 20.

27. D. Sylvester in conversation with the author, April 2000; see also *Richard Hamilton: Collected Words*, London 1983, p. 53.

28. R. Banham, 'Representations in Protest', written for *New Society*, 1969, reprinted in Paul Barker (ed.), *Arts in Society*, London 1977, pp. 61–66.

29. A. Seago, *Burning the Box of Beautiful Things*, Oxford 1995.

30. *Op. cit.* note 24.

31. *Victor Willing*, exhib. cat., ed. N. Serota and R. Kirby, London, Whitechapel Art Gallery, 1986, p. 57.

32. *Ibid.*

33. Myles Murphy in telephone conversation with the author, April 2001.

34. L. Mazzetti, 'Making a Film', *Ark* 17, pp. 30–33.

35. R. Melville, 'Exhibitions', *Architectural Review*, March 1958, p. 204.

36. *Victor Willing*, *cit.* note 31, p. 60.

37. *Ibid.*, p. 58.

38. *Ibid.*

39. R. Medley, *Drawn from the Life: A Memoir*, London 1983, p. 204.

40. *Ibid.*, p. 203.

41. *Ibid.*, p. 206.

42. *Ibid.*, p. 204.

43. *Kenneth Armitage*, exhib. cat. by A. Bowness, London, Whitechapel Art Gallery, 1959, p. 9.

44. R. Burstow, 'The Geometry of Fear: Herbert Read and British Modern Sculpture after the Second World War', in *Herbert Read: A British Vision of World Art*, exhib. cat., ed. B. Read and D. Thistlewood, Leeds City Art Galleries, 1993, pp. 119–32.

45. Patrick Heron, *The Changing Forms of Art*, London 1955, p. 229.

46. P. James (ed.), *Henry Moore on Sculpture*, London 1966, plates 33–35.

47. Banham, *op. cit.* note 28, p. 64.

48. Heron, *op. cit.* note 45, p. 226.

49. R. Melville, 'The New Sculptors', *Harper's Bazaar*, January 1952, p. 73.

50. R. Burstow, 'Butler's competition project for a Monument to the "Unknown Political Prisoner"; abstraction and Cold War politics', *Art History*, December 1989, pp. 472–96.

51. Melville, *loc. cit.* note 49.

52 R. Berthoud, *Henry Moore*, London 1987, p. 137.

53 Heron, *op. cit.* note 48, p. 229.

54 L. Alloway, 'Francis Bacon: A great, shocking, eccentric painter', American *Vogue*, 1 November 1963, pp. 136ff.

55 R. Butler, *Creative Developments*, London 1962, p. 28.

NEW REALISMS

1 J. Berger in *New Statesman*, 6 June 1959, quoted in *The Forgotten Fifties*, exhib. cat., ed. J. Spalding, Sheffield, Graves Art Gallery, 1984, p. 40.

2 D. Sylvester, 'The Kitchen Sink', *Encounter*, December 1954, pp. 61–64.

3 D. Sylvester, *About Modern Art*, London 1997, p. 19.

4 *Art News and Review*, 26 January 1952, p. 7.

5 Sylvester, *op. cit.* note 3, p. 151.

6 *The Listener*, 8 April 1954, p. 618.

7 *The Listener*, 12 August 1954, p. 252.

8 *New Statesman*, 19 January 1952.

9 J. Berger, *Permanent Red*, London 1960, p. 80.

10 *The Kitchen Sink Painters*, exhib. cat. by F. Spalding, London, Mayor Gallery/Julian Hartnoll, 1991, pp.10–11.

11 *Ibid.*, p. 7.

12 *Albert Herbert: Retrospective*, exhib. cat. by J. England, London, England & Co., 1991, p. 7.

13 *Ibid.*

14 Jacqueline Stanley in conversation with author, September 2000.

15 W.R. Sickert, 'Idealism', *Art News*, 12 May 1910.

16 Derrick Greaves interviewed by the author, November 2000.

17 J. Minton, 'Three Young Contemporaries', *Ark* 13, pp. 12–14.

18 J. Bratby, *Painters on Painting: John Bratby ARA on Stanley Spencer's 'Early Self-Portrait'*, London 1969, p. 6.

19 A. Clutton-Brock, *John Bratby*, London 1961, p. 10.

20 *Ibid.*

OPPOSING FORCES

1 Richard Lannoy in conversation with the author, August 2000.

2 *Art News and Review*, 24 February 1951, p. 6.

3 R. Banham, 'Representations in Protest', for *New Society*, 1969, reprinted in Paul Barker (ed.), *Arts in Society*, London 1977, p. 64.

4 *'An Unnerving Romanticism': The Art of Sylvia Sleigh and Lawrence Alloway*, exhib. cat., ed. A.I. Schlegel, Philadelphia, Philadelphia Museum of Art, 2001.

5 Richard Lannoy in conversation with the author, June 2001.

6 M. McLuhan, *The Mechanical Bride: Folklore of Industrial Man*, London 1967, p. 59.

7 L. Alloway, 'The Long Front of Culture', *Cambridge Opinion* 17, 1959, pp. 25–26.

8 Richard Hamilton interviewed for *Fathers of Pop*, Arts Council TV documentary, 1979.

9 L. Alloway, 'Personal Statement', *Ark* 19, p. 28.

10 M. Girouard, *Big Jim: The Life and Work of James Stirling*, London 1998, p. 56.

11 L. Alloway, *Nine Abstract Artists*, London 1954, p. 1.

12 Alloway, *op. cit.* note 9.

13 D.W. Thompson, *On Growth and Form*, Cambridge 1982, pp. 3, 326. Thompson's revised edition of 1942 was in wide circulation at this time.

14 *Nigel Henderson*, exhib. cat., London, Anthony d'Offay Gallery, 1977 (unpaginated).

15 *Ibid.*

16 L.L. Whyte (ed.), *Aspects of Form*, London 1951, p. 210.

17 **Op. cit.** note 8.

18 *The Independent Group: Postwar Britain and the Aesthetics of Plenty*, exhib. cat., ed. D. Robbins, London, ICA, 1990, p. 29.

19 This has been rectified by the recent publication of V. Walsh, *Nigel Henderson: Parallel of Life and Art*, London 2001.

20 R. Spencer (ed.), *Eduardo Paolozzi: Writings and Interviews*, Oxford 2000, p. 56.

21 *Nigel Henderson*, exhib. cat.,Norwich, Norwich School of Art Gallery, text by C. Mullen, p. 25.

22 *Nigel Henderson*, exhib. cat., *cit.* note 14 (unpaginated).

23 *Nigel Henderson: Recent Work*, exhib. cat., London, ICA, 1961 (folded sheet).

24 *Humphrey Jennings: Film-Maker/Painter/Poet*, exhib. cat., ed. Mary-Lou Jennings, London, British Film Instititute, 1982, pp. 50–51.

25 *Nigel Henderson*, *cit.* note 14 (unpaginated).

26 *Nigel Henderson: Photographs of Bethnal Green 1949–1952*, exhib. cat., Nottingham, Midland Group, 1978, p. 5.

27 *Ibid.*

28 *Nigel Henderson*, *cit.* note 21.

29 *Nigel Henderson*, *loc. cit.* note 26.

30 The dissemination of Henderson's photographs was mostly confined to his experimental images, rather than his 'documentary' photographs.

31 *Nigel Henderson*, *loc. cit.* note 26.

32 *Ibid.*

33 *Ibid.*

34 *Nigel Henderson*, *cit.* note 23.

35 W. Johnstone, *Points in Time*, London 1980, p. 247.

36 Ken Garland interviewed by the author, August 1999.

37 *Ibid.*

38 *The Independent Group*, *cit.* note 18, p. 25.

39 *Ibid.*, pp. 203–06.

40 R. Banham, 'The New Brutalism', *Architectural Review*, December 1955, pp. 354–61.

41 Spencer, *op. cit.* note 20, p. 59.

42 N. Ind, *Terence Conran: The Authorized Biography*, London 1995, p. 38.

43 R. Melville, 'Eduardo Paolozzi', *Horizon* 92, September 1947, pp. 212–13.

44 Spencer, *loc. cit.* note 41.

45 *Surrealism and After: The Gabrielle Keiller Collection*, E. Cowling (ed.), exhib. cat., Edinburgh, Scottish National Gallery of Modern Art, 1997, p. 108.

46 *Dada, Surrealism, and Their Heritage*, exhib. cat. by W.S. Rubin, New York, Museum of Modern Art, 1968, p. 115.

47 Spencer, *op. cit.* note 20, p. 72.

48 See *Architectural Design*, December 1953, p. 352.

49 M. Banham and B. Hillier (eds.), *A Tonic to the Nation*, London 1976, p. 50.

50 Other versions of *St Sebastian* are in the Solomon R. Guggenheim Museum, New York, and the Rijksmuseum Kröller-Müller, Otterlo.

51 Spencer, *op. cit.* note 20, p. 92.

52 *The Independent Group*, *cit.* note 18, p. 207.

53 William Turnbull interviewed by the author, August 2000.

54 L. Alloway, 'Sculpture as Walls and Playgrounds', *Architectural Design*, January 1957, p. 26.

55 L. Alloway, 'Re Vision', *Art News and Review*, 22 January 1955, p. 5.

56 *Richard Hamilton: Collected Words*, London 1982, p. 31.

57 R. Hamilton, 'Hommage à Chrysler Corp.', *Architectural Design*, March 1958, p. 120.

58 According to Peter Smithson, the letter was never received.

59 *Ark* 18, November 1956, pp. 49–50.

60 *Ibid.*

61 Author unknown, 'John McHale: Magda Cordell', *Uppercase* 1, 1958 (unpaginated).

62 Magda Cordell McHale in conversation with the author, March 2000.

63 *Ibid.*

64 *The Expendable Ikon: Works by John McHale*, exhib. cat., Buffalo NY, Albright-Knox Art Gallery, 1984, pp. 45–47.

65 J. McHale, 'Expendable Ikon 1', *Architectural Design*, February 1959, p. 82.

66 *Magda Cordell/John McHale*, exhib. cat., London, ICA, 1961 (folded sheet).

67 *The Expendable Ikon*, *cit.* note 64, p. 45.

CITIES/BODIES

1 *The Independent Group: Postwar Britain and the Aesthetics of Plenty*, exhib. cat., ed. D. Robbins, London, ICA, 1990, p. 25.

2 All three contributed to the magazine specially printed illustrations that were only marginally connected to architecture.

3 R. Banham, *A Critic Writes: Essays by Reyner Banham*, Berkeley and Los Angeles 1996, p. 1.

4 *Reg Butler*, exhib. cat., ed. by R. Calvocoressi, London, Tate Gallery, 1983, p. 59.

5 From typescript obituary by J. Rykwert, 1988.

6 N. Ind, *Terence Conran: The Authorized Biography*, London 1995, p. 10.

7 Author unknown, 'Alison & Peter Smithson', *Uppercase* 3, 1960, (unpaginated).

8 L. Alloway, 'Design as a Human Activity', *Architectural Design*, September 1956, p. 302.

9 M. Girouard, *Big Jim: The Life and Work of James Stirling*, London 1998, p. 86.

10 R. Banham, *The New Brutalism*, London 1966, p. 85.

11 Tate Archive: transcript of BBC Radio *Third Programme* broadcast, 17 August 1956.

12 C. Mullen: *Head-Lands*, London, Serpentine Gallery, 1983, p. 1.

13 N. Henderson, 'Images from a Scrapbook', *Uppercase* 3, 1960 (unpaginated).

14 R. Banham, in *Art News and Review*, 9 August 1952, p. 4, commented that Catleugh was one of 'the few English artists to see Jackson Pollock's qualities as a *designer*'.

15 R. Spencer (ed.), *Eduardo Paolozzi: Writings and Interviews*, Oxford 2000, p. 77.

16 N. Henderson in reply to C. Mullen's questionnaire, 1984.

17 *Things*, exhib. cat., ed. by K. Fijalkowski, Norwich, Norwich Gallery, 2000, pp. 47-57.

18 Author unknown, 'John McHale: Magda Cordell', *Uppercase* 1, 1958, (unpaginated).

19 Magda Cordell McHale in conversation with the author, May 2000.

20 See, for example, T.R. Fyvel, *The Insecure Offenders*, London 1961.

21 'Letters to the Editor', *Architectural Design*, June 1957, p. 220.

22 W. Lassally, *Itinerant Cameraman*, London 1987, pp. 57–58.

23 N. Pevsner, 'London Revisted', *Vogue*, 15 February 1961, pp. 45, 102, 104.

24 *Ibid.*, p. 102.

25 C. MacInnes, 'Reaching for Twenty', *Queen*, 22 December 1959, pp. 17–21.

26 R. Wollheim, 'Babylon, Babylone', *Encounter* 104, May 1962, pp. 25–36.

27 R. Melville, 'Action Painting: New York, Paris, London', *Ark* 18, pp. 30–33.

28 Magda Cordell McHale in conversation with the author, October 2000.

29 *The Other Story: Afro-Asian Artists in Post-War Britain*, exhib. cat., ed. G. Brett, London, Hayward Gallery, 1989, p. 39.

30 *The Fifties*, exhib. cat., ed. T. Woollcombe, London, The British Council, 1998, p. 28.

31 Reprinted in N. Wadley (ed.), *The Drawings of Franciszka Themerson*, Amsterdam 1991, pp. 20–31.

32 *Ibid.*

CONTINUUM

1   *New Vision 56–66*, exhib. cat. by M. Garlake, Jarrow, Bede Gallery, 1984, p. 3.

2   The rise of the London 'Situation' group was extensively documented in *The Sixties Art Scene in London*, exhib. cat. by D. Mellor, London, Barbican Art Gallery, 1993.

3   See Rumney's quotation from Guy Debord in R. Rumney, 'The Leaning Tower of VENICE', *Ark* 24, (unpaginated fold-out section).

4   Toni del Renzio interviewed by the author, January 1998.

5   *New Vision 56–66*, *cit.* note 1, p. 18.

6   Richard Smith interviewed by the author, October 2000.

7   L. Alloway, 'Eduardo Paolozzi', *Architectural Design*, April 1956, p. 133.

8   *Richard Hamilton: Collected Words*, London 1983, p. 31.

9   A. Seago, *Burning the Box of Beautiful Things*, Oxford 1995, p. 135.

10 P. Procktor, *Self-Portrait*, London 1991, p. 46.

11 P. Blake, 'Only Sixteen', *Ark* 25, p. 29.

12 R. Coleman, 'A Romantic Naturalist', *Ark* 18, pp. 60–61.

13 'Drawings by Peter Blake', *Ark* 20, pp. 10–11.

Photographer unknown: Photograph of Germano Facetti used in the catalogue for *This is Tomorrow (1956)*. Private collection

14 Peter Blake in conversation with the author, November 2000.

15 L.R. Lippard (ed.), *Pop Art*, London 1966, p. 41.

16 Richard Smith interviewed by the author, October 2000.

17 R. Denny in *Ready Steady Go*, exhib. cat., London, Royal Festival Hall, 1992, p. 24.

18 Lippard, *op. cit.* note 15, p. 53.

19 Richard Smith interviewed by the author, October 2000.

20 L. Alloway, 'Size Wise', *Art News and Review*, September 1960, p. 2.

21 R. Denny, 'Mosaic', *Ark* 16, pp. 18–20.

22 L. Alloway 'Pop Art Since 1949', *The Listener*, 27 December 1962, p. 1087.

23 *Allen Jones*, exhib. cat. by M. Livingstone, Liverpool, Walker Art Gallery 1979.

John Deakin: Michael Andrews, 1952 (no. 31)
Andrews was photographed for *Vogue* in his room at the Slade's student lodgings. Note the study for the head of the screaming woman in *A Man Who Suddenly Fell Over*.

Biographies are arranged alphabetically by artist's surname. Works featured in the exhibition are listed immediately after the text, in chronological order.

Dimensions are given in centimetres. For two-dimensional works, height is given before width; for three-dimensional works, height before width before depth. If a work is illustrated the page reference is given.

MICHAEL ANDREWS (1928–1995)

Born in Norwich, Andrews attended Norwich School of Art, East Anglia, in 1947 and the Slade School of Fine Art, London, from 1949 to 1953. He served in the Royal Army Ordnance Corps from 1947 to 1949. While at the Slade Andrews was taught by William Coldstream, who had been appointed Slade Professor of Fine Art in 1949. In the final examination for the Slade diploma Andrews submitted two paintings, one being *A Man who Suddenly Fell Over* (1952; no. 1), which was bought by the Tate Gallery, London, when it featured in Andrews's first solo exhibition at the Beaux-Arts Gallery, London, in 1958. In both paintings, the central figure was portrayed captured in a moment of uncertainty and discomfort in which time and narrative were suspended. This reflected Andrews's interest in existentialism, then prevalent among Slade students. In 1957 Andrews redecorated the Colony Room, a drinking club in Soho, and in 1962 he celebrated the club in two group portraits of the artist's drinking acquaintances.

Andrews taught at Norwich School of Art in 1959, Chelsea School of Art, London, in 1960 and at the Slade from 1963 to 1966. He moved back to Norfolk in 1977, living there until 1992, when he returned to London. Retrospective exhibitions were held at the Hayward Gallery, London, in 1980 (organized by the Arts Council), the Whitechapel Art Gallery, London, in 1991, and Tate Britain, London, in 2001.

1 (illus. p. 60)
A Man who Suddenly Fell Over, 1952
Oil on board, 120 × 172 cm
Tate, London (Purchased 1958)

2 (illus. p. 134)
Flats, 1959
Oil on board, 105.4 × 138.4 cm
Arts Council Collection, Hayward Gallery, London

KENNETH ARMITAGE (born 1916)

Born in Leeds, Armitage studied at Leeds College of Art from 1934 to 1937 and the Slade School of Fine Art, London, from 1937 to 1939. He served in the army during World War II. Like many artists Armitage took up a teaching post after the War: he was Head of Sculpture at Bath Academy of Art, Corsham, Wiltshire, from 1946 to 1956.

Armitage's interest in history, archaeology and modern architecture, coupled with his constant awareness of shapes – in particular, in the early 1950s, his memories of aircraft wings – influenced his work. He created groups of figures in plaster (later casted in bronze), engaged in everyday activities. He also started to join figures together, which enabled him to experiment with the placement of limbs to capture the sense of a crowd and movement. His first solo exhibition was held at Gimpel Fils Gallery, London, in 1952, and in the same year he represented Britain at the Venice Biennale, where he showed *People in the Wind* (1950; no. 3), which was bought by the Museum of Modern Art, New York. He held a solo exhibition at the Venice Biennale in 1958, for which he received the David E. Bright Foundation Award. Later he abandoned plaster and took up clay as a modelling material. The torsos of his figures were flattened into plaques from which reduced limbs protruded like sticks. He became aware of the relationship of his sculpture with the ground and placed many of his figures on their sides or backs, which gave them a greater sense of being isolated in their own space (see no. 4).

In the 1960s Armitage experimented with new materials such as wax, resin and aluminium, and highly polished or painted surfaces. The human figure was central to all his work, with the exception of his fascination with the oak trees in Richmond Park, Surrey, in the mid-1970s. Armitage first trained as a painter and throughout his career he made drawings in which he employed the expressive quality of line to capture the vitality of the human figure.

Armitage's international career was confirmed with his first solo exhibition in New York at the Bertha Schaefer Gallery in 1954. Retrospective exhibitions were held at the Whitechapel Art Gallery, London, in 1959, Artcurial, Paris, in 1985 and an eightieth-birthday survey at Yorkshire Sculpture Park in 1996–97. He became Visiting Professor, University of Caracas, Venezuela, in 1964, Visiting Professor, University of Boston, in 1970 and Visiting Tutor, Royal College of Art, London, from 1974 to 1979. He was made a CBE in 1969.

3 (illus. p. 67)
People in the Wind, 1950
Bronze, 64.8 × 40 × 34.3 cm
Tate, London (Purchased 1960)

4 (illus. p. 66)
Figure Lying on its Side No. 5, 1957
Bronze, 38.1 × 82.5 × 22.3 cm
Arts Council Collection, Hayward Gallery, London

FRANK AUERBACH [born 1931)

Born in Berlin, Auerbach moved to England in 1939 and acquired British citizenship in 1947. He studied at the Hampstead Garden Suburb Institute, north London, before entering the Borough Polytechnic, London, in 1947. Although he attended St Martin's School of Art, London, from 1948 to 1952 and the Royal College of Art, London, from 1952 to 1955 Auerbach continued to attend classes at the Borough until 1953. Auerbach stayed because of the charismatic teaching of David Bomberg (see p. 178), in whose classes Auerbach found the freedom to explore his own approach to painting, and the support and space to confirm the individuality that remained constant throughout his work.

Auerbach focused deliberately on a narrow range of motifs: essentially the buildings and parks of his immediate environment near Primrose Hill, north London (see no. 7), and portraits of the people close to him. He drew continuously from life, drawings that he worked up into oil paintings in his studio, where he also drew on his memory of the place and the experience. His first solo exhibition was held at the Beaux-Arts Gallery, London, in 1959, where he exhibited until the mid-1960s.

Auerbach taught part-time at numerous art schools, in Sidcup, Ealing, and Bromley as well as at Camberwell College of Arts and the Slade School of Fine Art, both in London, from 1956 to 1968. He represented Britain at the Venice Biennale in 1986. Retrospective exhibitions were held at the Hayward Gallery, London, in 1978, and the Royal Academy of Arts, London, in 2001.

5 (illus. p. 27)
Earl's Court Building Site, 1955
Oil on board, 91.5 × 122 cm
Royal College of Art Collection, London

6 (illus. p. 27)
Building Site, Victoria Street, 1959
Oil on board, 112.4 × 140.5 cm
Ferens Art Gallery, Hull City Museum and Art Gallery, Kingston upon Hull

7 (illus. p. 28)
Primrose Hill, 1959
Oil on board, 121.9 × 151.1 cm
Arts Council Collection, Hayward Gallery, London

MICHAEL AYRTON (1921–1975)

Born in London, Ayrton had a multidisciplinary career as a painter, sculptor, stage designer, book illustrator, critic, author and broadcaster. In the late 1930s he spent time in Paris, where he shared a studio with John Minton (see pp. 184–85). Forced back to England by World War II, Ayrton, along with Minton and Keith Vaughan (see p. 187), became involved with the English Neo-Romantics, reflecting Ayrton's allegiance to the resurgence of nationalism in British art at this time. He served in the Royal Air Force from 1941 to 1942. His first major commission was from Sir John Gielgud to design a production of *Macbeth*, staged in 1942. In 1947 Ayrton made his first trip to Italy, where he was inspired by the work of the Renaissance masters. His interest in form also led him to look at the work of Cézanne and the Cubists. Ayrton was involved in a number of Festival of Britain projects: a revival of Purcell's *The Fairy Queen* at Covent Garden, London, required new sets and costumes to be designed and restoration of the old ones he had produced four years earlier for the original production. He was commissioned to produce a mural for Kelvin Hall, Glasgow – *The Elements as Sources of Power*, which was destroyed after the festival – and also to produce sets and costumes for a mock-up of a typical production studio in the Television Pavilion. Ayrton also contributed *The Captive Seven* (1951) to the Arts Council's exhibition *60 Paintings for '51*.

Ayrton taught life drawing and stage design at Camberwell College of Arts, London, from 1942 to 1944. From 1944 to 1946 he was art critic of *The Spectator*. Retrospective exhibitions were held at the Whitechapel Art Gallery, London, in 1955 and at Agnew's, London, in 1984.

8 (illus. p. 134)
The Sweep and Others, 1951
Oil on canvas, 65 × 91 cm
Signed: *Michael Ayrton*
The Artworks Loan Scheme, Leicestershire Museums, Arts and Records Service, Leicester

FRANCIS BACON (1909–1992)

Born in Dublin, Bacon moved to London in 1920 and travelled to Berlin and Paris from 1927 to 1928. In Paris he saw an exhibition of work by Picasso that impressed him greatly and he began to make drawings and paintings in watercolour. On his return to London, Bacon set up as a furniture and textile designer while simultaneously working on oil paintings. At this stage Bacon's paintings were commercially unsuccessful. Discouraged when his work was rejected for inclusion in the International Surrealist Exhibition at the New Burlington Galleries, London, in 1936, he virtually ceased painting and destroyed nearly all his early work.

In 1944 Bacon painted *Three Studies for Figures at the Base of a Crucifixion*, which was shown at the Lefevre Gallery, London, in 1945. In the following years he exhibited frequently in London at the Lefevre and Redfern Galleries. Bacon made the first of a series of paintings based on reproductions of Velazquez's *Pope Innocent X* (1650) in 1949, which made up his first solo exhibition at the Hanover Gallery, London.

During the second half of the 1950s Bacon gained an outstanding international reputation. He represented Britain at the Venice Biennale in 1954 and had a retrospective at the Institute of Contemporary Arts, London, in 1955. He also had solo exhibitions in New York in 1953, Paris in 1957, Milan and Rome in 1958, and the Museum of Modern Art, New York, in 1959. In 1960 Bacon signed with Marlborough Gallery, London, who represented his work internationally for the rest of his life. During the following decades Bacon's increasing status led to many retrospectives and major exhibitions, including an exhibition at the Tate Gallery, London, and a subsequent European and American tour in 1962–64; a second exhibition at the Tate Gallery in 1985; the Tate Gallery Liverpool in 1990–91; and a retrospective at the Centre Georges Pompidou, Paris, which toured to Haus der Kunst, Munich, in 1996 and the Hayward Gallery, London, in 1998.

9 (illus. p. 51)
Untitled (Two Figures in the Grass), c. 1952
Oil on canvas, 147.3 × 132.2 cm
The Estate of Francis Bacon, courtesy of Faggionato Fine Arts,
London, and the Tony Shafrazi Gallery, New York

10 (illus. p. 53)
Man with Dog, 1953
Oil on canvas, 152.4 × 116.8 cm
Albright-Knox Art Gallery, Buffalo NY
(Gift of Seymour H. Knox, 1955)

JOHN BERGER (born 1926)

Born in London, Berger studied at Central School of Arts and
Crafts, London, from 1942 to 1943 and Chelsea School of Art,
London, from 1945 to 1947. He held exhibitions at the Lefevre
Gallery, London, and Leicester Galleries, London.

Berger taught at St Mary's Training College and wrote on
art for the *New Statesman* and *Tribune*. He became a controversial critic, advocating a Marxist approach to art and
supporting those artists he saw as being engaged with Social
Realism. He organized three exhibitions called *Looking
Forward*: the first was held at the Whitechapel Art Gallery,
London, in 1952, and included work by artists who responded
to their environments in various realist styles. The subsequent
exhibitions were held in 1953 and 1955.

He is a painter, art critic, teacher and author. His books
include *A Painter of Our Time* (1958), *Permanent Red* (1960)
and *Ways of Seeing* (1972).

11 (illus. p. 78)
Scaffolding: Festival of Britain, 1950
Oil on canvas, 76.2 × 50.8 cm
Signed bottom right: *Berger*
Arts Council Collection, Hayward Gallery, London

PETER BLAKE (born 1932)

Born in Kent, Blake attended Gravesend Technical College and
School of Art from 1946 to 1951 and the Royal College of Art,
London, from 1953 to 1956. He served in the Royal Air Force
from 1951 to 1953. Combining painting, collage and graphic
design, he created unique and bold works in which he layered
images from art history with those from popular culture. In
1956–57 Blake travelled throughout Europe on a Leverhulme
Research Award, studying folk and popular art.

Blake won a junior prize at the John Moores Liverpool
Exhibition in 1961 and in the same year he was featured in the
BBC Monitor programme *Pop Goes the Easel*. He held his first
solo exhibition at the Portal Gallery, London, in 1962. In 1967
his distinctive style of collage and humour led to a commission
to design the record sleeve for the Beatles album *Sergeant Pepper's
Lonely Hearts Club Band*. He taught at St Martin's School of Art,
London, Harrow School of Art, north-west London, and
Walthamstow School of Art, north-east London, from 1960 to
1964, and the Royal College of Art from 1974 to 1976.

Retrospective exhibitions were held at the City Art Gallery,
Bristol, in 1969 and the Tate Gallery, London, in 1983; the latter
toured to the Kestner Gesellschaft, Hanover. He was elected an
Associate of the Royal Academy in 1974 and and a Royal
Academician in 1981. He was a founder member of the
Brotherhood of Ruralists in 1975. He was awarded a CBE in
1983 and was involved in the Associate Artist scheme
organized by the National Gallery, London, in 1994.

12 (illus. p. 158)
Preparation for the Entry into Jerusalem, 1955–56
Oil on hardboard, 127 × 102 cm
Royal College of Art Collection, London

13 (illus. p. 160)
Got a Girl, 1960–61
Oil, wood, photo collage and record on hardboard, 92 × 153 cm
The Whitworth Art Gallery, University of Manchester, Manchester

Roger Mayne: *Sandra Blow*, 1959 (no. 68)

SANDRA BLOW (born 1925)

Born in London, Blow studied at St Martin's School of Art,
London, from 1942 to 1946, Royal Academy of Arts Schools,
London, from 1946 to 1947 and the L'Accademia de belle Arta,
Rome, from 1947 to 1948. Her experience of Renaissance art
and her meeting with fellow artist Alberto Burri during her stay
in Rome initiated her interest in the texture of materials and
collage and her awareness of abstract art. Blow also drew
inspiration from the energy of early American Abstract
Expressionism and developed her engagement with the
handling of paint. Her work was predominately abstract,
dealing with issues of space, movement and balance; however,
traces of the human figure can be seen in some of her work.

Blow held numerous exhibitions at Gimpel Fils Gallery,
London, from 1951 to 1960 and she represented Britain at the
Venice Biennale in 1958. In the late 1950s she moved away from
pure abstraction and became engaged in a discourse between
abstraction and landscape. Her friendship with Roger Hilton
(see p. 183) and visits to Cornwall marked a development in the
graphic freedom of her work. Blow won second prize at the
John Moores Liverpool Exhibition in 1961.

During the 1960s her work became more minimalist, with
a lightness of colour and texture. Later she used a variety of
materials and processes to create large-scale paintings. She
taught as a visiting lecturer in the Painting School at the Royal
College of Art, London, from 1961 to 1975. She was elected an
Associate of the Royal Academy in 1971 and and a Royal
Academician in 1978. A major solo exhibition of her work was
held at the Royal Academy of Arts, London, in 1994.

14 (illus. p. 145)
Oil Drawing, 1959
Oil and charcoal on paper, 119.4 × 110.5 cm
Collection of the artist

DAVID BOMBERG (1890–1957)

Born in Birmingham, Bomberg moved with his family to
London's East End in 1895. He studied at Central School of Arts
and Crafts, London, and Walter Sickert's evening classes at
Westminster School from 1908 to 1910, before studying at the
Slade School of Fine Art, London, from 1911 to 1913. Bomberg
enlisted in the Royal Engineers during World War I. He had his
first solo exhibition at the Chenil Gallery, London, in 1914 and
he exhibited alongside the Vorticist group in 1915. A founder
member of the London Group, Bomberg showed in their
annual exhibitions in 1914 and 1919, and on a regular basis
from the mid-1930s until his death. He moved to Palestine in
1923, and settled in Jerusalem until 1927.

During World War II Bomberg captured the blitzed London
cityscape and the enduring image of St Paul's Cathedral in his
charcoal drawings and oil paintings of 1944–46 (see no. 15).
From 1945 to 1953 he taught at Borough Polytechnic, London,
where Frank Auerbach (see p. 177) and Leon Kossoff (see p. 183)
were among his students. During this time Bomberg formed
the Borough Group, which held seven exhibitions between 1947
and 1950, and the Borough Bottega in 1953.

In 1954 Bomberg moved to Spain. In 1958 Helen Lessore
proposed a large retrospective at the Beaux-Arts Gallery, London,
but he declined. Posthumously major exhibitions were held at
the Whitechapel Art Gallery, London, in 1979 and the Tate
Gallery, London, in 1988.

15 (illus. p. 23)
Evening in the City of London, 1944
Oil on canvas, 69.8 × 90.8 cm
The Museum of London, London

JOHN BRATBY (1928–1992)

Born in Wimbledon, Bratby studied at Kingston School of Art,
south-west London, from 1948 to 1949 and the Royal College of
Art, London, from 1951 to 1954. He visited Italy on a travel
scholarship in 1954 and later that year had his first solo
exhibition at the Beaux-Arts Gallery, London. Through the
gallery Bratby became associated with fellow painters Derrick
Greaves (see p. 181), Edward Middleditch (see p. 184) and Jack
Smith (see p. 186). Bratby made the paintings used in the film
The Horse's Mouth (1957–58), based on a Joyce Cary novel.
During the 1960s he published four novels: *Breakdown* (1960);
Breakfast and Elevenses (1961); *Brake-Pedal Down* (1962) and
Break 50 Kill (1963).

Bratby represented Britain at the Venice Biennale in 1956
and exhibited at Zwemmer Gallery, London, from 1958 to 1966.
He taught at Carlisle College of Art in 1956 and the Royal
College of Art from 1957 to 1958. He was a regular exhibitor at the Royal
Academy of Arts, London, and was elected an Associate of the
Royal Academy in 1959 and a Royal Academician in 1971. He had
a retrospective of his portraits at the National Portrait Gallery,
London, in 1991 and a major show at the Catto Gallery, London,
in 1997.

16 (illus. p. 89)
Jean and Still Life in Front of Window, 1954
Oil on hardboard, 122 × 108.8 cm
Southampton City Art Gallery, Southampton

17 (illus. p. 75)
The Toilet, 1956
Oil on hardboard, 122 × 77.5 cm
Signed upper left: *Bratby*
Ferens Art Gallery, Hull City Museums and Art Gallery,
Kingston upon Hull

REGINALD BUTLER (1913–1981)

Born in Hertfordshire, Butler practised as an architect from 1936 to 1950. During World War II he was a conscientious objector and worked as a blacksmith in Sussex from 1941 to 1945. Butler started to explore his interest in sculpture in 1947, joining Henry Moore as an assistant. Early sculptures demonstrated Henry Moore's influence, but when Butler's first iron figures were shown at the Hanover Gallery, London, in 1949 they illustrated a significant departure.

Early public commissions included *Birdcage* (1951; see illus. p. 36) for the Festival of Britain and *Oracle* (1952; see illus. p. 124) for Hatfield Technical College. Butler represented Britain at the Venice Biennale in 1952, where he exhibited *Woman* (1949; no. 18), and in the same year he won a public sculpture competition for 'A Monument for an Unknown Political Prisoner'. The project was never realized, and his maquette (1951–52; no. 19) received criticism in the popular press of the time, and was even attacked while on display at the Tate Gallery, London.

Butler's works gradually became fuller and their surfaces more textured. During his time as a Gregory Fellow at Leeds University, he developed a new technique of casting in shell bronze, which enabled him to cast hollow figures. Butler's use of a framework within which he encased and grounded his figures reflected his fascination with the work of Francis Bacon (see pp. 177–78). Butler, Bacon and the French sculptor Germaine Richier showed together in *London – Paris* at the Institute of Contemporary Arts, London, in 1950. Butler was also interested in photography and took photographs of his works as he wanted them to be seen.

Butler taught at the Slade School of Fine Art, London, from 1950 to 1980. A posthumous retrospective was held at the Tate Gallery, London, from 1983 to 1984.

18 (illus. p. 69)
Woman, 1949
Forged steel, 221 × 71.1 × 48.3 cm
Tate, London (Purchased 1950)

19 (illus. p. 70)
Final Maquette for The Unknown Political Prisoner, 1951–52
Painted stone and painted bronze, 44.5 × 20.5 × 16.5 cm
Tate, London (Lent by Mrs Rosemary Butler, the artist's widow, 1986)

ANTHONY CARO (born 1924)

Born in Surrey, Caro studied engineering at Christ's College, Cambridge, from 1942 to 1944 and during vacations attended Farnham School of Art, Surrey. He studied sculpture at the Regent Street Polytechnic School of Art, London, in 1946 and the Royal Academy of Arts Schools, London, from 1947 to 1952. He served in the Royal Navy from 1944 to 1946. Caro worked as a part-time assistant to Henry Moore in 1951, an experience that broadened his understanding of both modern and African art.

Caro first showed his sculptures at the Institute of Contemporary Arts, London, in 1955. His first solo exhibition was in Milan at Galleria del Maviglio, 1956, followed by one at Gimpel Fils Gallery, London, in 1957. Caro's early figurative sculptures were modelled in clay and plaster (later cast in bronze). They explored the body contorted by everyday actions and reflected Caro's interest in the work of Francis Bacon (see pp. 177–78), Willem de Kooning and Jean Dubuffet.

During 1959 Caro met the American critic Clement Greenberg, whose friendship and criticism was a constant source of encouragement. He travelled to New York on a Ford Foundation grant, where he met leading American artists David Smith, Robert Motherwell and Kenneth Noland. He was also impressed by the work of Jackson Pollock, which he saw at the Museum of Modern Art, New York. On his return to London in 1960 Caro radically changed his approach, breaking away from figuration and making abstract works from steel girders and sheet metal. Many of these works were coated with industrial and household paints and placed directly on the ground. His first abstract work was *Twenty-Four Hours* (1960;

no. 21). His first solo exhibition of abstract steel sculpture was at the Whitechapel Art Gallery, London, in 1963. He represented Britain at the Venice Biennale in 1966, alongside Richard Smith (see p. 186), Harold Cohen (see p. 179) and Robyn Denny (see p. 180), and was awarded the David E. Bright Foundation Prize. He developed his work in steel, creating delicate table sculptures as well as more architectural pieces.

Caro taught at St Martin's School of Art, London, from 1952 to 1980, where he was a source of inspiration to a whole generation of British sculptors. His work has been shown throughout the world, in both gallery settings and open-air exhibitions. Major exhibitions have been held at the Hayward Gallery, London, in 1969; the Museum of Modern Art, New York, in 1975; the Tate Gallery, London, in 1991–92; and the new Metropolitan Museum of Art, Tokyo, in 1995. He was awarded a knighthood in 1987. Caro was part of the team that worked on the Millennium Bridge, London, in 2000, creating two monumental sculptures that serve as entrance gates to the bridge.

20 (illus. p. 67)
Woman Waking Up, 1956
Bronze, 30.5 × 66 × 38 cm
Arts Council Collection, Hayward Gallery, London

21 (illus. p. 129)
Twenty-Four Hours, 1960
Painted steel, 138.4 by 223.5 by 83.8 cm
Tate, London (Purchased 1975)

PRUNELLA CLOUGH (1919–1999)

Born in London, Clough studied at Chelsea School of Art, London, from 1937 to 1939 and Camberwell College of Arts, London, from 1946 to 1949. During World War II her graphic skills were employed for drawing maps and charts for the Office of War Information. Her first solo exhibition was at the Leger Galleries, London, in 1947.

Clough's humanized and individual perception of workers, be it the fishermen in East Anglia captured in her paintings of the late 1940s, or the workers of the London docks and factories in the 1950s, was central to her work. In her paintings she tried to capture the sense of the workers' integration with their environment, without making them seem subservient or consumed by industrialization.

In the 1960s Clough's work gradually became more abstract, but continued to be concerned with the traces of human presence in the urban environment. In 1999 she won the Jerwood Prize for Painting.

Clough taught part-time at Chelsea School of Art, London, from 1956 to 1969 and Wimbledon School of Art, south-west London, from 1966 to 1997. A retrospective of her work was held at the Whitechapel Art Gallery, London, in 1960. Major solo exhibitions include those held at the Fitzwilliam Museum, Cambridge, in 1982, Camden Art Centre, London, in 1996 and Kettle's Yard, Cambridge, in 1999. A memorial exhibition was held at Annely Juda Fine Art Gallery, London, in 2000.

22 (illus. p. 78)
Man with a Blowlamp, 1950
Oil on canvas, 55 × 45 cm
Board of Trustees of the National Museums and Galleries on Merseyside, Liverpool (Walker Art Gallery)

HAROLD COHEN (born 1928)

Born in London, Cohen served in the Royal Air Force before studying at the Slade School of Fine Art, London, from 1948 to 1952. He then spent six months in Italy on an Abbey Travelling Scholarship. Cohen had his first solo exhibition at the Ashmolean Museum, Oxford, in 1951, followed by several exhibitions at Gimpel Fils Gallery, London, the first being in 1954.

In his paintings Cohen used colour to express emotions, and he looked to the work of American painter Sam Francis for inspiration. In his early work Cohen used a grid to structure the paintings, but this gradually relaxed, and his work became

freer, as seen in his Garden series (1958). While in Spain in 1958 he introduced the use of black as an outline, reflecting his interest in the work of Alan Davie (see p. 180), which had been shown at Gimpel Fils Gallery the same year.

Taking up a Harkness Commonwealth Fellowship, Cohen spent two years in America, from 1959 to 1961. During this period he explored factors of symmetry and asymmetry and the spatial effects of colour fields. His interest was always in colour, form and communication.

Cohen taught art history at Camberwell College of Arts, London, from 1953 to 1955, and was elected Fellow in Fine Art at the University of Nottingham in 1956. In 1968 Cohen spent a year at the University of California, San Diego, where he became interested in computing and began a sustained investigation into its relationship to creativity.

23 (illus. p. 152)
Plan for a City, 1958
Oil on canvas, 130.5 × 130.5 cm
The Artworks Loan Scheme, Leicestershire Museums, Arts and Records Service, Leicester

ROBERT COLQUHOUN (1914–1962)

Born in Kilmarnock, Scotland, Colquhoun's initial apprenticeship was as an engineer. He studied at the Glasgow School of Art from 1933 to 1937, where he met Robert MacBryde (see pp. 183–84), with whom he began a life-long relationship. Colquhoun served in the Royal Army Medical Corps in 1940 before being invalided out the following year. In 1941 he moved to London with MacBryde and met fellow painters John Minton (see pp. 184–85), Michael Ayrton (see p. 177), Craxton and Keith Vaughan (see p. 187), as well as the poets Dylan Thomas and George Barker. In 1943 Colquhoun met Jankel Adler, a Polish émigré painter, when he moved into the house Colquhoun shared with MacBryde and Minton. Colquhoun had his first solo exhibition at the Lefevre Gallery, London, in 1943. He drew inspiration from his close friendships with Minton and Adler, as well as from the work of Picasso and German Expressionism. The sense of unease in Colquhoun's paintings led Bryan Robertson, director of the Whitechapel Art Gallery, London, to ask Samuel Beckett to write the introduction to Colquhoun's retrospective at the Whitechapel Art Gallery in 1958.

Colquhoun was also a printmaker and theatre designer. He worked at the Miller's Press, Lewes, East Sussex, from 1947 to 1948. In 1951 Colquhoun and MacBryde were commissioned to design the set and costumes for Massine's ballet *Donald of the Burthens* and for George Barker's *King Lear* in 1953.

24 (illus. p. 32)
Woman with a Birdcage, 1946
Oil on canvas, 101.5 × 75.5 cm
Signed and dated top right: *Colquhoun 46*
Bradford Art Galleries and Museums, Bradford

MAGDA CORDELL McHALE (born 1921)

Born in Hungary, the artist married Frank Cordell, musical director of EMI. She was a regular figure at the newly formed Institute of Contemporary Arts, London, and part of the Independent Group in the 1950s. Throughout the 1950s and early 1960s Cordell explored her interest in the creative processes and bodily iconography in a series of sculptural studies and mixed-media monoprints. Reyner Banham included a photograph of her sculpture *Figure* (1955) in his article 'The New Brutalism' in *Architectural Review* (December 1955), alongside work by Nigel Henderson (see p. 182), Eduardo Paolozzi (see p. 185) and the Smithsons.

Cordell held an exhibition of her monotypes and collages at the Institute of Contemporary Arts in 1955 and of her paintings at Hanover Gallery, London, in 1956. Cordell collaborated with Richard Hamilton (see p. 182), and John McHale (see p. 184) in *This is Tomorrow* at the Whitechapel Art Gallery, London, in 1956. Cordell married John McHale and they both moved to America in 1961.

25 (illus. p. 142)
Figure, 59, c. 1958
Oil and acrylic on masonite, 228.6 × 152.4 cm
Albright-Knox Art Gallery, Buffalo NY
(Gift of the artist, 1995)

26 (illus. p. 141)
Presence A, c. 1958–60
Pigment, coloured inks and polymer on canvas,
152.4 × 101.6 cm
Collection of the artist

27 (illus. p. 140)
Presence B, c. 1958–60
Pigment, coloured inks and polymer on canvas,
152.4 × 101.6 cm
Collection of the artist

ALFRED DANIELS (born 1924)

Born in London, Daniels studied at Woolwich Polytechnic, east London, from 1943 to 1944, and the Royal College of Art, London, from 1947 to 1950, followed by postgraduate studies in mural design from 1950 to 1952. He served in the Royal Air Force from 1943 to 1947.

Daniels was included in *Six Young Contemporaries* at Gimpel Fils Gallery in 1951, where he showed *Sunday on the Grass* (1951; no. 28), as well as numerous group shows at Zwemmer Gallery, London. He taught at Hornsey College of Art, north London, from 1951 to 1976, the Royal College of Art, London, from 1964 to 1969 and from 1984 to 1987, City of London Polytechnic from 1973 to 1988 and Middlesex Polytechnic from 1976 to 1980. He undertook several commissions, including an important set of murals for Hammersmith Town Hall, west London, in 1951.

28 (illus. p. 79)
Sunday on the Grass, 1951
Oil on board, 70.5 × 41.3 cm
Signed and dated bottom right: *Alfred Daniels, 1951*
Collection of Margot Hamilton Hill ARCA

ALAN DAVIE (born 1920)

Born in Stirling, Scotland, Davie attended Edinburgh College of Art from 1937 to 1941. While serving in the Royal Artillery from 1940 to 1946 he read Walt Whitman's *Leaves of Grass* (first published 1855) and was inspired by the poet's desire to capture emotions first hand. Davie briefly became a professional jazz musician in 1947. In 1948 he travelled to Paris and Italy, where he visited the first post-war Venice Biennale and saw work by European Surrealists and contemporary American artists from the Peggy Guggenheim Collection. Impressed by the work of Klee and Picasso, he also looked to the writer James Joyce, music and ancient and non-Western art. Davie had his first solo exhibition in London with Gimpel Fils Gallery in 1950.

Like many artists in the mid-1950s Davie became interested in Zen Buddhism, as well as the Jungian idea of 'archetypal symbols' and a collective unconscious, as part of his search for a more intuitive approach to creativity. Symbols began to appear in Davie's work in the 1950s, as well as words and, later in the 1960s, short pieces of text. The work of the 1950s was gestural and calligraphic, and the titles served as poetic markers that hinted at ritual and narrative.

Davie taught at Central School of Arts and Crafts, London, from 1953 to 1956 and from 1959 to 1960. He was Gregory Fellow at Leeds University from 1956 to 1959, where he developed his approach to creating paintings in series.

In 1960 he took up gliding and also enjoyed sailing and diving. Through these activities he was brought into direct contact with natural forces beyond his control, an experience he wanted to communicate in his work. In 1972 he received the CBE. Retrospective exhibitions were held at the Stedelijk Museum, Amsterdam, in 1962, McLellan Galleries, Glasgow, in 1992 and Barbican Gallery, London, in 1993.

29 (illus. p. 40)
The Saint, 1948
Oil on paper, 122 × 89 cm
Scottish National Gallery of Modern Art, Edinburgh
(Purchased with support from the National Heritage
Memorial Fund and the National Art Collections Fund, 1997)

30 (illus. p. 41)
Woman Bewitched by the Moon no. 2, 1956
Oil on masonite, 152.8 × 122 cm
Signed and dated on reverse: *Alan Davie '56/Woman
Bewitched By the Moon No. 2/New York No. 3*
Scottish National Gallery of Modern Art, Edinburgh
(Purchased 1987)

JOHN DEAKIN (1912–1972)

Born in Cheshire, Deakin settled in London in the early 1930s; his initial passion was for painting and travel, and he held an exhibition at the Mayor Gallery, London, in 1938. His paintings were in the 'primitive' style and have been described as inspired by Rouault and Gauguin. Deakin returned to painting in the late 1950s and held an exhibition at the St George's Gallery, London, in 1956. In the 1960s he experimented with collage and sculpture. However, Deakin is best known as a photographer, with a substantial body of work dating from the late 1940s to the mid-1950s.

During World War II he joined the Army Film and Photography Unit and was posted to Milan in 1942. For eighteen months he recorded the aftermath of the siege of the island. After the war, Deakin came to the attention of the editor of British *Vogue,* Audrey Withers, and he was employed as a staff photographer in 1947. His relationship with the magazine was fraught, as Deakin did not fit into the fashion industry and was notorious for losing or breaking equipment. He was sacked in 1948, though re-employed by Withers in 1951. He stayed with *Vogue* until 1954, when he was sacked for a second time. During this period he photographed writers, fashion models, Hollywood stars and artists.

Deakin also worked relentlessly as a documentary photographer of European cities and urban life. In 1949 he completed *London Today,* a book of his London urban landscapes. Christopher Kinmonth's travel book *Rome Alive* (1951) contained forty of Deakin's street photographs. Deakin held two exhibitions at David Archer's London bookshop, *John Deakin's Paris* and *John Deakin's Rome,* both in 1956.

Soho's pubs and clubs and their artistic inhabitants were among Deakin's most famous subjects. He photographed numerous artists, such as Francis Bacon (see pp. 177–78), Lucian Freud (see p. 181) Eduardo Paolozzi (see p. 185) Robert Colquhoun (see p. 179) and John Minton (see pp. 184–85), and many of his photographs have become defining images of the period.

In 1984 an exhibition mostly of portraits, *The Salvage of a Photographer,* was held at the Victoria and Albert Museum, London. Deakin's first large-scale retrospective was held at the National Portrait Gallery, London, in 1996.

31 (illus. p. 176)
Michael Andrews, 1952
Silver gelatin print, 19 × 19.2 cm
Private collection

32
William Turnbull, January 1952
Vintage silver gelatin print, 30.5 × 30.5 cm
The Condé Nast Publications Ltd, London

33 (illus. p. 49)
Francis Bacon (original contact sheet), 1952
Vintage silver gelatin print, 40.6 × 30.5 cm
The Condé Nast Publications Ltd, London

34
Isabel Lambert, c. 1953
Vintage silver gelatin print, 40.6 × 35.5 cm
The Condé Nast Publications Ltd, London

35
Eduardo Paolozzi, c. 1953
Vintage silver gelatin print, 30.5 × 27.9 cm
The Condé Nast Publications Ltd, London

36
Robert Colquhoun, April 1958
Vintage silver gelatin print, 27.9 × 25.4 cm
The Condé Nast Publications Ltd, London

ROBYN DENNY (born 1930)

Born in Abinger, Denny studied at St Martin's School of Art, London, from 1951 to 1954, and the Royal College of Art, London, from 1954 to 1957. He had his first solo exhibition at Gallery One, London, in 1958, in which he showed a group of mosaic images made over the previous two years.

Within the Royal College of Art Painting School Denny was part of a small group, along with Richard Smith (see p. 186) and Roger Coleman, who were inspired by American culture and the exhibition *Modern Art in the United States* at the Tate Gallery in 1956, and who believed in the creative inspiration of their urban surroundings. Although taught by John Minton (see pp. 184–85), whom he admired as a figure, Denny rejected what he saw as Minton's traditionalism, based in nostalgia for a pastoral England long since gone. For Denny art was to be forward looking, urban, gestural and abstract. He summed up his ideas in his Royal College of Art thesis (1957), entitled 'Language, symbol, image, an essay in communication'. It sought to show how signs constructed the environment and human behaviour. The layering of signs, symbols and images was central to Denny's work. He used fragments of newsprint, coloured paper and bitumen to explore the creative possibilities of materials outside the traditional sphere of painting, as well as to engage more directly with his urban environment.

In 1959 Denny was commissioned to create two murals, one for the Austin Reed shop on Regent Street, London, and the other for Abbey Wood Primary School, London. In both, Denny overlaid bold collaged letters and numerals.

Denny wrote on art for *Art International* from 1963 to 1964, and taught at Bath Academy of Art, Corsham, Wiltshire, and the Slade School of Fine Art, London. He represented Britain at the Venice Biennale, 1966. A retrospective exhibition was held at the Tate Gallery, London, in 1973.

37 (illus. p. 163)
Red Beat 6, 1958
Oil on masonite, 121.9 × 182.9 cm
Albright-Knox Art Gallery, Buffalo NY
(Gift of Seymour H. Knox Jr, 1958)

38 (illus. p. 164)
Abbey Wood No. 1, 1958–59
Mixed media and gouache on paper, 26.4 × 28.3 cm
Signed and dated: *Denny 59*
Tate, London (Presented by the artist, 1973)

39 (illus. p. 165)
Baby is Three, 1960
House paint on canvas, 213.4 × 365.8 cm
Tate, London (Purchased 1973)

JOAN EARDLEY (1921–1963)

Born in Sussex, Eardley studied briefly at Goldsmiths College, London, from 1938 to 1939 and then at Glasgow School of Art from 1940 to 1943, followed by a post-diploma scholarship year in 1948–49. In 1947 she spent six months at the Patrick Allen-Fraser School of Art, Hospitalfield, Scotland, where she was taught by James Cowie. After travelling to France and Italy in 1948–49, Eardley had her first solo exhibition at Glasgow School of Art in 1949. In 1951 she showed *Street Kids* (c. 1949–51; no. 40) at the Royal Scottish Academy summer exhibition in Edinburgh. At this period Eardley was considered one of the most important of young Scottish painters.

While interested in Jackson Pollock, Willem de Kooning and Tachisme, Eardley felt that subject-matter was more important than abstract expression. Deeply aware of the lives and atmosphere of her immediate environment, Eardley made studies and paintings of Glasgow children. In her search for the inner character of Glasgow, children were a symbolic representation of the city. Other principal subjects in her work were kitchen interiors and landscapes. In 1956 Earley moved to Catterline, a small fishing village on the Scottish coast, where she often worked outdoors, painting marine and landscape scenes that captured the powerful and changing weather.

Eardley taught as a guest teacher at the Patrick Allen-Fraser School of Art in 1960. Her work was widely exhibited in Scotland and in group shows in London. A retrospective was held at Talbot Rice Centre and Royal Scottish Academy, Edinburgh, in 1998.

40 (illus. p. 81)
Street Kids, c. 1949–51
Oil on canvas, 101.6 × 73.7 cm
Signed bottom right: *Joan Eardley*
Scottish National Gallery of Modern Art, Edinburgh
(Purchased with funds given by two anonymous donors, 1964)

John Deakin: Lucian Freud, 1952.
The Condé Nast Publications Ltd, London

LUCIAN FREUD (born 1922)

Born in Berlin, Freud and his family moved to England in 1933, and he received British citizenship in 1939. He studied at the Central School of Arts and Crafts, London, from 1938 to 1939, the East Anglian School of Drawing and Painting at Dedham under Cedric Morris and Lett Haines from 1939 to 1942 and then part-time at Goldsmiths College, London, from 1942 to 1943. He had his first solo exhibition at Lefevre Gallery, London, in 1944.

At the heart of Freud's work was portraiture of people he knew well and found interesting. His meticulous observation, poetic perception and sense of unease and tension within the painting, led, in the late 1940s, to Herbert Read describing Freud as the 'Ingres of Existentialism'. Freud was one of five artists to receive an Arts Council purchase prize – for his painting *Interior, Paddington* (1951; see illus. p. 63) – in the Festival of Britain exhibition *60 Paintings for '51*. In 1952 he was included in *Recent Trends in Realist Painting* at the Institute of Contemporary Arts, London, and in 1954 he represented Britain at the Venice Biennale, along with Ben Nicholson and Francis Bacon (see pp. 177–78).

In the late 1950s Freud started to use hog brushes, which allowed for freer brush strokes, and he used more ochre, umber and red in his palette, in order to capture the feeling of flesh. From the mid-1960s the female nude became a principal theme in his work.

Freud showed with various London galleries, including the Hanover Gallery, the Marlborough Fine Art Gallery and the Anthony d'Offay Gallery. Freud's position as one of the leading painters of portraits has been celebrated in numerous national and international solo exhibitions. Retrospective exhibitions were held at the Hayward Gallery, London, in 1974; the Tate Gallery Liverpool in 1992; and the Whitechapel Art Gallery, London, in 1993; the last toured to the Metropolitan Museum of Art, New York, and the Museo Nacional Reina Sofia, Madrid. He was created a Companion of Honour in 1983 and was awarded the Order of Merit in 1993.

41 (illus. p. 62)
Juliet Moore Asleep, 1943
Conté pencil on paper, 34 × 46.3 cm
Collection of Annie Freud

42 (illus. p. 62)
Chicken in a Bucket, 1944
Pastel and pencil on paper, 38 × 39.3 cm
Private collection, courtesy of Faggionato Fine Arts, London

WILLIAM GEAR (1915–1997)

Born in Scotland, Gear studied at Edinburgh College of Art from 1932 to 1937 and Edinburgh University from 1936 to 1937, before travelling for a year through Europe on a scholarship. He served in the Royal Corps of Signals from 1940 to 1945. Gear settled in Paris from 1947 to 1950, where he integrated himself into the Parisian and international art world. He became associated with the CoBrA group (an acronym of Copenhagen, Brussels and Amsterdam, the cities where the group was based, though it had a strong focus in Paris), with whom he exhibited. Like such Ecole de Paris painters as Jean-Michel Atlan, Gear used heavy black outlines around patches of colour to define the forms within his paintings.

When Gear returned to London in 1950 he had a wide experience of the international avant garde. He exhibited *Autumn Landscape* (1950; no. 43) in *60 Paintings for '51*, for which he received one of five Arts Council purchase prizes; this lead to a public outcry against the work because of its perceived extreme degree of abstraction. Gear referenced forms in nature, as the title of this work indicates, while also using his forms to express his emotional identification with his environment. Gear gradually replaced his heavy black outlines with a softer, more organic framework and more Tachiste brushwork.

Gear had his first solo exhibition at Gimpel Fils Gallery, London, in 1953. He represented Britain at the Venice Biennale in 1954 and was featured in *Metavisual, Tachiste, Abstract* at the Redfern Gallery in 1957. Retrospective exhibitions were held at the Whitechapel Art Gallery, London, in 1954, Gimpel Fils Gallery in 1961, the RBSA Gallery, Birmingham, in 1976 and the Redfern Gallery, London, in 1997. He was appointed curator of Towner Art Gallery, Eastbourne, Sussex, in 1958 and Head of Fine Art, Birmingham College of Art, in 1964. He was elected Senior Royal Academician in 1995.

43 (illus. p. 39)
Autumn Landscape, 1950
Oil on canvas, 183.2 × 127 cm
Signed and dated bottom centre: *Gear 50*
Laing Art Gallery, Tyne and Wear Museums, Newcastle-upon-Tyne

DERRICK GREAVES (born 1927)

Born in Sheffield, Greaves was an apprentice signwriter from 1943 to 1948. He attended the Royal College of Art, London, from 1948 to 1952. Greaves exhibited in *Young Contemporaries* at Gimpel Fils Gallery, London, where John Berger (see p. 178) singled out his work, along with that of Edward Middleditch (see p. 184), as representing politically committed work. Greaves studied and exhibited in Italy from 1952 to 1953 while on an Abbey Major Scholarship. His first solo exhibition was at the Beaux-Arts Gallery, London, in 1953; he became a notable member of the Kitchen Sink School, with whom he exhibited at the Venice Biennale in 1956. In many of his paintings, Greaves focused on his home town of Sheffield, in which he captured the harsh reality of derelict industrial buildings.

In 1958 Greaves held the first of several solo exhibitions at the Zwemmer Gallery, London. Retrospective exhibitions were held at the Whitechapel Art Gallery, London, in 1977 and the Graves Art Gallery, London, in 1980. He taught for several years at St Martin's School of Art, London, and later became Head of Printmaking at Norwich College of Art, East Anglia, in 1983.

44 (illus. p. 87)
Dog, 1955
Oil on canvas, 118.1 × 78.7 cm
Signed top right: *Derrick Greaves*
Arts Council Collection, Hayward Gallery, London

WILLIAM GREEN (born 1934)

Born in Greenwich, Green attended Sidcup School of Art, Kent, from 1952 to 1954 and the Royal College of Art, London, from 1955 to 1958, before which he spent three months in prison as a conscientious objector. In his early years Green was influenced by German Expressionism, but, like fellow Royal College of Art students, he was inspired by the Abstract Expressionism he saw at *Modern Art in the United States* at the Tate Gallery, London, in 1956. Green knew about the French Action Painter Georges Mathieu, but felt his own inspiration came more from America: he was strongly influenced by Jackson Pollock's work, which he had seen in reproductions. It was not until 1958 that Green saw many of these works, in the major Jackson Pollock exhibition at the Whitechapel Art Gallery, London. By his second year at the Royal College of Art Green was creating purely abstract work. Like Pollock, Green placed his hardboard sheets directly on the floor and physically immersed himself in the process of creating his paintings. He also decided to use only black paint, usually bitumen or enamel, which he threw at the hardboard. Green's approach to Action Painting was made notorious by Ken Russell's film *Making an Action Painting* (1957), in which Green was shown hurling bitumen and paraffin at a sheet of hardboard, before cycling across the picture, skidding across it in plimsolls and finally scorching the surface with fire.

Green exhibited in *New Trends in British Art*, organized by Lawrence Alloway for the Rome–New York Foundation, Rome, in 1957 and *Dimensions: British Abstract Art 1948–57* at the O'Hana Gallery, London. In 1958 he had his first solo exhibition at the New Vision Centre Gallery, London. He also showed at the first *Situation* exhibition at the RBA Galleries, London, in 1960.

Green taught at a working men's college from 1957 to 1958, and also at various other schools, including Harrow School of Art, north-west London; Walthamstow School of Art, north-east London; Goldsmiths College, London; and later at Havering Technical College, Essex, from which he retired in 1981. Having not exhibited since the mid-1960s, Green held an exhibition at England & Co. Gallery, London, in 1993.

45 (illus. p. 147)
Nude, 1958
Oil on board, 75 × 62 cm
England & Co. Gallery, London

Roger Mayne: Victor Pasmore and Richard Hamilton, 1957
(no. 65)

RICHARD HAMILTON (born 1922)

Born in London, Hamilton studied at Westminster Technical
College and, in the evenings, at St Martin's School of Art in
1936, the Royal Academy of Arts Schools in 1938 and 1946 and
the Slade School of Fine Art from 1948 to 1951. During World
War II he served as an engineering draughtsman in the Royal
Engineers. At the Slade he met Nigel Henderson (see p. 182),
Eduardo Paolozzi (see p. 185) and William Turnbull (see p. 187)
and became interested in Marcel Duchamp.

Hamilton created all or part of five major environmental
exhibitions between 1951 and 1958: *Growth and Form* at the
Institute of Contemporary Arts, London, in 1951; *Man, Machine
and Motion* at the Hatton Gallery, Newcastle-upon-Tyne, and
the Institute of Contemporary Arts, London, in 1955; *This is
Tomorrow* at the Whitechapel Art Gallery, London, in 1956; *An
Exhibit* at the Hatton Gallery and the Institute of Contemporary
Arts in 1957 and *A Gallery for a Collector* at the *Daily Mail*
Ideal Home Exhibition at Olympia, London, in 1958. These
exhibitions enabled Hamilton to explore a wide range of issues
that he also pursued in his work, including popular culture,
science, technology and the influence of the mass media on the
communication of imagery.

Hamilton's interest in Duchamp led him to reconstruct
the latter's *Large Glass*, which was shown in the exhibition
The Almost Complete Works of Marcel Duchamp, curated by
Hamilton himself at the Tate Gallery, London, in 1966. He was
a prize winner at the John Moores Liverpool Exhibition in 1969.

Hamilton was appointed lecturer in the Fine Art
Department at the University of Durham from 1953 to 1966 and
he taught interior design at the Royal College of Art, London,
from 1957 to 1961. A retrospective exhibition was held at the
Tate Gallery, London, in 1970. In 1982 *Collected Words* was
published, which brought together the full range of Hamilton's
writings and lectures.

46 (illus. p. 115)
Reaper (o), 1949
Lift-ground and colour aquatint from three plates,
198 × 148 cm (plate size)
Edition 20
Collection of Rita Donagh

47 (illus. p. 116)
Hommage à Chrysler Corp., 1957
Oil, metal foil and collage on wood, 122 × 81 cm
Tate, London (Purchased with assistance from the
National Art Collections Fund and the Friends of the
Tate Gallery, 1995)

NIGEL HENDERSON (1917–1984)

Born in London, Henderson attended Stowe School from 1931
to 1933 and through his mother became associated with the
Bloomsbury Group in the mid-1930s. During World War II he
served as a pilot. At the Slade School of Fine Art, London,
from 1945 to 1949, he formed friendships with fellow students
Richard Hamilton (see p. 182) and Eduardo Paolozzi (see p.
185), with whom he stayed in Paris, where he met Brancusi,
Giacometti, Braque and Arp.

With his wife, Judith Stephen, an anthropologist,
Henderson moved to Bethnal Green in the East End of London
in 1945. His photographs of the working-class community
aroused the interest of Alison and Peter Smithson, who were
themselves exploring the relationships between communities
and their urban habitat. Henderson also experimented with
collage, creating photograms using material from bomb sites
and other found items. Henderson and Paolozzi established
Hammer Prints Ltd, which ran from 1955 until 1961.

A key figure in the Independent Group, Henderson
contributed to *Parallel of Life and Art* at the Institute of
Contemporary Arts, London, in 1953 and *This is Tomorrow* at the
Whitechapel Art Gallery, London, in 1956. His first major solo
show was held at the Institute of Contemporary Arts in 1961.
In the early 1950s Henderson taught creative photography at
Central School of Arts and Crafts, London, as well as producing
posters for jazz musician Ronnie Scott. He later taught at
Colchester School of Art, Essex, from 1957 to 1960 and
Norwich School of Art, East Anglia, from 1965 to 1968. A
retrospective exhibition was held at Kettle's Yard, Cambridge,
in 1977 and a touring exhibition was organized by Norwich
School of Art Gallery in 1982–83. A major retrospective, *Nigel
Henderson: Parallel of Life and Art*, began a British tour in
September 2001 at Gainsborough's House, Sudbury, Suffolk.

48 (illus. p. 102)
Cecil Collins, 1951
Gelatin silver print, 25.5 × 18.8 cm
Private collection

49
Gillian Alexander Skipping, 1951
Gelatin silver print, 50.5 × 40.4 cm
The Estate of Nigel Henderson

50 (illus. p. 99)
Untitled, c. 1956
Screenprint with collage and ink on paper, 22.7 × 19.8 cm
The Estate of Nigel Henderson

ALBERT HERBERT (born 1925)

Born in London, Herbert attended St Martin's School of Art in
1942, Wimbledon School of Art from 1947 to 1949 and the
Royal College of Art from 1949 to 1952. During World War II he
served in the army, from 1943 to 1945.

At the Royal College of Art he initially exhibited with fellow
students John Bratby (see p. 178), Peter Coker, Derrick Greaves
(see p. 181), Edward Middleditch (see p. 184) and Jack Smith
(see p. 186). Impressed by a slide lecture on New Realism
given by David Sylvester in 1951 and featuring work by Francis
Bacon (see pp. 177–78) and Alberto Giacometti, and developing
an interest in psychoanalysis, Herbert decided to make
figurative, emotive and symbolic paintings. In 1952–53 he
visited Spain and Ibiza on a travel scholarship before moving
to Paris. He won the Abbey Major Scholarship to the British
School in Rome in 1953–54, where he met Italian realist painters.

From the mid-1950s Herbert's work became increasingly
inspired by his interest in Catholicism and its imagery and
rituals. He taught part-time at Leicester College of Art in 1954,
full-time at Birmingham College of Art from 1956 to 1964 and
was a tutor and later principal lecturer at St Martin's School of
Art, London, from 1964 to 1988.

51 (illus. p. 80)
Children Playing, 1952
Oil on canvas, 91.5 × 122 cm
Royal College of Art Collection, London

JOSEF HERMAN (1911–1999)

Born in Warsaw, Poland, Herman studied at the School of Art
and Decoration, Warsaw, from 1930 to 1932. In 1938 he left
Poland for Brussels. Two years later he moved to Glasgow,
where he met Jankel Adler. In 1944 Herman moved to a Welsh
mining village, Ystradgynlais, where he lived until 1955. During
this period he made a series of sombre-hued paintings and
drawings of miners and their environment. Subsequently
Herman's palette juxtaposed passages of strong, bright
colours with the darker tones.

Herman had his first London exhibition at Reid and Lefevre
in 1943. From 1946 until 1981 he showed at Roland, Browse and
Delbanco Gallery, London. As part of the Festival of Britain in
1951, Herman exhibited a mural of miners, for which no. 52 is a
study. A retrospective exhibition was held at the Whitechapel Art
Gallery, London, in 1956. Herman published an autobiography,
Related Twilight, in 1975. He was awarded an OBE for services to
British art in 1981 and elected a Royal Academician in 1990.
Among recent publications, Robert Heller's *Josef Herman*
(London 1998), which accompanied a major retrospective at
Flowers East Gallery, London, is the most comprehensive.

52 (illus. p. 37)
Miners, 1950
Oil on paper laid on board, 52.5 × 121.3 cm
Signed, dated and inscribed on reverse: *Study for Mural/
Festival of Britain/ 1951/ Josef Herman*
Scottish National Gallery of Modern Art, Edinburgh
(Purchased 1972)

PATRICK HERON (1920–1999)

Born in Leeds, Heron was a painter, designer and writer on the
arts. He spent his early years in Cornwall, from 1925 until 1929,
when his family moved to Welwyn Garden City, Hertfordshire.
His father set up Cresta Silks, and Heron produced his first
textile design for the company in 1934, continuing to do so until
1951. Heron registered as a conscientious objector and from
1940 to 1943 he undertook agricultural work until exempted on
medical grounds. He then moved to Cornwall and worked at the
Leach Pottery in St Ives from 1944 to 1945, where he became
friendly with the community of artists who had settled there. In
1943 Heron saw Matisse's *The Red Studio* (1911) at the Redfern
Gallery, London, which formed the basis of his approach to
colour and space, as did the work of Braque, which he saw in
an exhibition at the Tate Gallery, London, in 1946. Heron
developed his interest in French and European painters and
visited France and Paris numerous times, writing about
Soulages and de Staël among others. He also praised the
American Abstract Expressionist painters whose work was part
of the exhibition *Modern Art in the United States* at the Tate
Gallery in 1956. However, by the late 1960s and 1970s he
published a number of articles in which he questioned the
perceived ascendancy of American artists.

In 1947 Heron held his first London exhibition at the
Redfern Gallery. His paintings up until the mid-1950s were
predominantly figurative or still lifes with complex and
ambiguous spatial relationships (see no. 53). After this point
they became increasingly abstract, although there were traces
of references to his environment: the sea and the garden at
his home. He had bought Eagle's Nest in Zennor, Cornwall, in
1955 and moved there the following year, where he lived until
his death.

Heron was art critic of the *New Statesman* from 1947
to 1950 and London correspondent of the New York journal
Arts from 1955 to 1958. His early ideas about painting were
collected in *The Changing Forms of Art* (1955). In 1953 he
organized, wrote the catalogue for and exhibited in *Space in
Colour*, an exhibition of ten of his British contemporaries at the
Hanover Gallery, London. He also exhibited in *Metavisual,
Tachiste, Abstract* at the Redfern Gallery, London, in 1957.

He won the Grand Prize at the second John Moores
Liverpool Exhibition in 1959. He taught one day a week at
Central School of Arts and Crafts, London, from 1953 to 1956.
Retrospective exhibitions were held at the Whitechapel Art

Gallery, London, in 1972; the Barbican Gallery, London, in 1985; and the Tate Gallery, London, in 1998. In 1977 he was created a CBE and from 1980 to 1987 he was a Trustee of the Tate Gallery.

53 (illus. p. 19)
Two Women in a Café, 1950
Oil on canvas, 114 × 95 cm
The Artworks Loan Scheme, Leicestershire Museums,
Arts and Records Service, Leicester

ROGER HILTON (1911–1975)

Born in Middlesex, Hilton attended the Slade School of Fine Art, London, from 1929 to 1931 and the Royal Academy of Arts Schools, London, in 1933 and spent the intervening years studying in Paris. Hilton joined the army in 1939 but was captured in 1942 and remained a prisoner of war until 1945.

In 1951 he took part in *Abstract Paintings, Sculptures and Mobiles*, the first post-war abstract exhibition in England, at the Artists International Association, London. A year later he held his first post-war solo exhibition at Gimpel Fils Gallery, London. Contemporary Parisian art had a strong influence on his own, freer, calligraphic style. In 1953 he met the Dutch artist Constant, who was living in London. They travelled to Paris and Amsterdam together to look at paintings by Mondrian and debated how abstract paintings might become purely spatial objects integrated into architecture. As a result, Hilton's work became simpler, and he reduced his palette. While some of Hilton's work made no reference to the visible world, others included traces of the human body (see no. 54).

Hilton was included in Lawrence Alloway's book *Nine Abstract Artists* (1954). He exhibited in *Statements*, organized by Alloway at the Institute of Contemporary Arts, London, in 1957, *Metavisual, Tachiste, Abstract* at the Redfern Gallery, London, in 1957 and had a solo exhibition at the Institute of Contemporary Arts in 1958. In 1963 he won first prize at the John Moores Liverpool Exhibition and exhibited at the Venice Biennale in 1964. Retrospective exhibitions were held at the Serpentine Gallery, London, in 1974; the Gruenebaum Gallery, New York, in 1976; the Hayward Gallery, London, in 1993; and Tate St Ives, Cornwall, in 1997–98.

Hilton taught at the Central School of Arts and Crafts, London, from 1954 to 1956, during which time he visited St Ives to stay with Patrick Heron. In 1956 he rented a studio in Newlyn, Cornwall, where he spent the next four summers. He finally settled in Cornwall in 1965. He was awarded the CBE in 1968.

54 (illus. p. 143)
Grey Figure, 1957
Oil on board, 174 × 122 cm
Southampton City Art Gallery, Southampton

DAVID HOCKNEY (born 1937)

Born in Bradford, Hockney studied at Bradford School of Art from 1953 to 1957 and the Royal College of Art, London, from 1959 to 1962. A conscientious objector, he spent his National Service working in a hospital.

Encouraged by fellow Royal College of Art student R.B. Kitaj, Hockney looked to his own environment and situation as sources for inspiration, an approach that was reflected in the titles of his work. One significant aspect of this was his homosexuality, which he began to incorporate into his work from the early 1960s. Hockney was particularly impressed by Picasso's versatility of style and his freedom to borrow from any source. Hockney was a prize winner at the John Moores Liverpool Exhibition in 1961 and 1967.

In 1961 Hockney visited New York and was struck by the freedom of American society. On his return he produced his first major series of etchings, *A Rake's Progress* (1961–63). He produced other series of etchings, including *Illustrations of Fourteen Poems from C.P. Cavafy* (1966), *Illustrations of Six Fairy Tales from the Brothers Grimm* (1968–69, published 1970) and *The Blue Guitar* (1977).

Hockney moved to Los Angeles at the end of 1963, where he began to use acrylic rather than oil paint to achieve his distinctive flat surfaces. He also developed an interest in photography, which was to broaden and inform his work. He had his first solo exhibition in New York at the Kasmin Gallery in 1963.

Hockney continually experimented with styles and processes. In the 1980s and 1990s he incorporated the technology of mass communication, including the photocopier, fax machine, video and computer, into his work, challenging conventional definitions of what constituted an 'original' work of art while still infusing the piece with his own subjectivity.

His first retrospective was held at the Whitechapel Art Gallery, London, in 1970, followed by one at the Los Angeles County Museum of Art in 1988 that toured to the Tate Gallery, London. A retrospective of his drawings was held at the Royal Academy of Arts, London, in 1995–96.

55 (illus. p. 149)
Doll Boy (study), 1960
Oil, pencil and black chalk on hardboard, 75.2 × 60.7 cm
Signed and inscribed on reverse: *David Hockney, R.C.A*
Collection of Brian Clarke

56 (illus. p. 169)
Going to be a Queen for Tonight, 1960
Oil on board, 122 × 92 cm
Royal College of Art Collection, London

57 (illus. 172)
I'm in the Mood for Love, 1961
Oil on board, 123 × 99 cm
Royal College of Art Collection, London

ALLEN JONES (born 1937)

Born in Southampton, Jones studied at Hornsey College of Art, north London, from 1955 to 1959 and the Royal College of Art, London, from 1959 until 1960, when he was expelled for rebellious behaviour. After he was expelled he returned to Hornsey College of Art and took a teacher-training course. He taught lithography at Croydon College of Art, south London, and, later, drawing at Chelsea School of Art, London. In his work of the early 1960s Jones responded to everyday elements of London life, such as the buses on which he travelled. In 1961 he exhibited in *Young Contemporaries* at the RBA Galleries, London. His success in this exhibition led to a commission from Courtaulds Ltd for a large mural painting designed to hang in the restaurant at the firm's headquarters in the City of London (no. 58).

Jones moved to New York in 1964 and travelled throughout the USA. In New York he looked to the imagery of mass-produced consumer goods and advertising. These sexy, colourful, bold images fed into his paintings and fibreglass-and-aluminium sculptures, which usually incorporated the eroticized and simplified female form. Jones also designed posters and a calendar for Pirelli, as well as undertaking work for stage and screen. Jones also produced a number of public commissions, including a steel sculpture at the Chelsea and Westminster Hospital, London.

Jones had his first solo exhibition at the Arthur Tooth & Sons Gallery, London, in 1963 and also showed at the Richard Feigen Gallery in New York in 1964. Retrospective exhibitions have been held at the Walker Art Gallery, Liverpool, in 1979 and the Barbican Centre, London, in 1995.

58 (illus. pp. 166–67)
City, 1961
Oil on canvas, 152 × 398 cm
Museum Kunst Palast, Düsseldorf

LEON KOSSOFF (born 1926)

Born in London, Kossoff returned to studying at St Martin's School of Art from 1949 to 1953, after a period of military service from 1945 to 1948. Encouraged by Frank Auerbach (see p. 177) Kossoff attended evening classes given by David Bomberg (see p. 178) at Borough Polytechnic, London, from 1950 to 1952; he then studied at the Royal College of Art, London, from 1953 to 1956.

Kossoff's continuous source of inspiration was the areas of London that he knew intimately, including Bethnal Green, the City, Willesden Junction, York Way and Dalston. His subject-matter has ranged over time from bomb sites to building sites, railways, a children's swimming pool in Willesden, Christ Church, Spitalfields, and the Embankment, as well as portraits of friends and family. In the early 1950s he worked on paintings of St Paul's Cathedral and City building sites. He joined the Beaux-Arts Gallery, London, in 1956 and had his first solo exhibition there in 1957.

Kossoff taught at Chelsea School of Art, London, and Regent Street Polytechnic School of Art, London, from 1959 to 1964 and St Martin's School of Art from 1966 to 1969. He represented Britain at the Venice Biennale in 1995, and the same year he had his first solo exhibition on the Continent. A retrospective was held at the Tate Gallery, London, in 1996.

59 (illus. p. 26)
St Paul's Building Site, 1954
Oil on board, 152.4 × 121.9 cm
Private collection

60
City Building Site, 1956
Oil on canvas, 76 × 63.5 cm
Royal College of Art Collection, London

61 (illus. p. 25)
City Building Site, 1959
Oil on board, 124.5 × 152.4 cm
Private collection

RICHARD LANNOY (born 1928)

Born in Surrey, Lannoy attended Guildford School of Art and Heatherley School of Art. He was a painter, photographer and writer and was among those who founded the Independent Group at the Institute of Contemporary Arts, London, in the early 1950s. He travelled widely as a reportage photographer in the 1950s and 1960s and published several books of photographs, including *India* (1956) and *The Speaking Tree* (1971). Lannoy resumed his career as a painter in the 1980s.

62 (illus. p. 14)
Lee Miller with Richard and Terry Hamilton at a party at the Penroses', 1951
Digital enlargement from original contact sheet,
20.3 × 13.2 cm
Private collection

63 (illus. p. 54)
Henri Cartier-Bresson Exhibition, ICA, London, 1957
Gelatin silver print, 23.1 × 15.4 cm
Collection of the artist

ROBERT MacBRYDE (1913–1966)

Born in Ayrshire, Scotland, MacBryde studied at Glasgow School of Art from 1932 to 1937, where he met Robert Colquhoun (see p. 179) with whom he began a life-long relationship. They travelled together to France and Italy on Colquhoun's scholarship in 1937–39, and on their return they worked together in a studio in Ayrshire. Although exempt from national service on medical grounds, MacBryde decided to go with Colquhoun to Edinburgh and then Leeds, where Colquhoun had been posted as part of his service in the Royal Army Medical Corps. In 1941, after Colquhoun had been discharged, they both moved to London and shared a house with John Minton (see pp. 184–85) and in 1943 with Jankel Adler.

In 1947 MacBryde made a series of monotypes and lithographs at the Miller's Press, Lewes, East Sussex. In 1948, along with Colquhoun, he designed sets for Massine's ballet *Donald of the Burthens*, produced in 1951.

MacBryde was a bold colourist who often enclosed his rich colours in thick black lines. In London he adopted the lyrical style of the Neo-Romantic painters, but later developed a style that was more influenced by European painters such as Klee, Picasso and Adler. References to Celtic designs and patterns were also evident in his work.

MacBryde and Colquhoun briefly moved to Essex to live in the house of the poet George Barker, but they returned to London in 1954 and travelled to Italy and Spain. After Colquhoun died in 1962 MacBryde moved to Dublin, where he was killed in a car accident in 1966.

64 (illus. p. 33)
Still Life, c. 1947
Oil on canvas, 41.5 × 87 cm
Signed bottom left: *MacBryde*
Scottish National Gallery of Modern Art, Edinburgh
(Bequeathed by Miss Elizabeth Watt, 1989)

ROGER MAYNE (born 1929)

Born in Cambridge, Mayne studied chemistry at Oxford, but in 1951 he became fascinated with photography. He first visited St Ives, Cornwall, in 1953, becoming friendly with many of the artists there. In 1954 he moved to London, where he began to document people at play in the close-knit communities living in the decaying Victorian terraces of North Kensington. His photographs were exhibited at the Institute of Contemporary Arts, London, in 1956, to critical acclaim. His vivid Social Realism recorded a way of life that was soon to pass away for ever.

After moving to Dorset in 1975 he continued to photograph children (often his own family), as well as landscapes and the people he encountered on his visits abroad, with the improvisational skills and quick eye that characterize all his work. The Victoria and Albert Museum, London, mounted a retrospective of his 1950s photographs in 1986. The Tate Gallery St Ives exhibited his photographs in *St Ives Artists: 1953–1965* in 2001, and a major monograph, *Roger Mayne: Photographs*, was also published in 2001.

65 (illus. p. 182)
Victor Pasmore and Richard Hamilton, 1957
Gelatin silver print, 25.4 × 20.2 cm
Collection of the artist

66 (illus. p. 138)
Leeds, 1958
Gelatin silver print, 18.3 × 24.2 cm
Collection of the artist

67 (illus. p. 123)
Queue for *The Fly*, West End, 1958
Gelatin silver print, 23.2 × 17.4 cm
Collection of the artist

68 (illus. p. 178)
Sandra Blow, 1959
Silver gelatin print, 25.2 × 16.7 cm
Collection of the artist

69 (illus. pp. 170–71)
Harrow Road Looking towards Clarendon Crescent with slum clearance in background, 1960
Gelatin silver print, 19 × 25.3 cm
Collection of the artist

JOHN McHALE (1922–1978)

Born in Glasgow, McHale was part of the Independent Group that met at the Institute of Contemporary Arts, London, in the early 1950s. His interest in science, technology and communication theory found expression in a series of collages called Transistors (see no. 70) and in his collage books, which he produced and exhibited in *Collages and Objects* at the Institute of Contemporary Arts in 1954.

A study trip to Yale in 1955 on a scholarship galvanized McHale's interest in popular culture. He brought back glossy magazines that provided material for a series of collages McHale produced between 1956 and 1958 in which he used the head as a motif, and which comprised printed images that were organic, mechanical or technological.

McHale participated in *This is Tomorrow* at the Whitechapel Art Gallery, London, in 1956, and also exhibited at the Institute of Contemporary Arts throughout the 1950s. A retrospective exhibition was held there in 1962. McHale married Magda Cordell (see pp. 179–80) and they moved to America in 1961, where he published a number of books, including *Buckminster Fuller* (1962) and *The Future of the Future* (1969).

70 (illus. p. 119)
Transistor, 1954
Collage, 46 × 59 cm
Scottish National Gallery of Modern Art, Edinburgh
(Purchased 1995)

71 (illus. p. 120)
Suited Figure, 1956
Collage, 77 × 52 cm
Signed and dated bottom right: *McHale/'56*
Scottish National Gallery of Modern Art, Edinburgh
(Presented by Magda Cordell, 1995)

72 (illus. p. 120)
Virginia Imported, 1956
Collage, 61 × 38 cm
Signed and dated bottom centre: *McHale/'56*
Scottish National Gallery of Modern Art, Edinburgh
(Presented by Magda Cordell, 1995)

73 (illus. p. 121)
First Contact, 1958
Collage on canvas, 122 × 183 cm
Albright-Knox Art Gallery, Buffalo NY
(Gift of Magda Cordell McHale, 1995)

ROBERT MEDLEY (1905–1994)

Born in London, Medley studied at Byam Shaw School from 1923 to 1924, briefly at the Royal Academy of Arts Schools, London, in 1924 and the Slade School of Fine Art, London, from 1924 to 1926, where he met Duncan Grant, Roger Fry and the Bloomsbury Group. Medley lived and worked in Paris from 1926 to 1927 and looked to the work of Cézanne and Bonnard for inspiration.

Through his contact with Diaghilev's Ballet Russes, Medley made many studies and compositions of figures in movement. He was also a designer for numerous theatre productions in the 1930s and was a co-founder of a new and experimental Group Theatre. In 1936 he established the Artists International Association with Misha Black and others. He moved away from the ideals of the Bloomsbury Group as he become more involved with Henry Moore, Graham Sutherland and Paul Nash. During World War II he worked as an official war artist and served in the Royal Engineers. During the 1950s and 1960s he exhibited at the Hanover Gallery, London, and the Leicester Galleries, London.

Medley held posts at several art schools, including Chelsea School of Art, London, from 1932 to 1939 and from 1946 to 1950; the Department of Theatre Design at the Slade School of Fine Art, London, from 1949 to 1950; Head of Department of Fine Art, Camberwell College of Arts, London, from 1958 to 1965; and visiting tutor at Newcastle-upon-Tyne School of Art from 1965 to 1966. He was Chairman of the Faculty of Painting

at the British School in Rome from 1967 to 1977. In 1970 he co-founded the 'Artists' Market', with whom he exhibited regularly until 1979. A retrospective exhibition was held at the Whitechapel Art Gallery, London, in 1963 and at the Museum of Modern Art, Oxford, in 1984. In 1982 he was awarded the CBE and in 1986 he was elected a Royal Academician.

74 (illus. p. 64)
Bicyclists Against a Blue Background, 1951
Oil on canvas, 155 × 136 cm
Signed and dated bottom right: *C. RO. M./2/51*
York City Art Gallery, York
(Presented by the Arts Council, 1952)

EDWARD MIDDLEDITCH (1923–1987)

Born in Essex, Middleditch served in the army from 1942 to 1947 and was awarded the Military Cross in 1945. He studied at the Regent Street Polytechnic School of Art, London, in 1948 and the Royal College of Art, London, from 1949 to 1952, where he was taught by Ruskin Spear (see p. 186) and John Minton (see pp. 184–85), both of whom influenced his work. Middleditch held his first solo exhibition at the Beaux-Arts Gallery, London, in 1954. He became associated with fellow artists labelled as the Kitchen Sink School, and together they represented Britain at the Venice Biennale in 1956. Middleditch showed landscapes or landscape-inspired paintings, including *Pigeons in Trafalgar Square* (1954; no. 75). His direct approach to the subject-matter, presenting it in the centre of the picture space, and his handling of the paint led Helen Lessore, the owner of the Beaux-Arts Gallery, to call him a 'poet of appearances'. In 1957 he travelled to Blanes, a small fishing village in Spain where the sharpness of the light and the spiky quality of the vegetation was reflected in his paintings. These paintings were shown in an exhibition at the Beaux-Arts Gallery in 1958.

Middleditch moved into a large house in Buckinghamshire with Derrick Greaves (see p. 181) and his family in 1957. In 1962 he moved to Suffolk. Middleditch taught at Chelsea School of Art, London, from 1958 to 1963; Regent Street Polytechnic School of Art, London, in 1960; and Cambridge School of Art and St Martin's School of Art, London, in 1961. He was appointed Head of Fine Art at Norwich School of Art, East Anglia, from 1964 to 1984. When the Beaux-Arts Gallery closed in 1965 Middleditch exhibited regularly at the Royal Academy of Arts, London, and from 1969 at the New Art Centre, London. A retrospective exhibition and tour was organized by the Arts Council at Castle Museum, Norwich, in 1987–88. He was elected an Associate of the Royal Academy in 1968 and a Royal Academician in 1973, as well as Keeper of the Royal Academy of Arts Schools from 1984 to 1986.

75 (illus. p. 77)
Pigeons in Trafalgar Square, 1954
Oil on board, 180 × 118.5 cm
The Artwork Loan Scheme, Leicestershire Museums, Arts and Records Service, Leicester

JOHN MINTON (1917–1957)

Born in London, Minton was a painter, illustrator and teacher. He studied at St John's Wood Art School, London, from 1935 to 1938. He shared a studio in Paris with Michael Ayrton (see p. 177) from 1938 to 1939, during which period he became aware of the Paris-based Neo-Romantics. At the outbreak of World War II Minton returned to London and registered as a conscientious objector. He later joined the Pioneer Corps and while stationed in north Wales he saw a copy of *Horizon* that contained Graham Sutherland's essay 'Welsh Sketch Book'. He was impressed by Sutherland's ability to infuse the landscape with a sense of disquiet. Discharged from the army on medical grounds in 1943 he resumed painting. He had his first solo exhibition at the Redfern Gallery, London, in 1945.

Minton travelled to Corsica in 1947, Spain in 1949 and Jamaica in 1950, which offered him new subject-matter and changed his palette. Minton was aware of but tried to reject the changes of pace and the increasing focus on Tachisme, Abstract Expressionism and hard-edge abstraction occurring in the later 1950s.

Minton also illustrated more than a dozen books, as well as designing posters, lithographs, linocuts, wallpaper designs, stage sets and theatrical costumes. He taught at Camberwell College of Arts, London, from 1943 to 1946; the Central School of Art and Crafts, London, from 1946 to 1948; and the Royal College of Art, London, from 1946 to 1957. The Arts Council toured a major exhibition in 1958–59, and a retrospective was held at Reading Museum and Art Gallery in 1974 and the Royal College of Art in 1994.

76 (illus. p. 31)
Children of the Gorbals, 1945
Watercolour on paper, 54 × 75 cm
Signed and dated upper right: *John Minton 1945*
Northampton Town and County Art Society, Northampton

EDUARDO PAOLOZZI (born 1924)

Born in Leith, Scotland, Paolozzi studied at Edinburgh College of Art in 1943 and at the Slade School of Fine Art, London, from 1944 to 1947. He had his first solo exhibition at the Mayor Gallery, London, in 1947 and that summer he went to live in Paris. During his stay he met with, among others, Fernand Léger and Alberto Giacometti. Paolozzi was fascinated by the machine imagery and Dadaist wit of Francis Picabia and was greatly inspired by the work of Jean Dubuffet, which informed his richly encrusted sculptures in the 1950s.

A key figure in the Independent Group, Paolozzi gave a screening of his Bunk collages and tearsheets in 1952. Paolozzi explored his interest in found objects, technology and popular culture through paintings, collage, screenprints and sculpture. During the 1960s and early 1970s he published several books with Surrealist-inspired collage texts and explored his kaleidoscopic view of contemporary life through film.

Paolozzi was involved in a number of group exhibitions, including *Parallel of Life and Art* at the Institute of Contemporary Arts, London, in 1953; *This is Tomorrow* at the Whitechapel Art Gallery, London, in 1956; and *New Images of Man* at the Museum of Modern Art, New York, in 1959. He represented Britain at the Venice Biennale in 1952 and 1960, when he was awarded the David E. Bright Foundation Award. From the late 1970s until the present day Paolozzi has undertaken a number of public commissions in Britain and Europe. They are monumental public statements based on his private vocabulary, which include such elements as the mechanized head or figure and geometric murals.

Paolozzi taught textile design at Central School of Arts and Crafts, London, from 1949 to 1955; sculpture at St Martin's School of Art, London, from 1955 to 1958; and ceramics at the Royal College of Art, London, from 1968 to 1969. He was also visiting professor at art schools in Hamburg, Cologne, Munich and the University of California, Berkeley, in the 1960s. Retrospective exhibitions have been held at the Tate Gallery, London, in 1971; the Nationalgalerie, West Berlin, in 1975; and the Royal Scottish Academy, Edinburgh, in 1984, the last touring to Munich and Cologne in 1985. The Scottish National Gallery of Modern Art, Edinburgh, holds the main archive of his work, with a reconstruction of his studio, at the Dean Gallery, Edinburgh. He was elected an Associate of the Royal Academy in 1972 and a Royal Academician in 1979. He was knighted in 1989.

77 (illus. p. 104)
Cocks Fighting, 1948
Pen and ink wash on paper, 25 × 37 cm
Signed and dated bottom centre: *Paolozzi 1948*
Government Art Collection, London

78 (illus. p. 105)
Two Forms on a Rod, 1948–49
Bronze, 51 × 65 × 32.5 cm
Stamped: *Eduardo Paolozzi London* and *cast by Morris Singer Co. London SW8*
Scottish National Gallery of Modern Art, Edinburgh
(Purchased 1988)

79 (illus. p. 106)
Forms on a Bow, 1949
Brass, 48.3 × 63.5 × 21.6 cm
Tate, London (Presented by the Contemporary Art Society, 1958)

80 (illus. p. 105)
Growth (Table Sculpture), 1949
Bronze, 80 × 60.5 × 39 cm
Stamped: *3/6 Eduardo Paolozzi*
Scottish National Gallery of Modern Art, Edinburgh
(Bequeathed by Gabrielle Keiller 1995)

81 (illus. p. 107)
Untitled, 1951
Watercolour on paper, 46 × 60 cm
Signed and dated bottom centre: *Eduardo Paolozzi 1951*
Government Art Collection, London

82 (illus. p. 109)
Robot, c. 1956
Bronze, 123 × 30 × 20 cm
Collection of Brian Clarke

83 (illus. p. 109)
St Sebastian 1, 1957
Bronze, 214.5 × 72 × 35.5 cm
Scottish National Gallery of Modern Art, Edinburgh
(Purchased 1993)

BERNARD PERLIN (born 1918)

Born in Richmond, Virginia, Perlin studied at the New York School of Design in 1934. He worked in the Office of War Information Graphics Division from 1942 to 1943 and began to paint full-time in 1946. His work was included in *Symbolic Realism in American Painting* at the Institute of Contemporary Arts, London, in 1950. Perlin represented America at the Venice Biennale in 1956.

84 (illus. p. 79)
Orthodox Boys, 1948
Tempera on board, 76.2 × 101.6 cm
Tate, London (Presented by Lincoln Kirstein through the Institute of Contemporary Arts, London, 1950)

PETER ROSE PULHAM (1910–1956)

Born in London, Pulham studied at the Architectural Association School of Architecture, London, in 1927–28 and Oxford University. During the 1930s Pulham worked as a photographer for *Harper's Bazaar*. His interest in and connections with Surrealist art circles in Paris led him to take up painting full-time in 1938. His first solo exhibition was at the Redfern Gallery, London, in 1947, with another at the Hanover Gallery, London, in 1950. He exhibited in *Recent Trends in Realist Painting* at the Institute of Contemporary Arts, London, in 1952.

85 (illus. p. 55)
Grisaille Figure, 1947
Oil on canvas, 79 × 98.5 cm
Andrée and Oscar Quitak Collection

ISABEL RAWSTHORNE (LAMBERT) (1912–1992)

Born in London, the artist attended the Royal Academy of Arts Schools, London, in 1930 and L'Académie de la Grande Chaumière, Paris, in 1934. She modelled in London for Jacob Epstein and in Paris she sat for André Derain, Alberto Giacometti and others. She was both a painter and a stage designer. She held an exhibition at the Hanover Gallery, London, in 1948, and designed a number of ballet productions for the Royal Opera House in Covent Garden, London. No. 86 was painted while she was married to Constant Lambert. She was subsequently married to Alan Rawsthorne.

86 (illus. p. 35)
Skeleton of Two Birds and a Fish, 1948
Oil on canvas, 78 × 60 cm
Collection of Biddy Noakes

CERI RICHARDS (1903–1971)

Born in Dunvant, near Swansea, Wales, Richards attended Swansea School of Art from 1921 to 1924 and the Royal College of Art, London, from 1924 to 1927. Richards had his first solo exhibition at the Glynn Vivian Gallery, Swansea, in 1930. He exhibited with the Objective Abstractionists at Zwemmer Gallery, London, in 1934 and with the Surrealists at the London Gallery in 1936–37.

Richards taught at Chelsea School of Art, London, before the outbreak of World War II, when he moved to Cardiff. He was Head of Painting at Cardiff School of Art from 1940 to 1944. In 1943 he was commissioned by the Ministry of Information to make drawings of tin-plate workers, which were exhibited at the National Museum of Wales. During this time Richards looked for inspiration to the poetry of Dylan Thomas, whose themes fed into many of his works.

At the end of the War Richards moved back to London and exhibited regularly at the Redfern Gallery. Through his work Richards wanted to communicate the intensity of his engagement with the subject, as well as the material substance and physical quality of painting. He looked to the work of European masters such as Picasso, Ernst and Matisse and drew on the creative agency of chance, which he felt gave tension to his work. He worked in different media, creating constructions, collages and prints, as well as experimenting by incorporating found objects and materials into his paintings.

Richards exhibited a variation of *Trafalgar Square* (see illus. p. 38) in *60 Paintings for '51* at the Institute of Contemporary Arts, London, in 1951 and represented Britain at the Venice Biennale in 1962. From 1963 he exhibited regularly at the Marlborough Fine Art Gallery, London. He taught at Chelsea School of Art, London, from 1947 to 1957; the Slade School of Fine Art, London, from 1955 to 1958; and the Royal College of Arts, London, from 1958 to 1960. A retrospective exhibition was held at the Whitechapel Art Gallery, London, in 1960 and a major exhibition at the Tate Gallery, London, in 1981. He was awarded the CBE in 1960 and the following year he was made an Honorary Fellow of the Royal College of Art, London.

87
Trafalgar Square II, 1951
Oil on canvas, 114.5 × 152.5 cm
Board of Trustees of the National Museums and Galleries on Merseyside, Liverpool (Walker Art Gallery)

RALPH RUMNEY (born 1934)

Born in Halifax, West Yorkshire, Rumney studied at Halifax School of Art, but left in disillusionment and travelled to the Continent, partly to avoid conscription (he was a conscientious objector). In 1956 Rumney had a solo exhibition in Milan and his first solo exhibition in London at the New Vision Centre Gallery.

He was the only British participant in the founding of *Internationale Situationniste* in 1957, from which its main spokesman, Guy Debord, later expelled him in 1959. He presented himself as the delegate from the 'London Psychogeographic Committee', which drew upon the techniques of the *derivé*: an uncontrolled drift through the urban landscape (often under the influence of alcohol or drugs), following the subconscious 'pull' of the architecture encountered, and 'psychographology', which involved mapping the patterns of the derivé in an attempt to lay the blueprint of new utopian urban environments. Rumney mapped his own *derivé* through the back streets of Venice, following the unpredictable wanderings of his friend the American Beat writer Allan Ansen (alias 'A').

By the early 1960s Rumney became disillusioned by what he saw as the stifling atmosphere of the gallery system. For the next decade and a half Rumney worked as a writer and broadcaster, mainly in France. In the mid-1970s Rumney taught art history, theory and film-making at Canterbury College of Art, Kent. Rumney began to create artworks again in 1983, and held a solo exhibition at the Transmission Gallery, Glasgow, in 1985. A retrospective exhibition was held at England & Co. Gallery, London, in 1989.

88 (illus. p. 151)
Untitled, 1956
Oil on board, 104.5 × 71.5 cm
England & Co. Gallery, London

JACK SMITH (born 1928)

Born in Sheffield, Smith studied at Sheffield College of Art from 1944 to 1946, St Martin's School of Art, London, from 1948 to 1950 and the Royal College of Art, London, from 1950 to 1953. He served in the Royal Air Force from 1946 to 1948. Smith had his first solo exhibition at the Beaux-Arts Gallery, London, in 1952, where he exhibited regularly until 1958.

He became associated with the Kitchen Sink School of John Bratby (see p. 178), Derrick Greaves (see p. 181) and Edward Middleditch (see p. 184), who were seen as a new generation of British realists. In 1949 Smith moved into a shared house with Greaves and George Fullard. This household became the main subject-matter of his paintings.

Smith represented Britain at the Venice Biennale in 1956. He was awarded first prize at the John Moores Liverpool Exhibition in 1957. After a trip to Spain in 1954 Smith became more interested in the play of light on shapes. Initially he retained a recognizable subject-matter, but gradually his work became more abstract.

Smith taught part-time at the Bath Academy of Art, Corsham, Wiltshire, in 1953, where he met William Scott, Peter Lanyon, Bryan Wynter and Terry Frost. From 1957 he taught part-time at Chelsea School of Art, London; Hornsey School of Art, north London; Wimbledon School of Art, London; and then at the Royal College of Art, London. Retrospective exhibitions were held at the Whitechapel Art Gallery, London, in 1959 and Sunderland Arts Centre in 1977 (the latter touring nationally) and a major exhibition was held at the Serpentine Gallery, London, in 1978. In 1986 he designed sets and costumes for the Ballet Rambert.

89 (illus. p. 73)
Interior with Child, 1953
Oil on board, 122 × 122 cm
Royal College of Art Collection, London

90 (illus. p. 91)
Shirt in Sunlight, 1956
Oil on board, 155.5 × 125.5 cm
Signed and dated: *Jack Smith '56*
The Artworks Loan Scheme, Leicestershire Museums, Arts and Records Service, Leicester

91
Still Life in Shadow, 1959
Oil on canvas, 91.5 × 91.5 cm
Signed on reverse: *Jack Smith 1959*
Collection of the artist

RICHARD SMITH (born 1931)

Born in Hertfordshire, Smith studied at Luton School of Art, Bedfordshire, from 1948 to 1950, St Albans School of Art, Hertfordshire, from 1952 to 1954 and the Royal College of Art, London, from 1954 to 1957. He served in the Royal Air Force from 1950 to 1952.

In 1957 he spent a short time in Italy on a scholarship and visited New York, where he admired the painterly quality of work by Sam Francis and Mark Rothko. Smith lived in America on a Harkness Fellowship from 1959 to 1961, where he looked to the work of Ellsworth Kelly for inspiration and mixed with the younger generation of New York artists. Smith was part of the emerging Pop Art world: part of Ken Russell's television programme *Pop Goes the Easel* was filmed in his studio.

Smith represented Britain at the Venice Biennale in 1966. He had solo exhibitions at the Green Gallery, New York, in 1961; the Kasmin Gallery, New York, in 1963, 1967, 1969 and 1972; and the Galleria dell'Ariete, Milan, in 1969. These six exhibitions were re-created for a retrospective exhibition at the Tate Gallery, London, in 1975. An earlier retrospective was held at the Whitechapel Art Gallery, London, in 1966.

He taught mural decoration at Hammersmith College of Art, London, in 1957–58, and St Martin's School of Art, London, from 1961 to 1963, during which time he made a film called *Trailer*. He was awarded the CBE in 1972.

92 (illus. p. 153)
Yellow, Yellow, 1957
Oil on canvas, 127 × 102 cm
Royal College of Art Collection, London

93 (illus. p. 161)
Penny, 1960
Oil on canvas, 226.1 × 210.8 cm
Signed, dated and inscribed on reverse: *R. Smith 1960 Penny*
The Trustees of the Museums and Galleries of Northern Ireland (Ulster Museum)

FRANCIS NEWTON SOUZA (born 1924)

Souza was born in Goa. Three months after his birth his father died, and Souza moved with his mother to Bombay in 1928. He attended the Sir JJ School of Art, Bombay, from 1940 to 1945, when he was expelled by the school's English director, who was suspicious of Souza's left-wing views. He began to enjoy some success in Bombay, and in 1947 he founded the Progressive Artists Group there.

In 1949 Souza emigrated with his first wife, Maria, to London. At first he found little support for his painting, and existed through his wife's work as a couturier and the sale of occasional articles. Krishna Menon, Indian High Commissioner in London, was a patron and commissioned Souza to paint murals for the Indian Students Bureau (the murals were subsequently destroyed). Following two exhibitions in Paris, Souza had the first of many one-man shows at Gallery One, London, in 1955, and became a successful and respected artist in the capital.

In 1967 Souza settled in New York, leaving in London a wife, a mistress, and four daughters. Shortly afterwards Souza separated from his second wife and became a recluse. He still lives and works in New York.

94 (illus. p. 16)
The Emperor, 1958
Oil on board, 101.5 × 61 cm
Signed and dated: *Souza '58*
The Artworks Loan Scheme, Leicestershire Museums, Arts and Records Service, Leicester

AUGUSTUS JOHN RUSKIN SPEAR (1911–1990)

Born in Hammersmith, London, Spear studied at Hammersmith School of Art from 1926 to 1929 and the Royal Academy of Arts Schools, London, from 1930 to 1934. He was elected President of the London Group in 1949. Spear held his first solo exhibition at the Leicester Galleries, London, in 1951. He exhibited at the Pushkin Museum, Moscow, in 1957.

His first teaching post was at Croydon School of Art, south London, in 1935 and he later taught at St Martin's School of Art, London, and Hammersmith School of Art from 1941 to 1945 and at the Royal College of Art, London, from 1948 to 1975. His colleagues included Carel Weight (see p. 187), Rodrigo Moynihan and John Minton (see pp. 184–85). He was elected a Royal Academician in 1954 and was awarded the CBE in 1979. He held a retrospective at the Royal Academy of Arts, London, in 1980.

95 (illus. p. 83)
Haute Couture, 1954
Oil on board, 213 × 122 cm
Collection of Mrs Mary Spear

96 (illus. p. 84)
Catching the Night Train, 1959
Oil on canvas, 223 × 116.5 cm
Collection of Mrs Mary Spear

FRANCISZKA THEMERSON (1907–1988)

Born in Warsaw, Poland, Themerson attended Warsaw Academy of Fine Art from 1924 to 1931. She lived in Paris from 1937 to 1940 and after that in London. Painter, designer, publisher and illustrator, Themerson worked in several fields. Collaborating with her husband, the writer Stefan Themerson, she worked on experimental films, illustrated children's books, which her husband wrote, and with him founded the Gaberbocchus Press in 1948. Themerson also created theatre designs for productions that included *Ubu roi* and *Ubu enchainé* by Alfred Jarry and *The Threepenny Opera* by Berthold Brecht and Kurt Weill. In the 1960s she taught theatre design at Wimbledon School of Art, London, and Bath Academy of Art, Corsham, Wiltshire. Themerson's work was shown in a number of group and solo exhibitions, including Gallery One, London, in 1957 and 1959 and the Whitechapel Art Gallery, London, in 1975. In 1968 Themerson designed the exhibition *Cybernetic Serendipity*, organized by Jasia Reichardt for the Institute of Contemporary Arts, London.

The catalogue *The Drawings of Franciszka Themerson*, edited by N. Wadley, accompanied an exhibition at the Nordjyllands Kunstmuseum, Aalborg, Holland, in 1991. The exhibition *Franciszka Themerson: Unposted Letters 1940–42* was mounted at the Imperial War Museum, London, in 1996.

97 (illus. p. 146)
Comme la vie est lente, comme l'espérance est violente, 1959
Oil on canvas, 105.5 × 156 cm
Collection of Jasia Reichardt

DAVID TINDLE (born 1932)

Born in Huddersfield, West Yorkshire, Tindle studied at Coventry School of Art, West Midlands, from 1945 to 1947. He exhibited at the Summer Exhibitions at the Royal Academy of Arts, London, from the early 1950s. Tindle's realism was firmly located in the immediacy of his own surroundings. He painted portraits, interiors and landscapes that were subtle and delicate and placed importance on surface and texture.

Tindle taught at Hornsey College of Art, north London, from 1959 to 1974 and the Royal College of Art, London, from 1972 to 1983, being made a fellow of the Royal College of Art in 1981. He was Ruskin Master of Drawing at Oxford University from 1985 to 1987. Tindle was included in numerous group shows at the Royal Academy of Arts throughout his career. He was elected an Associate of the Royal Academy in 1973 and a Royal Academician in 1979. In 1986 he was commissioned by the National Portrait Gallery, London, to paint a portrait of Sir Dirk Bogarde and in 1990 commissioned to paint one of Lord Sainsbury. A retrospective was held at the Herbert Art Gallery, Coventry, in 1957.

98 (illus. p. 133)
Shell Site: South Bank, 1959
Oil on canvas, 77.5 × 69 cm
Signed and dated: *Tindle '59*
The Artworks Loan Scheme, Leicestershire Museums, Arts and Records Service, Leicester

JULIAN TREVELYAN (1910–1988)

Born in Surrey, Trevelyan read English Literature at Trinity College, Cambridge, from 1929 to 1931, and while there published 'Dreams', a Surrealist manifesto, in the magazine *Transition*. He left in 1931 and decided to move to Paris. He attended classes at S.W. Hayter's experimental workshop Atelier 17, Paris, where leading avant-garde artists including Miró, Giacometti, Ernst and on occasion Picasso worked. Trevelyan developed a Surrealist style of painting and etching. In 1934 he returned to London, where he exhibited in the International Surrealist Exhibition at the New Burlington Galleries, London, in 1936. He became a member of the English Surrealist Group. Trevelyan served with the Royal Engineers from 1940 to 1943. During the War he worked with Carel Weight (see p. 187) on a selection committee of the Artists International Association.

In his work Trevelyan looked to the complex relationship between the domestic, the industrial and nature. His work of the 1940s was lyrical, but by the early 1950s there was a shift towards a more simplified, decorative style through which the colours conveyed a sense of place and the emotions of the artist. Etching also played a vital rôle in his work, allowing him to adopt a more abstract approach to painting.

He taught etching and art history at Chelsea School of Art, London, from 1950 to 1955 and became Tutor in Engraving and later Head of the Etching Department at the Royal College of Art, London, from 1955 to 1963. A retrospective was held at Watermans Arts Centre, Brentford, West London, in 1986, followed by an exhibition at Bohun Gallery, Henley-on-Thames, in 1988. Trevelyan was awarded Senior Fellowship of the Royal College of Art in 1986 and in 1987 was appointed Associate Royal Academician. He published his autobiography, *Indigo Days*, in 1957.

99 (illus. p. 133)
Hyde Park, 1956
Oil on canvas, 75 × 75 cm
Signed and dated bottom right: *Trevelyan 56*
Arts Council Collection, Hayward Gallery, London

100 (illus. p. 135)
Picadilly Circus at Night, 1957
Oil on canvas, 46 × 61 cm
Signed and dated: *Trevelyan 57*
Collection of Sarah Braun

WILLIAM TURNBULL (born 1922)

Born in Dundee, Scotland, Turnball studied art in the evenings and found employment as a magazine illustrator. During World War II he served as a pilot in the Royal Air Force, from 1941 to 1945. Turnbull studied at the Slade School of Fine Art, London, from 1946 to 1948, where he met Eduardo Paolozzi (see p. 185). He lived in Paris for two years, between 1948 and 1950, when he met fellow young British artists as well as leading Modernists, especially Constantin Brancusi and Alberto Giacometti, who inspired him. Turnbull had his first solo exhibition at the Hanover Gallery, London, in 1950, followed by a second in 1952. In 1953 he moved away from linear structures

to solid three-dimensional forms that included masks and totemic figures, and, later, abstract metal constructions. In his work Turnbull experimented with a combination of materials, drawing influences from high and low art, Western and non-Western forms.

Turnbull also explored issues of language and process through his paintings. From the early 1950s he used the head as a recurring motif. In 1957 his paintings became purely abstracted, the focus being on the brush marks, and the canvases became larger and more uniformly coloured. Turnbull regarded his paintings as environmental art, objects that activated the space they occupied. This change coincided with his experience of American Abstract Expressionism as seen at the Tate Gallery, London, in 1956.

Turnbull represented Britain at the Venice Biennale in 1952. He had a solo exhibition of sculpture and painting at the Institute of Contemporary Arts, London, in 1957 and exhibited in *This is Tomorrow* at the Whitechapel Art Gallery, London, in 1956 and *Situation* at the RBA Galleries, London, in 1960. A retrospective was held at the Tate Gallery, London, in 1973, and a major exhibition was held at the Serpentine Gallery, London, in 1995–96. He taught at the Central School of Arts and Crafts, London, from 1951 to 1961 and from 1964 to 1972.

101 (illus. p. 113)
Acrobat, 1951
Bronze on stone base, 132.1 × 81.2 × 55.9 cm
Collection of the artist, courtesy of Waddington Galleries, London

102 (illus. p. 114)
Head-form, c. 1955
Mixed media on paper, 76.5 × 56 cm
England & Co. Gallery, London

103 (illus. p. 114)
Mask, 1955–56
Oil on canvas, 111.8 × 86.4 cm
Signed, dated and inscribed on reverse: *Turnbull 1955–1956* 'Mask'
Swindon Museum and Art Gallery, Swindon Borough Council

104 (illus. p. 111)
Idol 2, 1956
Bronze, 161.3 × 43 × 49.5 cm
Tate, London (Purchased 1990)

KEITH VAUGHAN (1912–1977)

Born in Sussex, Vaughan had no formal art training but developed his interest in Italian Renaissance art and painted in his spare time. He was initially a conscientious objector, but later served in the Pioneer Corps from 1941 to 1946. During this period he came into contact with Neo-Romantic painters such as Graham Sutherland and John Minton (see pp. 184–85), which markedly affected his work.

Vaughan had his first solo exhibition of drawings at the Lefevre Gallery, London, in 1942, and four years later a solo exhibition of his oil paintings was held at the same gallery. In 1951 he painted the Theseus mural in the Festival of Britain's Dome of Discovery. Throughout his career, his subject-matter remained constant: a male nude in a landscape, the image becoming increasingly abstracted in his later work.

Vaughan held a number of teaching posts, including Camberwell College of Arts, London, from 1946 to 1948; Central School of Arts and Crafts, London, from 1948 to 1957 and the Slade School of Fine Art, London, from 1954 to 1977. Retrospective exhibitions were held at the Hatton Gallery, University of Durham, in 1956 and the Whitechapel Art Gallery, London, in 1962. A posthumous exhibition was held at the Geffrye Museum, London, in 1981. Agnew's, London, took the estate over from Waddington, London, in 1985 and held a major exhibition in 1990.

105 (illus. p. 34)
Assembly of Figures 1, 1952
Oil on board, 142.2 × 116.8 cm
Signed and dated centre right: *Vaughan/52*
Private collection

BRIAN WALL (born 1931)

Born in London, Wall worked as a glass-blower from 1945 to 1950. While serving in the Royal Air Force he attended Luton College of Art, Bedfordshire, from 1951 to 1952. Wall then lived in Paris and London until 1954 when, prompted by his interest in the work of Ben Nicholson, he moved to St Ives, Cornwall. In the late 1950s he became a part-time assistant to Barbara Hepworth. Wall's first sculptures were architectonic, made in wood. He was one of the first British sculptors to make welded-steel abstracted constructions.

Wall returned to London in 1960. He taught at Ealing College of Art, west London, from 1961 to 1962 and St Martin's School of Art, London, from 1962 to 1972. He visited America in the late 1960s and taught at the University of California, Berkeley, where he became Professor of Art.

106 (illus. p. 128)
Landscape Sculpture, 1958
Iron, 50.8 × 38.1 × 25.4 cm
Arts Council Collection, Hayward Gallery, London

CAREL WEIGHT (1908–1997)

Born in London, Weight studied part-time at Hammersmith School of Art, London, from 1928 to 1930 and then part-time at Goldsmiths College, London, from 1930 to 1933. He held his first solo exhibition at Cooling Galleries, London, in 1943. In the 1930s he was a member of the Artists International Association. When his studio was bombed in 1941 he lost a large body of his early work. Conscripted into the army in 1942, Weight became an official war artist in 1945.

He taught at Beckenham School of Art, south-east London, from 1932 to 1942. He was tutor in the Painting School of the Royal College of Art, London, from 1947 to 1957 and Professor of Painting from 1957 to 1973. At the college he wanted to create an environment where young artists could develop their own individual vision. Weight advocated working from life, and his own paintings were concerned with the human condition, captured in the microcosmic settings of the south London streets and parks that surrounded him. He also painted portraits of friends, often set in their own environment. He painted a mural for the Festival of Britain's Country Pavilion in 1951, and another for Manchester Cathedral in 1963. During the 1960s he painted numerous religious works.

He was elected an Associate of the Royal Academy in 1955 and a Royal Academician in 1965. He was made Honorary Fellow of the Royal College of Art in 1955, awarded the CBE in 1962 and created a Companion of Honour in 1995. A retrospective was held at the Royal Academy of Arts, London, in 1982 and a touring exhibition was organized by the Newport Museum and Art Gallery, Gwent, Wales, in 1993.

107 (illus. p. 65)
Anger, 1955
Oil on canvas, 91.5 × 122 cm
Signed and dated bottom right: *Carel Weight '55*
The Museum of London, London

GERALD WILDE (1905–1986)

Born in London, Wilde attended Chelsea School of Art from 1926 to 1935. He served in the Pioneer Corps from 1940 to 1941. Wilde held his first solo exhibition at the Hanover Gallery, London, in 1948.

During the 1960s Wilde ceased to paint, and in 1970 a case of mistaken identity led to his death being announced in the press. After this Wilde began to paint again and exhibited in a number of group and solo exhibitions. A retrospective was held at the Institute of Contemporary Arts, London, in 1955. In 1972 Alan Yentob produced a documentary on Wilde for BBC 2 that included an interview with David Sylvester, who commented on the importance of, though lack of recognition for, Wilde. The catalogue *Gerald Wilde*, edited by C. Hawes (London 1988), accompanied a retrospective at the October Gallery, London.

108 (illus. p. 45)
Piccadilly Circus, 1946
Gouache on paper, 55.8 × 78.7 cm
Private collection

109 (illus. p. 43)
The Alarm, 1947
Gouache on paper, 54.5 × 75.7 cm
Signed and dated bottom right: *Gerald Wilde 47*
Arts Council Collection, Hayward Gallery, London

110 (illus. p. 44)
Beast in Landscape, 1949
Oil on board, 83.8 × 111.8 cm
Collection of Mr and Mrs A.H. Sandford-Smth

VICTOR WILLING (1928–1986)

Born in Alexandria, Willing and his family moved to England in 1932. He studied at the Slade School of Fine Art, London, from 1949 to 1954. Willing sought to capture the essentials of perception and engaged in popular contemporary discussions on phenomenology and existentialism. In particular, the notion of 'vertigo' – the abandonment of the self to the call of the abyss – was captured in his work. Through inviting Francis Bacon (see pp. 177–78) to give a talk at the Slade, Willing met David Sylvester, a prominent critic and champion of modern art, who felt Willing was particularly alert to the current mental atmosphere.

Willing held his first solo exhibition at the Hanover Gallery, London, in 1955. He briefly changed his style in response to Abstract Expressionism. However, this was not received well, so he reintroduced the human figure to his work.

The development of Willing's career was interrupted when he moved to Portugal, living there from 1957 to 1974 with the painter Paula Reguo, whom he married, and their child. During this period he did little painting but read widely, including such works as Nietzsche's *The Birth of Tragedy* (1871). He taught at Bath Academy of Art, Corsham, Wiltshire; the Slade School of Fine Art, London; and Chelsea School of Art, London, from 1964 to 1967.

On his return to London in 1974 Willing devoted himself exclusively to painting, but his style had changed, and he looked to the work of de Chirico, Matisse and Picasso for inspiration. His work drew on memory and visionary scenarios, including a brief period of painting and drawing directly from hallucinations.

A retrospective was held at the Whitechapel Art Gallery, London, in 1986. He died later the same year from multiple sclerosis, which had been diagnosed in 1966.

111 (illus. p. 61)
Act of Violence, 1952
Oil on board, 152.6 × 182.5 cm
College Art Collections, University College London

EDWARD WRIGHT (1912–1988)

Born in Liverpool, where his father was the Ecuadorian Vice-Consul, Wright studied at Liverpool School of Art from 1930 to 1931 and Bartlett School of Architecture, London University, from 1933 to 1936. Wright refused to accept boundaries between different media, and was a painter, typographer and graphic designer, latterly specializing in lettering for architectural environments; one of his last commissions was for the illuminated lettering at the Tate Gallery Liverpool in 1988.

Photographer unknown: Edward Wright at the Café Torino, *c.* 1955. Collection of Anna Yandell

He taught at the Central School of Arts and Crafts, London, with Anthony Froshaug from 1952; at the Royal College of Art, London, from 1956; and at Chelsea School of Art, London, where he became Head of Graphic Design, from 1963. Robin Kinross described Wright as more than a teacher: 'a culture-carrier who helped a lot of people.' A retrospective exhibition, *Edward Wright: Graphic Work and Painting*, was toured by the Arts Council in 1985.

112 (illus. p. 125)
Letter Collage, 1947
Collage, 18 × 15.9 cm (image size)
Collection of Anna Yandell

113 (illus. p. 125)
Bunsen Burners, 1948
Ink and gouache, 32.6 × 23.7 cm
Collection of Anna Yandell

Selected Bibliography

There are substantial monographs devoted to most – though not all – of the artists represented in *Transition*. Among the most useful volumes dealing with the period from a broader perspective are:

From London: Bacon, Freud, Kossoff, Andrews, Auerbach, Kitaji, exhib. cat., ed. R. Calvocoressi and P. Long, British Council, London, in association with the Scottish National Gallery of Modern Art, Edinburgh, 1995

L. Alloway, *Nine Abstract Artists, Their Work and Theory: Robert Adams, Terry Frost, Adrian Heath, Anthony Hill, Roger Hilton, Kenneth Martin, Mary Martin, Victor Pasmore, William Scott*, London 1954

D. Robbins (ed.), *The Independent Group: Postwar Britain and the Aesthetics of Plenty*, Cambridge MA and London 1990

A. Massey, *The Independent Group: Modernism and Mass Culture in Britain 1945–59*, Manchester and New York 1995

Paris Post War: Art and Existentialism 1945–55, exhib. cat., ed. F. Morris, London, Tate Gallery, 1993

The Sixties art scene in London, exhib. cat. by David Mellor, London, Barbican Art Gallery, in association with Phaidon Press Ltd, London, 1993

A. Seago, *Burning the Box of Beautiful Things: The Development of a Postmodern Sensibility*, Oxford 1995

The Kitchen Sink Painters, exhib. cat., intro. by F. Spalding, London, The Mayor Gallery, in association with Julian Hartnoll, 1991

British Art in the 20th Century: The Modern Movement, exhib. cat., ed. S. Compton, London, Royal Academy of Arts, 1987

Exhibition Road: Painters at the Royal College of Art, exhib. cat., ed. P. Huxley, London, Royal College of Art, 1988

The Forgotten Fifties, exhib. cat. by J. Spalding, Sheffield, Mappin Gallery, 1984

M. Garlake, *New Art New World: British Art in Postwar Society*, New Haven and London 1998

The literature of British Art of the 1950s continues to expand at an encouraging rate. The Michael Andrews retrospective at Tate Britain in the summer of 2001, was followed, in October of that year, by a major Frank Auerbach exhibition at the Royal Academy of Arts, London. As this catalogue went to press, James Hyman, *The Battle for Realism: Figurative Art in Britain During the Cold War 1945–1960* (London 2001) was published: it promises to be an essential and invaluable study of the period.

Index

Abstract Expressionism 11, 18, 42, 74, 90, 140, 150, 152, 162
Abstract Expressionism (exhibition) 152, 162
Action Painting 18, 147, 150, 154, 181
Adams, Robert 127, 129
Adler, Jankel 16, *30*, 30–1, 33, 144, 179
Adsetts, Ernest 86
Alberts, The 132
Alloway, Lawrence 12, 15, 29, 45, 50, 71, 92, 94–5, 96, 97–8, 99, 111, 117, 119, 120, 124, 127, 140, 150, 152, 154, 160, 162, 163, 165–6, 168
Anderson, Lindsay 59, 74
Andrews, Michael 12, 59, *60*, *60*, 61, 66, 131, 133, *134*, 176, 177
Anglo-French Art Centre 14, *15*, 125
Antal, Frederick 76
Archer, David 135, 136
Architectural Design (magazine) 124, *131*
Architectural Review (magazine) 94, 98, 120, 124
Ark (magazine) 118, 132, 154, 162, 163
Armitage, Kenneth 66, *66*, 67, 68, 177
Art News and Review (magazine) 76, 95, 124
Artists International Association (AIA) 15, 76, 82
Arts Council 14, 36, 37, 42
Ashburner, Geoffrey 96, 97
Atlan, Jean-Michel 181
Auerbach, Frank 12, 16, 25, *27*, *28*, 28–9, 133, 177
Ayrton, Michael 12, 30, 35, *35*, 37, 133, *134*, 177

Bacon, Francis 12, 13, 14, 16, 18, 29, 35, 46, 48, *48*, 49, 50, 51, 52, *52*, *53*, 54, 60, 65, 71, 74, 76, 80–1, 94, 130, 133, 136, 168, 177–8, 179
Balla, Giacomo 52
Balthus, 74, 76
Banham, Mary 96, 124, 130
Banham, Peter Reyner 56, 68, 92, 94, 95, 98, 99, 103, 115, 117, 119, 120, 124, 129, 130, 179
Beaton, Cecil 29, 54
'Beaux-Art Quartet' 74, 78, 86
Belcher, Muriel 133
Bell, Graham 100
Benjamin, Walter 20, 52
Berger, John 14, *18*, 42, 66, 72, 74, 76, 78, *78*, 144, 178, 181
Berman, Eugene 30, 35
Bernal, J.D. 96, 100, 130
Bernard, Bruce and Jeffrey 133
Berry, Arthur 86
Bisley, Anthony 10
Black Eyes and Lemonade (exhibition) 155, *156*
Blake, Peter 22, 78, 154–7, *157–60*, 159–60, 165, 178
Blow, Sandra 144, *145*, 178, *178*
Bomberg, David 12, *23*, 24–5, 28, 43, 177, 178
Bomberg, Lilian 25
Bombois, Camille 78
Boshier, Derek 154, 165
Boty, Pauline 154
Bowen, Denis 150
Bowling, Frank 144
Bragaglia, Anton and Arturo 52
Braithwaite, Barbara 59, *59*
Brandt, Bill 54
Bratby, John 12, *12*, 14, 20, 72, 74, *75*, 76, 78, 85, 86, 88, *89*, 178
Brausen, Erica 94
Bridgwater, Emmy 94
Brown, Denise Scott 103
Brutalism/New Brutalism 15, 36, 103, 104, 124, 130, 131, 137
Buffet, Bernard 74, 76, 82
Buhler, Robert 56, 82
Burn, Rodney 56
Burra, Edward 31, 88
Burri, Alberto 103, 178
Butler, Reg 36, 46, 68, 68–71, *69*, *70*, 71, 124, *124*, 126, 179

Capa, Cornell 55
Caro, Anthony 66, *67*, 129, *129*, 179
Carter, Peter 130
Cartier-Bresson, Henri *54*, 55
Castellanos, Julio 78
Catleugh, Jon 130, *131*
Caulfield, Patrick 154

Central School of Arts and Crafts *38*, 82, 102, 105, 124
Chadwick, Lynn 86
Chagall, Marc 167
Chamberlin, Powell & Bon 138
Chelsea School of Art 42, 125
Chillingworth, John 139, *139*
Clark, Sir Kenneth 29
Clough, Prunella 37, 78, *78*, 179
Clutton-Brock, Alan 88
CoBrA group 37, 181
Cohen, Bernard 11
Cohen, Harold 152, *152*, 179
Coker, Peter 86
Coldstream, William 16, 46, 60–1, 65, 74, 82, 101, 177
Coleman, Roger 152, 154
Collins, Cecil 102, *102*
Colony Room, London 133, *133*, 135
Colquhoun, Alan 130
Colquhoun, Ithell 94
Colquhoun, Robert 30, *32*, 33, 37, 105, 133, 179, 183, 184
Conran, Terence 107, 126
Constant 183
Constructivism 127, 129, 150, 152
Cooper, D.E. 122
Cordell, Frank 120, 132, *132*, 154, 179
Cordell (McHale), Magda 119, 120, 121, 132, *132*, 140–1, 140–2, 150, 179–80
Craxton, John 29, 46
Creme, Benjamin 135
Crooke, Pat 124, *137*
Crosby, Theo 12, 13, 46, 122, 124, 127, 138, 160

Daniels, Alfred 72, 78, 79, 80, 156, 180
Darwin, Robin 82
Davenport, John 55
Davie, Alan 37, 40, 41, 42, 102, 126, 150, 168, 180
Deakin, John 2, 48, 49, 95, 133, 136, 156, 176, 180, 181
Deighton, Len 56, 132, 139
de Kooning, Willem 20, 150, 162
del Renzio, Toni 36, 42, 92, 94, 95, 99, 107, 124, 150, 154
de Maistre, Roy 48
Denny, Robyn 10, 11, 147, 150, 152, 154, 162–3, 163–5, 165, 168, 180
Diamond, Harry 65
Dickinson, Thorold 59
Dicks, Ted 132
Dimensions (exhibition) 150, 152
Dominguez, Oscar 125
Dorfles, Gillo 119–20
Drew, Jane 36, 107
Drury, Paul 29
Dubuffet, Jean 103, 105, 140, 185
Duchamp, Marcel 20, 99, 100, 115, 117, 182
Duxbury, Leslie 66, 86

Eardley, Joan 78, *81*, 180–1
EMI Records 132
Encounter (magazine) 76
Euston Road School 74, 80, 85
existentialism 81–2

Facetti, Germano 124, 126, 135, *175*
Faith, Adam 137, *137*
Farson, Daniel 133, 135, 136
Feaver, William 43–4, 107
Festival of Britain (1951) 14, 22, 24, 36, *36*, 68, 97, 107
Festival Pattern Group 97
Fifties, The (exhibition) 12
Forgotten Fifties, The (exhibition) 12, 20–1
40 Years of Modern Art (exhibition) 96
Frame, Robert 135
Freedman, Barnett 155
Freud, Lucian 12, 29, *29*, 48, 54, 59, *62*, *63*, 65, 74, 133, 136, 181, *181*
Froshaug, Anthony 124
Frost, Terry 150
Froy, Martin 96
Fullard, George 66, 86
Fuller, Peter 21

Gallery One 136, *136*, 144
Garlake, Margaret 12, 42, 150
Garland, Ken 102–3, 124, 126
Gear, William 12, 14, 16, 18, 37, *39*, 52, 150, 181
Giacometti, Alberto 35, 74, 80, 104, 108, 111, 147
Giedion, Sigfried 97, 98, 111, 115, 167
Gimpel Fils Gallery 130
Glass, Douglas 55
Gombrich, E.H. 97
Gooding, Peter 156
Goodman, Lea 136
Gowing, Lawrence 46, 124
Gradidge, Roderick 137
Graham, Sidney 135
Greaves, Derrick 14, 66, 72, 74, 76, 85, 86, *87*, 88, 181
Green, Alfred Rozelaar 14
Green, Terry 154
Green, William 147, *147*, 181
Greenberg, Clement 179
Gregory, Eric C. 68, 69
Greville, Edmond T. 137
Growth and Form (exhibition) 96, 97, 99, 103
Gruber, Francis 74, 82, *82*
Guggenheim, Peggy 99, 100, 130
Guttuso, Renato 78

Hamilton, Richard 9, 11, *14*, 94, 95, 96, 97, 99, 102, 115, *115*–17, 117–18, 120, 124, 129, 148, 154, 182, *182*
Hamilton, Terry 11, *14*
Hammarsköld, Hans 17
Hampson, Frank 98
Hanover Gallery 65, 68, 78, 94, 108, *110*, 111, 115, 117, 140
Hayes, Colin 56, 82
Heath, Adrian 14, 127
Henderson, Judith (*née* Stephen) 100, 107, 108, 126
Henderson, Nigel 14, 22, 54, 59, 93, 94, 96, 97, *97*, 99, 99–103, 104, 105, 107, 108, *110*, 126, *126*, 127, *127*, 129–30, *130*, 131, 132, *133*, 182
Henderson, Wyn 100, 102
Henry, Pierre 132
Hepworth, Barbara 13, 36, 68, 187
Herbert, Albert 80, 80–1, 182
Herman, Josef 16, 36, 37, 182
Heron, Patrick 12, 16, 18, *19*, 37, 68, 102, 144, 150, 182–3
Herron, Ron 103
Hill, Anthony 127, 129
Hilton, Roger 18, *143*, 144, 150, 178, 183
Hitchens, Ivon 37, 86
Hockney, David 11, 35, 148, *149*, 154, 165, 168, *169*, 172, 183
Hodgkins, Frances 29, 52
Hogarth, Paul 74, 76, 102
Hoppe, John 130
Horizon (magazine) 94, 104
House and Garden (magazine) 126
Hunstein, Don 124
Hurry, Leslie 35

ICA *see* Institute of Contemporary Arts
Independent Group 15, 16, 92, 94–8, 99, 105, 106, 120–1, 124, 127, 130, 131, 137, 140–1, 154
Ingham, Bryan 138
Institute of Contemporary Arts (ICA) 14, 15, 55, 56, 70, 94, 98, 132, 154; exhibitions 14, *17*, 18, *54*, 55, 74, 78, 96, 98, 103, 107, 115, 120, 124, 130, 140, 150, 152, 160
Ironside, Robin 22, 29–30

Jay, William 146
Jeffress, Arthur 94
Jennings, Humphrey 13, 100
Johnson, Charles 94–5
Johnstone, William 82, 102
Jones, Allen 154, 165, 166–7, 183
Jones, Barbara 22
Juda, Hans and Elsbeth 11

Kaner, Sam 131
Kapp, Helen 168
Kar, Ida 136, *136*
Kitaj, R.B. 12, 148, 155, *155*, 165

'Kitchen Sink School' 74, 76, 82, 85, 86, 159
Klee, Paul 31, 81, 98, 103, 105, 146
Kline, Franz 16, 150
Klingender, Francis D. 76
Kneale, Bryan 16, 17, 129
Kokoschka, Oskar 86
Kooning, Willem de *see* de Kooning
Kossoff, Leon 12, 25, *25*, *26*, 28–9, 133, 183

Lacey, Bruce 132
Lambert (Rawsthorne), Isabel 35, *35*, 55, 74, 105, *133*, 136, 185
Lannoy, Richard 9, 14, *14*, *54*, 58, 92, *117*, 124, 130
Lanyon, Peter 37, 150
Larkins, William 29
Lassally, Walter 59, 137
Latham, John 160
Le Brocquy, Louis 102
Le Corbusier 130
Lefevre Gallery 13, 33, 36, 52
Léger, Fernand 14, 37, 125
Lessore, Helen 74, 184
Lett-Haines, Arthur 48
L'Hôte, André 14, 102
Lichtenstein, Roy 20
Life (magazine) 55
Livingstone, Marco 148
Locker, Eric 136
London Group 12, 24
Looking Forward (exhibition) 66, 74
Lowry, L.S. 36
Lurçat, Jean 14
Lye, Len 102
Lyttleton, Humphrey 130, 131

MacBryde, Robert 30, 33, *33*, 37, 133, 179, 183–4
McHale, John 9, 99, 118, 119–21, *119–21*, 124, 127, 131, 132, *132*, 154, 179, 184
MacInnes, Colin 137, 139
McLuhan, Marshall 95, 162
Maddox, Conway 94
Mahoney, Charles 56
Man, Machine and Motion (exhibition) 115, 117
Manessier, Alfred 18
Martin, Kenneth and Mary 127, 129
Marx, Enid 155
Mason, Raymond 14, 104
Mathieu, Georges 18
Matta, Roberto 98, *98*
Mayne, Roger 122, *123*, 138, *138*, 139, *171*, *182*, 184
Mayor Gallery 104, 125
Mazzetti, Lorenza 59, *59*, 74
Medley, Robert *64*, 65, 100, 184
Mellor, David 35, 146–7
Melly, George 122, 130, 131
Melville, John 94
Melville, Robert 14, 48, 50, 60, 69, 70, 74, 94, 95, 104, 105, 140, 154
Mesens, E.L.T. 14, 94, 131
Meynell, Vera 100
Middleditch, Edward 14, *38*, 72, 74, 76, *77*, 86, 181, 184
Middleton, Michael 55, 126
Miller, Lee *14*
Minaux, André 74
Minton, John 11, 14, 16, 29, *29*, 30, 31, *31*, 35, 37, 56, 74, 80, 82, 86, 131, 133, 147, 150, 177, 179, 180, 184–5
Modern Painters (magazine) 21
Modernism 48, 50, 96
Moholy-Nagy, Laszlo 96, 103
Moore, Henry 13, 16, 29, 30, 42, 68, 71, 179
Moraes, Henrietta 133, 136
Moreton, Rex *132*
Morley, Malcolm 11
Morris, Cedric 48
Moynihan, Rodrigo 37, 54, 55–6, *56*, 59, 82
Murphy, Myles 59
Musgrave, Victor 136, 144

Nalecz, Halima 150
Nash, Paul 13, 16, 29

Neo-Romanticism 13, 14, 16, 29–30, 33, 35, 37, 42
New Brutalism *see* Brutalism
New Vision Centre Gallery 90, 144, 150
Nicholson, Ben 13, 29, 36, 37, 96

O'Hana Gallery 150
Ono, Yoko 20
Op Art 20

Palmer, Samuel 29, 30
Paolozzi, Eduardo 13, *13*, 14, 35, 36, 59, 68, 92, *93*, 94, 96, 97, 99, *100*, 101, 103, 103–9, 104–8, 111, 124, 126, 127, 129, 130, 131, 132, 150, 154, *185*
Pasmore, Victor 36, 37, 102, 127, *182*
Peake, Mervyn 102
Penn, Irving 56, *57*
Penrose, Roland 13, 14, 94, 99, 130
Perlin, Bernard 78, *79*, 1*56*, 185
Permeke, Constant 36
Pevsner, Nikolaus 138
Phillips, Peter 154, 165
Picasso, Pablo 14, 31, 33 48, 104, 130, 148
Pidgeon, Monica 124
Piper, John 13, 16, 29, 3c, 36, 96
Place (exhibition) 150, 1*52*, 163
Pollock, Jackson, 37, 74, 98, 130, 150, 179, 181
Pop Art 11, 16, 20, 80, 8*5*, 106, 117, 118, 144, 154, 155, 159, 160, 162, 165, 167, 168, 171
Price, Cedric 124
Procktor, Patrick 72, 154
Pulham, Peter Rose 54–5, *55*, 74, 185
Pursuit of the Real, The (exhibition) 21

Race, Steve 130
Raine, Kathleen 100, *101*
Rawsthorne, Isabel *see* Lambert
RCA *see* Royal College of Art
Rea, Betty 74
Read, Sir Herbert 13, 14 52, 68, 94, 95–6, 150, 168, 181
realism 72, 74, 76; *see also* Social Realism; Symbolic Realism
Rebeyrolle, Paul 74
Recent Trends in Realist Paintings (exhibition) 74, 76, 82
Redfern Gallery 150
Reichardt, Jasia 165
Reilly, Sir Charles 25
Reisz, Karel 74
Richard, Cliff 137, 168
Richards, Ceri 12, 29, *38*, 42, 65, 185
Richardson, Albert 25
Richardson, Tony 74
Richier, Germaine 14
Riesman, David 95
Roberts, William *38*, 72
Robertson, Bryan 12, 13, 16, 33, 179
Rogers, Claude 37, 59
Rowntree, Kenneth 56
Royal College of Art 11, 54, 56, *56*, 59, 78, 80, 82, 85, 86, 98, 125, 131, 132, 147, 150, 154, 159, 165, 171
Rumney, Ralph 150, *151*, 152, 185–6
Rykwert, Joseph 124, 1*25*, *126*

Sadler, Sir Michael 52
St Ives artists 12, 144, ¯50
Schaeffer, Pierre 132
Schwitters, Kurt 16, *16*, 165
Scott, Ronnie 131
Scott, William 37
Sewell, John 132
Shahn, Ben 156
Sharrer, Honoré 78, 15*5*, 159
Sickert, Walter 16, 85
Situationists 150, 163
Sixties Art Scene in London (exhibition) 146–7
60 Paintings for '51 (exhibition) 36, 37, *38*, 42
Slade School of Fine Art 16, 46, 54, 59, 60, 65, 82, 98, 99, 101, 104, 125
Smith, Jack 12, *12*, 14, *56*, *73*, 74, 76, 78, 86, 88, 90, *90*, 91, 186

Smith, Richard *10*, 11, *147*, 152, *153*, 154, 157, 160, *161*, 162, 165, 186
Smithson, Alison and Peter 103, 118, *118*, 124, *124*, 125, 126–7, *127*, *131*, 132, 138, 154, 182
Smithson, Robert 118, *118*
Soane, Sir John 21
Social Realism 11, 12, 14, 16, 66, 74, 76, 78, 82, 86, 90
Soulages, Pierre 18, 37
Souza, Francis Newton 16, 144, *144*, 146
Spear, (Augustus John) Ruskin 13, *13*, 56, *56*, 72, 74, 82, *82*, *83*, 84, 85, *85*, 186
Spencer, Stanley 29, 88
Spender, Humphrey 100
Staël, Nicolas de 18, *18*
Stanley, Eric 56, *56*
Stanley, Jacqueline 82
Statements: A Review of British Abstract Art in 1956 (exhibition) 150
Stevens, Sam 124
Stirling, James 124, 127, 130
Summerson, John 55
Surrealism 13–14, 16, 29, 94, 102, 104
Sutherland, Graham 13, 29, 30, 36, 42, 46, 52, 54, 58, 74, 184
Swingler, Humphrey 101
Sylvester, David 12, 14, 18, 42, 54, *54*, 56, 59, 60, 74, 76, 80, 81, 94, 98, 105, 148, 167, 188
Symbolic Realism 78, 156

Tachisme 18, 37, 90, 150
Taine, Hippolyte 11
Tate Gallery, London 16, 90, *107*, 162
Tchelitchew, Pavel 30, 35, 78
Themerson, Franciszka 16, 144–5, 146, *146*, 186
Themerson, Stefan 144–6
This is Tomorrow (exhibition) 9, 13, *107*, *117*, 118, 120, 125, 127, *127*, 129, 130, *130*
Thomas, Mark Hartland 97
Thompson, D'Arcy Wentworth 96
Tindle, David 133, *133*, 186–7
Titchell, John 78
Tobey, Mark 16
Tomorrow's Furniture (exhibition) 130
Trevelyan, Julian 12, 13, 14, 100, 133, *133*, *135*, 187
Turnbull, William *2*, 14, 68, 94, 95, 96, *96*, 101, 102, 104, 105, *111*, 111–12, *112–14*, 114, 127, 130, 150, 187
Tzara, Tristan 125

Usill, Harley 130

Vaughan, Keith 12, 18, 29, 30, 34, 35, 37, 102, 177, 187
Venice Biennale 37 (1948), 68 (1952), 86 (1956)
Vezelay, Paule 127
Voelcker, John 9, 118, 120, 131
Vorticism 12, 24, 38

Waddington, C.H. 96–7
Wall, Brian 12, *128*, 129, 187
War Artists Advisory Committee 24
Watson, Peter 14, 74
Weekes, John 127
Weight, Carel 12, 56, 82, 187
Whitechapel Art Gallery 16, *18*, 33, 74, 136, 155, *156*; *see also This is Tomorrow*
Whyte, Lancelot Law 96, 97
Wickham, Michael 126
Wilde, Gerald 42–5, *43*, *44*, *45*, 133, 187–8
Willing, Victor 46, *47*, 59, 60–1, *61*, 188
Wilson, Colin St John 124, 126, 129, 130
Wilson, Frank Avray 150
Wollheim, Richard 139
Wols (Wolfgang Schulze) 21, 140
Woolf, Virginia 50, 100
Wright, Edward 102, 124–5, *125*, 126, *137*, 154, 188, *188*
Wyeth, Andrew 78
Wynter, Bryan 37

Young Contemporaries (exhibition) 165, 166

Zwemmer Gallery 42, 86

Picture Credits

Barbican Art Galleries would like to thank all those who have kindly supplied photographic material for the book and given permission to use it. The publishers have made every effort to trace and contact copyright holders of the illustrations reproduced in this book; they will be happy to correct in subsequent editions any errors or omissions that are brought to their attention.

Page 9: © Richard Lannoy
Page 13 (top): © Courtesy of the Estate of Ruskin Spear/Bridgeman Art Library
Page 13 (btm): Photograph by Nigel Henderson/photograph © Janet Henderson/© Eduardo Paolozzi 2001. All Rights Reserved, DACS
Page 14: © Richard Lannoy
Page 16 (top): © DACS 2001
Page 16 (btm): © Francis Newton Souza
Page 17: © The Condé Nast Publications Ltd
Page 18: Photograph courtesy Walker Art Center/© ADAGP, Paris and DACS, London 2001
Page 19: © Estate of Patrick Heron 2001. All Rights Reserved, DACS
Page 20: Photograph © 1991 The Metropolitan Museum of Art/© ARS, NY and DACS, London 2001
Page 21: Photograph by Hester & Hardaway, Houston/© ADAGP, Paris and DACS, London 2001
Page 23: Photograph © The Museum of London/© The Family of David Bomberg
Page 25: © Leon Kossoff
Page 26: © Leon Kossoff
Page 27 (top): © Frank Auerbach
Page 27 (btm): Photograph © Ferens Art Gallery, Hull/© Frank Auerbach
Page 28: © Frank Auerbach
Page 29: © Lucian Freud
Page 30: Photograph © David Harris, The Israel Museum, Jerusalem/© DACS 2001
Page 31: © Royal College of Art
Page 32: © Courtesy of the Estate of Robert Colquhoun/Bridgeman Art Library
Page 35 (top): © Estate of Michael Ayrton
Page 35 (btm): Photograph © Tig Cockburn/© Buddy Noakes
Page 36: Photograph courtesy of Rosemary Butler/© Estate of Reg Butler
Page 38: Photograph © Tate, London 2001/© Estate of Ceri Richards 2001. All Rights Reserved, DACS
Page 39: © Estate of William Gear, RA
Page 40: © Alan Davie
Page 41: © Alan Davie
Page 43: © October Gallery
Page 44: © October Gallery
Page 45: © October Gallery
Page 47: © Paula Rego
Page 48: Photograph © 2001, The Art Institute of Chicago. All Rights Reserved/© Estate of Francis Bacon/ARS, NY and DACS, London 2001
Page 49: © The Condé Nast Publications Ltd
Page 51: © Estate of Francis Bacon/ARS, NY and DACS, London 2001
Page 52: © Estate of Francis Bacon/ARS, NY and DACS, London 2001
Page 53: © Estate of Francis Bacon/ARS, NY and DACS, London 2001
Page 54 (btm): © Richard Lannoy
Page 55: © George Melly
Page 56 (top): Photograph © Tate, London 2001
Page 57: Photograph by Irving Penn/© 1949 (renewed 1977) by Condé Nast Publications, Inc.
Page 58: © The Estate of Graham Sutherland
Page 59 (top): © Barbara Braithwaite
Page 60: Photograph © Tate, London 2001/© The Estate of Michael Andrews
Page 61: © Paula Rego
Page 62 (top): © Lucian Freud
Page 62 (btm): © Lucian Freud
Page 63: © Lucian Freud
Page 64: © The Robert Medley Estate
Page 65: Photograph © The Museum of London/© Estate of Carel Weight
Page 66: © Kenneth Armitage
Page 67 (top): © Anthony Caro
Page 67 (btm): Photograph © Tate, London 2001/© Kenneth Armitage
Page 68 (top): Photograph courtesy of Rosemary Butler/© Estate of Reg Butler

Page 68 (btm): Photograph courtesy of Rosemary Butler/© Estate of Reg Butler
Page 69: Photograph © Tate, London 2001/© Estate of Reg Butler
Page 70: Photograph courtesy of Rosemary Butler/© Estate of Reg Butler
Page 71 (top): Photograph courtesy of Rosemary Butler/© Estate of Reg Butler
Page 71 (btm): Photograph courtesy of Rosemary Butler/© Estate of Reg Butler
Page 73: © Jack Smith courtesy Angela Flowers Gallery
Page 75: © Estate of John Bratby
Page 77: © The Family of Edward Middleditch
Page 78 (btm): © The Estate of Cara Prunella Clough Taylor deceased
Page 79 (top): © Alfred Daniels
Page 79 (btm): Photography © Tate, London 2001/© Bernard Perlin
Page 80: © Albert Herbert
Page 81: © The Family of Joan Eardley
Page 82 (top): Photography © Tate, London 2001/© ADAGP, Paris and DACS, London 2001
Page 83: © Courtesy of the Estate of Ruskin Spear/Bridgeman Art Library
Page 84 (left): © Courtesy of the Estate of Ruskin Spear/Bridgeman Art Library
Page 84 (right): © Courtesy of the Estate of Ruskin Spear/Bridgeman Art Library
Page 87: © Derrick Greaves
Page 89: © Estate of John Bratby
Page 90: Photograph © Tate, London 2001/© Jack Smith courtesy Angela Flowers Gallery
Page 91: © Jack Smith courtesy Angela Flowers Gallery
Page 93: Photograph Tate Archive Photograph Collection/© Janet Henderson
Page 95: © The Condé Nast Publications Ltd
Page 96 (top): © William Turnbull 2001. All Rights Reserved, DACS
Page 97 (top): © Janet Henderson
Page 99: © Janet Henderson
Page 100: © Eduardo Paolozzi 2001. All Rights Reserved, DACS
Page 101: © Janet Henderson
Page 102 (top): © Janet Henderson
Page 102 (btm): © Janet Henderson
Page 103: © Janet Henderson
Page 104: Photograph © Crown copyright: UK Government Art Collection/© Eduardo Paolozzi 2001. All Rights Reserved, DACS
Page 105 (top): © Eduardo Paolozzi 2001. All Rights Reserved, DACS
Page 105 (btm): © Eduardo Paolozzi 2001. All Rights Reserved, DACS
Page 106: Photograph © Tate, London 2001/© Eduardo Paolozzi 2001. All Rights Reserved, DACS
Page 107 (top left): © Janet Henderson
Page 107 (top right): Photograph Tate Archive Photograph Collection
Page 107 (btm): Photograph © Crown copyright: UK Government Art Collection/© Eduardo Paolozzi 2001. All Rights Reserved, DACS
Page 108: Photograph by Nigel Henderson/photograph © Janet Henderson/© Eduardo Paolozzi 2001. All Rights Reserved, DACS
Page 109 (left): © Eduardo Paolozzi 2001. All Rights Reserved, DACS
Page 109 (right): © Eduardo Paolozzi 2001. All Rights Reserved, DACS
Page 110: © Janet Henderson
Page 111: Photograph © Tate, London 2001/© William Turnbull 2001. All Rights Reserved, DACS
Page 112: Photograph © Tate, London 2001/© William Turnbull 2001. All Rights Reserved, DACS
Page 113: © William Turnbull 2001. All Rights Reserved, DACS
Page 114 (left): © William Turnbull 2001. All Rights Reserved, DACS
Page 114 (right): © William Turnbull 2001. All Rights Reserved, DACS
Page 115 (left): Photograph courtesy of Richard Hamilton and Alan Cristea Gallery/© Richard Hamilton 2001. All Rights Reserved, DACS
Page 115 (right): Photograph © Tate, London 2001/© Richard Hamilton 2001. All Rights Reserved, DACS
Page 116: Photograph © Tate, London 2001/© Richard Hamilton 2001. All Rights Reserved, DACS
Page 117 (top): © Richard Hamilton 2001. All Rights Reserved, DACS
Page 117: © Richard Lannoy
Page 118: © Alison and Peter Smithson, Architects
Page 119: © Magda Cordell McHale
Page 120 (top): © Magda Cordell McHale
Page 120 (btm): © Magda Cordell McHale
Page 121: © Magda Cordell McHale

Page 123: © Roger Mayne
Page 124 (top): © Alison and Peter Smithson, Architects
Page 124 (btm): Photograph courtesy of Rosemary Butler/© Estate of Reg Butler
Page 125 (left): © Estate of Edward Wright
Page 125 (right): © Estate of Edward Wright
Page 126 (top): © Estate of Edward Wright
Page 126 (btm): © Janet Henderson
Page 127 (top): © Alison and Peter Smithson, Architects
Page 127 (btm): © Richard Lannoy
Page 129: Photograph © Tate, London 2001/© Anthony Caro
Page 130: © Janet Henderson
Page 131 (top): Photograph courtesy of Jon Catleugh
Page 131 (btm): © Alison and Peter Smithson, Architects
Page 132 (btm): © Magda Cordell McHale
Page 133 (top right): Photograph Tate Archive Photograph Collection/© Janet Henderson
Page 133 (btm): © David Tindle courtesy the Redfern Gallery
Page 134 (top): © Estate of Michael Andrews
Page 134 (btm): © Estate of Michael Ayrton
Page 137 (top): © Patrick Crooke
Page 137 (centre): © Estate of Edward Wright
Page 138 (top): © Roger Mayne
Page 138 (btm): © Estate of Bryan Ingham
Page 139 (top): © John Chillingworth
Page 140 (top): © Magda Cordell McHale
Page 140 (btm): © Magda Cordell McHale
Page 141: © Magda Cordell McHale
Page 142: © Magda Cordell McHale
Page 143: © Estate of Roger Hilton 2001. All Rights Reserved, DACS
Page 144: © Francis Newton Souza
Page 145: © Sandra Blow
Page 146: © Estate of Franciszka Themerson
Page 147: © William Green
Page 149: © David Hockney
Page 151: © Ralph Rumney
Page 153: © Richard Smith
Page 155: Photograph © Tate, London 2001/© R. B. Kitaj
Page 157: © Peter Blake 2001. All Rights Reserved, DACS
Page 158: © Peter Blake 2001. All Rights Reserved, DACS
Page 159 (left): Photograph © Tate, London 2001/© Peter Blake 2001. All Rights Reserved, DACS
Page 160: © Peter Blake 2001. All Rights Reserved, DACS
Page 161: Photograph reproduced with the kind permission of the Trustees of the Museums & Galleries of Northern Ireland/© Richard Smith
Page 163: © Robyn Denny
Page 164: © Robyn Denny
Page 165: © Robyn Denny
Page 166–67: © Allen Jones
Page 169: © David Hockney
Page 170–71: © Roger Mayne
Page 172: © David Hockney
Page 176: © The Condé Nast Publications Ltd
Page 178: © Roger Mayne
Page 181: © The Condé Nast Publications Ltd
Page 182: © Roger Mayne
Page 188: © Estate of Edward Wright

Barbican Art Galleries are also grateful to the following who undertook photographic work for catalogue reproduction use:

Black'n'White'n'Colour
Jonathan Morris-Ebbs
Woodley & Quick Photography